SOCIAL POLICY, POLITICAL ECONOMY AND THE SOCIAL CONTRACT

Jonathan Wistow

First published in Great Britain in 2022 by

Policy Press, an imprint of
Bristol University Press
University of Bristol
1–9 Old Park Hill
Bristol
BS2 8BB
UK
t: +44 (0)117 374 6645
e: bup-info@bristol.ac.uk

Details of international sales and distribution partners are available at policy.bristoluniversitypress.co.uk

© Bristol University Press 2022

British Library Cataloguing in Publication Data
A catalogue record for this book is available from the British Library

ISBN 978-1-4473-5260-0 hardcover
ISBN 978-1-4473-5261-7 paperback
ISBN 978-1-4473-5263-1 ePub
ISBN 978-1-4473-5262-4 ePdf

Cover design: Liam Roberts
Front cover image: iStock/OvochevaZhanna

To Carol, thanks for all your help and support.

Contents

1	Introduction	1
2	The political economy	22
3	Globalisation and devolution	52
4	Place: uneven geographies and spatial inequalities	72
5	Health and health inequalities	94
6	Social mobility	113
7	The intergenerational contract	130
8	Conclusion	145

Notes	154
Bibliography	157
Index	177

1

Introduction

> Policy and politics are increasingly seen as no longer making a difference to people's lives. (Streeck, 2016)

I tend to agree with Streeck but before exploring the implications of this it is, first, worth considering whether this actually matters. After all, we are living longer (on average[1]); we can attend more university courses than ever before; and we have access to new and exciting technologies, which for example provide access to a wide range of cultural material (both contemporary and archive), and leisure and recreation activities, and have the potential to free large parts of the population from exploitative wage-labour relations through the development of artificial intelligence and automation.[2] There has also been positive change in terms of how women, Black and minority ethnic groups and lesbian, gay, bisexual and transgender (LGBT) people are viewed compared with when I was growing up in the 1980s and 1990s. However, our public services across health, social care, education, tax and benefits, and criminal justice, for example, are stretched to the limit, and decent housing and labour market opportunities can be very difficult to access, with inequalities in wealth, class, gender, ethnicity and sexualities all playing a role to varying degrees. Alongside these, the spectre of climate change and COVID-19 (both the virus and the aftermath) loom over us. From a cultural sociology perspective, the emergent celebrity culture (see, for example, Hyde, 2019, 2020a, 2020b, 2021) has never been so vacuous, reflecting a highly individualistic consumer culture, placing the project of the self at the heart of consumption and even social activism. In relation to social contract theory, Thompson (2017) would describe this as a 'me', rather than 'we', intentionality, which as we shall see is significant in terms of the nature and character of the society in which we live and for the possibility of changing direction. These broadly positive and negative developments co-exist and co-evolve alongside one another and are all aspects of the wider trajectory of English society.

Society is continuously progressing (but with complex trajectories that cut across different places and systems), which influences the distribution of the resources, services, opportunities, experiences and outcomes that are available to individuals, communities and places. However, progress does not occur in isolation from existing patterns of inequalities in social relations and/or the social divisions of welfare. The social contract in

England, for example, obviously has elements of racism, sexism, patriarchy, homophobia and the like. These are present currently and, significantly, are locked into the history of society, through capital (of different types) accumulated across generations (Bourdieu, 1986) forming part of the trajectory and, in complexity theory language, the 'possibility space' of the present day. Sinfield's (1978: 141) argument about the social divisions of welfare legitimating (visible and concealed) patterns of the allocation and reallocation of resources, implies a tendency for social policy to limit the possibility for a radical change in trajectory. In thinking about the status quo in societies it is useful to consider the role of Gross Domestic Product (GDP) as a measure of success. This is an economic measurement of society and one that both simplifies *and* distorts and corrupts social processes. The problem (as we shall see) is that the largely economically driven model of defining and measuring growth and success is also linked to the type of political economy we are locked into and that has produced significant economic and social inequalities. Streeck (2016) argues that there is a unique role for sociology here, provided it refocuses on the crucial issue of our time: the rapidly changing relationship between economy and society. In writing this book I want to respond to Streeck's (2016) call to 'haul the economy back into society' through a new form of political economy – a 'socioeconomics' that seeks to make the economic subservient to the social. As Srnicek and Williams (2016) argue, many of the basic demands of the left (for example, less work, an end to scarcity) are materially more possible now than at any point but we remain wed to an obsolete set of social relations that produce insecure jobs, increasing debt, stagnant pay and widespread social inequalities.

An important role for social policy, then, is to understand and respond to the inequalities and inequities produced through the economy. Titmuss (1968) makes a very significant contribution in this respect by focusing on the notion of progress and the fact that it is not equally shared across society. He argues that socially caused 'diswelfares' – social costs and insecurities – are the price some people pay for other people's progress and as a consequence we need to take account of 'loss allocation' in society as well as 'benefit allocation' through welfare states. The significance of this framing is that it essentially emphasises collective responsibility for a relatively high degree of equality in social outcomes and that a priori we need to focus on limiting inequalities as well as providing policy solutions to mitigate against these. Titmuss' argument, in this respect, both resonates with my political philosophy[3] and has been influential in shaping the development of this book, that is, that social policy should be considered alongside wider debates about the nature of the political economy. However, and as we shall see, Titmuss' framing has been much less successful in influencing and shaping the direction of the English social contract and the political economy, which brings us back to Streeck's rather pessimistic view about the potential for policy and politics. Consequently, one aim of this book is to question the efficacy of social policy within the social contract, as it currently exists. In so doing, England provides the primary empirical case for discussion, although the theoretical framework developed here has wider international application. The use of social contract theory will connect questions about individual and social outcomes in societies with debates about the role and purpose of social policy within the broader political economy. Social policy has an important role to play in influencing the nature of the social contract but it will be argued here that social policy is more constrained and shaped by the social contract than the other way around.

Before considering the nature of the political economy and the interrelationships between this and the policies and the social reality it corresponds to, I want to spend a little time outlining the approach to understanding these. In doing so I follow David Byrne's work around complexity theory and the links he makes to both Bhaskar's (2008) ontology of critical realism and Reed and Harvey's (1992) development of this into complex realism. Taken together, these approaches understand the world as hierarchically layered, in which reality is stratified between, for example, the micro, meso and macro. In this respect, as Byrne (2005: 97) argues, reality is 'composed of complex open systems with emergent properties and transformational potential'. In expanding on the nature and characteristics of complex systems within the complex realist ontology, he later (2019: 5) describes these as 'an emergent product of complex interactions among their components, which may themselves be complex, of the components with the system as a whole and of the system with other systems at multiple levels which have significant relationships with it'. Consequently, an important contribution of complexity theory (and of particular relevance to the framing of this book) is, as Suteanu (2005: 117) argues, that it generates 'insights about the way in which the different parts relate to each other at different scales'.

Complexity theory, then, is both ontologically significant in terms of how it aligns with the approach *to understanding the way the world actually is* that develops throughout this book and, as Callaghan (2008) puts it succinctly, also provides an epistemology (that is, the way the world may be known[4]) for understanding the interactions between structure and agency. To me, at least, this is important because, first, it aids interpretation of the world that social policy is designed to influence, and even shape, and second, it enables us to consider this within a wider narrative about the trajectory of the political economy and the social contract. Political economy is understood here as an important component of the macro context, and structure, that influences both the types of social problems social policy is designed to respond to and the nature and capacity of social policy itself (that is, social policy delivery and implementation, which is increasingly outside of the public sector, albeit resourced largely through taxation). There is real agency in this structure and it interacts with other systems at meso (for example, regional and local) and micro (for example, ward, neighbourhood and individual) levels, which also have their own agency. A final contribution of complexity theory to the framing of this book is what Byrne (2019: 5) calls the 'complexity frame of reference language of trajectory, possibility space and attractor', to describe the path dependency of systems. These 'have trajectories through time and those trajectories happen in the possibility space ... movement in the possibility space is a movement to a different attractor, a shift to being a different kind of thing'.

Let us turn now to the macro trajectory of England; a key feature of this – and the United Kingdom (UK) as a whole – is the steep rise in income inequalities from the late 1970s onwards (Crouch, 2016; Sayer, 2016; Streeck, 2016). By the end of the 1980s it reached about 0.34 (up from 0.24 in 1978) on the Gini coefficient for 'disposable income'[5] and has fluctuated, generally above but occasionally below, this level ever since (see, for example, Belfield et al, 2016). To sum this up we can use complexity language again and call it a 'phase shift'[6] in levels of inequality that took place over the course of the 1980s. While the more recent fluctuations are not unimportant, the sharp increase throughout the 1980s represents a real step-change (a movement to a different attractor) in not only the extent of inequalities, but also the nature and composition of the society that this measures. As we shall see in Chapter 2, there has been a marked departure from the more equal society that the welfare state helped to foster in the third quarter of the 20th century. The post-war growth of the welfare state is associated with this period of relative equality and has been described as a 'golden age' of welfare based on secure growth, full employment, moderate welfare needs and national politicoeconomic autonomy (Taylor-Gooby, 2002). Taylor-Gooby (2002) continued to characterise a shift to a 'silver age' of labour market restructuring, demographic transition and economic globalisation. While these arguments, and those in the broad and contested literature on 'welfare state retrenchment' (see, for example, Pierson, 1996; Starke, 2006), draw attention to a significant trajectory influencing both the nature and extent of the welfare state, a longer historic perspective might suggest that the post-war period of welfare state growth and relative equality was no more than a 'blip'. In other words, are debates about welfare states and equality more realistically framed around *a reversion to type*, rather than as *retrenchment from the norm*? We will pick this issue up in more detail in the next chapter but, for now, it is better to not be too pessimistic about the possibilities for state intervention (through the welfare state) to shape society and contribute to equality and social rights.

With growing inequality, differences between people and households in society grow and experiences diverge.[7] Given that income inequalities are widely considered to significantly underestimate differences in wealth, the significance of this divergence becomes more urgent. Inequalities in wealth have increased at twice the rate of income since the 1970s (Atkinson, 2013), and concentrations of wealth are back to pre-First World War levels and heading towards those of the 19th century, when the brute luck of inheritance dominated economic and social life (Hutton, 2015). At the extremes, the collective wealth of the UK's 1,000 richest people equalled £547 billion *or* the equivalent of 3.7 years of the nation's pensions, 4.7 years of the public health system or 9.8 years of the welfare bill (Sayer, 2016). In other words, many of the most important needs of 63.9 million people could be met several times over by 0.00156 of the population (Sayer, 2016). A common argument to justify this kind of distribution is that we all benefit from the kinds of wealth creation generated by the exceptional talents and efforts of those at the 'top' of society. However, it is simply not the case as the extremely rich have been taking a larger share of slower growth (see Streeck, 2016), which leads Sayer (2016: 9) to suggest that we need to question the legitimacy of their wealth and the rules, situations and institutions they are allowed to take advantage of. Here the UK provides an internationally significant example, given that it is considered by many to be a forerunner of a certain type of capitalist political economy, whether that be best characterised as neoliberal (see, for example, Fevre, 2016; Christophers, 2018), post-industrial (see, for example, Nelson, 1995; Byrne, 2019) or post-Fordist (see, for example, Jessop, 1996). In fact, each of these definitions contributes to an overlapping (but not interchangeable) and generally complementary understanding of the political economy, which will be discussed more fully in Chapter 2.

Christophers (2018) usefully distinguishes neoliberalism from liberalism by focusing on privatisation: he argues that financialisation, market rule, economisation and entrenched class power all existed in liberalism, but privatisation did not (largely due to there being no substantive public sector to privatise). Post-industrialism, according to Byrne (2019: 18–19), is concerned with places that used to be characterised by the industrial production of material commodities and are now 'by the production of immaterial commodities on a primarily non-industrial basis but still under capitalist wage labour relations'. Post-Fordism (see Jessop, 2000) is concerned with the shift from the Keynesian welfare national state to a Schumpeterian workfare post-national regime in which a key role for the state is to make its labour force competitive in a global marketplace and social policy both is subordinated to economic competitiveness and has a key role in contributing to this. The notion of a regime here centres on the state as one player alongside corporations, international bodies, local agencies and not-for-profits that are all deployed in formerly state activities. Each of these 'isms' gained prominence from the mid to late 1970s onwards, has had a very significant effect on the make-up of English (and British) society ever since and can be considered to have made a substantial contribution to the changing nature of the complex systems comprising the political economy and the localised and regionalised manifestations of this. They represent changes in kind and nicely illustrate movements in 'possibility space/s' to different attractor/s. As such, they are also interpreted here as being central to changes in the nature of the social contract in England.

We will explore social contract theory more in the next section. For now, Hiley (1990: 170) provides a useful summary: '[T]he purpose of social contract theories is to provide justification for the State through the consent of individuals.' In so doing, political authority is legitimated on a premised contract or contracts relating to the obligations of rulers and subjects (and the limits thereof) (Lessnoff, 1990). It will be argued here that the notion of the social contract can be used to frame the 'possibility space', that is, the nature of the political economy *and* the scope, role and purpose of social policy in responding to social problems arising from this. As Gough (1957: 244) argues, 'it is a theory of political obligation, to explain the nature and limits of the duty of allegiance owed by subjects to the state, and of the right on the part of the state or its government to control the lives of its citizens'.

A key purpose of this book will be to challenge current policy, practice and thinking about the capacity and role of social policy in England and to be both critical and explicit about the social contract that produces these. In so doing, it is necessary to *identify*, *challenge* and *redefine* the social contract in order to achieve the kind of *phase shift* needed in the systems that produce profoundly unequal social outcomes in England. In identifying the social contract, we need to be clear about what is considered to be the more or less accepted status quo in terms of both the types of policy that relate and respond to and, therefore, affect broad policy issues such as spatial and health inequalities and social mobility *and* the wider political economy of post-industrial/Fordist English neoliberal capitalism that these policies have been framed within over the past 40 years or so. By bringing together social policy and the social contract, an argument will be extended about the nature of the existing social contract, the types of social outcomes this produces and the implications this has for the role of social policy.

The social contract

A core idea in social contract theory is that the best way for individuals to fulfil their self-interested ends is through a political community, thereby accepting some restrictions on our natural liberty (Hartz and Nielsen, 2015). Consequently, as citizens we enter into a conditional agreement in which some of our sovereignty is transferred to government on the basis that it will act in all our best interests. We can, therefore, use the idea of a social contract, for example, to frame how much inequality is tolerated in society and where, and to what extent, it is legitimate for the state to intervene to address these. If enough individuals and groups begin to question whether social outcomes are sufficiently equal across society, this may pose a threat to the legitimacy of the social contract and could ultimately lead to a breakdown in social cohesion. In the work of contractual theorists such as Hobbes and Locke, this loss of individual freedom is a pragmatic and self-interested response to the disadvantages associated with the lack of rules and stability in the 'state of nature'. However, Rousseau's view of the social contract went beyond this by arguing that entering into a society also contributes to new forms of human freedom associated with absolute normative equality as the basis of the civil state (Hartz and Nielsen, 2015), which leads to 'a new understanding of human individuality read as an association of equal, interdependent and autonomous individuals' (Thompson, 2017: 267). Indeed, Varoufakis (2017: 183) succinctly summarises the notion of a contract in the spirit of Rousseau as 'a mutually beneficial contract between equals'. Before we move on to develop and apply this type of application of social contract theory, it is useful to briefly consider the history of, and wider debates about, this concept.

Gough (1957) identifies two types of social contract. First, the 'social contract proper' is concerned with the origins of the state, in which some individual natural rights, derived from living in a 'state of nature', are surrendered to the state in exchange for a guarantee of the existence of the remaining rights. In so doing, individuals agree to come together to form an organised society. The second type of contract Gough (1957: 3) calls the 'contract of government' or the 'contract of submission'. This kind of contract presupposes that a state exists and seeks to determine the conditions and terms on which it is governed, that is, the obedience of people is secured in exchange for the protection and good governance of the ruler, or ruling body. Given the focus on contemporary society and social policy in this book, we will be much more concerned with applying the second type of social contract theory here. It is also debatable whether focusing on the origins of society marks the best use of social contract theory. For example, Polanyi (2018: 173) argued that Rousseau used the:

> construct Social Compact or Social Contract as any scientist would use a hypothesis ... in order to explain the facts ... it does not show the origin of the thing [society] but describes it as it is. It answers the chief question, in what situation does a person in a free society find himself?

The concept of the social contract will, therefore, be principally employed throughout the book in this way, as we are concerned with the role of social policy in relation to the situation people find themselves in, in England.

It is necessary, by way of background, to go into some depth about the differing nature and uses of social contract theory but in so doing it is equally important to not lose sight of this 'chief question' that builds upon an already recurrent theme in the discussion – that of the significance of linking individual to social outcomes. This section now explores three ways of using social contract theory, drawing on Hiley's (1990) work. This is followed by an outline of a preliminary contemporary understanding of the English social contract, in which the significance of the political economy is emphasised. Chapter 2 extends this framing of the social contract and the remaining chapters seek to develop this further through its application to specific social policy issues and areas.

Hiley (1990) identifies three distinct ways that a social contract can be thought to justify the social institutions it produces:

- first, individuals voluntarily and autonomously exchange freedom for security (for example, Hobbes);
- second, legitimacy stems from a recognition of equal interests and reciprocal benefits from association (for example, Rawls); and
- third, equality is a necessary condition (and an irreducible communal value) for entering the contract and transforms private and particular wills into public and general ones (for example, Rousseau).

The first approach that Hiley classifies would be characterised by Hartz and Nielsen (2015) as a clear, pragmatic and self-interested focus linked to the development of a stable political order that protects the interests of citizens much more effectively than possible in the state of nature. The other two approaches retain this element and add what Hartz and Nielsen (2015) describe as a normative aim to explain the degree to which it is legitimate to restrict the equal freedom found in the state of nature through a political community.

All three of the forms of social contract Hiley identifies are important and could be considered to be overlapping (or co-evolving) while also competing for position in complex and diverse contemporary democracies. People of influence, including the public, advocate for different conceptions of the political economy and types of policy that align more or less with one of these approaches. This creates a confusing and often contradictory notion of the social contract in England. But should we expect anything different in what is a confusing and contradictory society with a wide range of interests and preferences about the nature and design of the social order? However, this is not to say that there is not a dominant strand within the social contract. My argument is to employ the third approach (following Rousseau) to both understand and make a case to shift the balance of the social contract to this kind of understanding. Before we move on to consider this approach, we need to consider the first two in more detail, particularly because these are much more closely aligned to the social contract in England, as I interpret it at least.

8

Hobbes developed an argument for the social contract as a pragmatic and self-interested response to protect people from the harm that others might do to them in the state of nature (Meslin et al, 2014). In this view, limited material and social resources, combined with both the insatiable wants and needs driving humans and the absence of normative restrictions on human actions, lead to a state of competition in which every person is for themselves (Hartz and Nielsen, 2015). Hobbes (1985: 196) concludes that 'in such a condition there is no place for Industry, because the fruit thereof is uncertain'. Hobbes, therefore, is concerned with ensuring both stability and productivity through the social contract and the development of social institutions. Lessnoff (1990: 10) describes Hobbes as the 'great exception' among social contract theorists because the theory is usually invoked to justify resistance to rulers, whereas Hobbes argues that only an unchallengeable sovereign can create a stable or tolerable social structure. Hobbes in the *Leviathan* seeks to explain why humans would willingly give up their freedom by choosing to leave the state of nature, given it has no social or normative restrictions on human action (Hart and Nielsen, 2015). The reason given is that entering into a political community is the best way for individuals to achieve their self-interested ends.

However, Hartz and Nielsen (2015: 10) question whether 'appeals to self-interest are the right sort of arguments to justify the authority and legitimacy of the political order?' They argue that by interpreting freedom negatively as freedom from external constraints, including normative constraints imposed by a political community, then why would people be motivated to accept and act in accordance with these norms and principles? This raises two important issues for the argument being developed here. First, to what extent is Hobbes right about the self-interested tendency across human nature? Second, if, as a consequence, negative conceptions of freedom are central to the nature of the social contract then what are the implications for not only the participation of citizens in the social contract but also for the nature of the political/policy elite making up the political community.[8] To what extent, as a logical corollary, will they act in their own self-interest and from a privileged position? Indeed, Poulantzas' (2014: 12) argument, that 'we are hemmed in more and more tightly by a State whose most detailed practices demonstrate its connections with particular, and extremely precise, interests', chimes with the work of Sayer (2016) and Streeck (2016) in this respect.

Rawls effectively revived social contract theory in the 1970s through his 1971 book *The theory of social justice*, which linked the idea of social justice to debates about the legitimacy of social and political institutions (Lessnoff, 1990). Lessnoff (1990) argues that prior to Rawls the social contract was viewed as an outcome of common interests (in escaping the state of nature) but not as a method for settling these disputes. Rawls wanted our ethical system to be based on maximum freedom and maximum fairness, guaranteed through social and economic rights (Mason, 2019). In so doing, Rawls (1999) famously constructed a thought experiment based on the notion of a 'veil of ignorance' in which we do not know our position in society relative to such things as class, assets or ability. As Rawls (1990: 152) outlined, the aim of the veil of ignorance was to 'nullify the effects of special contingencies which put men at odds and tempt them to exploit social and natural circumstances to their own advantage'. Behind the veil it is established that society is subject to the circumstances of justice but the differences between parties is unknown to them and, therefore, they have no basis for bargaining in the usual sense (Rawls, 1990). In so doing, Rawls constructs an original position from which we can critically evaluate our deepest moral beliefs about self-interest and from which we will conclude that, as Lessnoff (1990: 18) summarises, 'inequalities in social distribution are just if and only if they would be acceptable to all in an original position of equality as defined by the veil of ignorance'. Rawls (1999) also argued that social and economic inequalities could only be justified if they gave the greatest benefit to the least advantaged – what became known as the 'difference principle'. For libertarians like Nozick, the redistribution implied in Rawls' theory of justice means that the poorly endowed will effectively exploit the well-endowed (Lessnoff, 1990), whereas those on the political left have been critical about the application of the difference principle to justify 'trickle-down' economics that blighted many regional and local redevelopment strategies under Conservative and New Labour governments.

We now turn to Rousseau's social contract theory and a necessarily selective discussion given available space. In fact, the approach here is to meditate on what Rousseau got right (following Castellani's, 2018, approach to Freud) and use these insights to be applied to debates about contemporary society. In developing his notion of a social contract, Rousseau acknowledged there are good pragmatic reasons that may motivate self-interested individuals to establish a political community. However, Hartz and Nielsen (2015) argue that Rousseau's primary focus was not on the prudential advantages of the social contract but on how it provides an enabling condition for human freedom, which offers a crucial step in the moral development of human beings. Indeed, justifying civil society through appeals to self-interest is to cede to forces outside of one's own control (that is, wants and desires) and, therefore, cannot in any meaningful sense promote or secure human freedom (Hartz and Nielsen, 2015). In this respect, Thompson (2017: 272) states that Rousseau argued for a new and expanded form of cognition 'that incorporates the values of interdependent, non-dominating, non-exploitative, and egalitarian social relations', and only through this will freedom be achieved. Rousseau's theory was, then, profoundly social in its focus. He developed the idea of the 'social tie' as the common element cutting across different interests and, therefore, 'it is solely on the basis of this common interest that every society should be governed' (Rousseau, 1993: 199). Critically, as Polanyi (2018) argues in discussing Rousseau's work, when the conditions are the same for all, no one has any interest in making them burdensome for all. This, in turn, leads Thompson (2017: 279) to describe the social contract as a process of 'autonomous rule-following' obtained through the 'social-ontological condition of living in interdependence with others'.

Rousseau's 'general will' is an important part of his theory, which according to Thompson (2017) provides a form of 'we thinking', leading to a new pattern of cognition, interpretation and action in a coordinated way with others. Rousseau (1993: 204) himself stated that 'the general will ... must be general in its objects as well as its essence; that it must both come from all and apply to all; and that it loses its natural rectitude when it is directed to some particular and determinant object'. This is a very important point in terms of how Rousseau's work will be employed here. However, in contemporary capitalist democracies such as England and the wider UK, this is clearly an ideal because, as we shall see, particular wills are very evident and well established in the (inequitable) organisation of society. Nevertheless, Rousseau's (1993: 191) argument, that 'each of us puts his person and all his power in common under the supreme direction of the general will, and, in our cooperative capacity, we receive each member as an indivisible part of the whole', has an important heuristic value in terms of the lens it provides on the distribution of social outcomes and as an appeal to thinking about the collective rather than as self-interested individuals. Therefore, the general will connects us as individuals to an interdependent and cooperative political community, which Thompson (2017) argues distinguishes the general will from the will of all, that is, it is more than an aggregation of wills as it involves thinking in terms of membership of a community with a common interest in public welfare and individual autonomy derived from a 'we intentionality'. In this respect the government is the servant of the will of the people.

The general will must promote the human good based on core-value concepts such as equality, autonomy and general welfare that Rousseau saw as foundational to freedom and, as such, includes rules that carry normative social content that seek to negate inegalitarian, exploitative egoistic forms of social relations and self (Thompson, 2017). Hartz and Nielsen (2015: 24) therefore argue that a conception of justice as equality can 'explicate the substantial normative structures inherent in our existing political communities, and show how and to what extent these structures support and enable particular normative conceptions of equality and freedom'. This is a crucial point in employing the social contract in relation to the political economy and social policy as it helps to theorise how these are interrelated and combine in the production of social outcomes such as health inequalities and social mobility. In turn, equality becomes a necessary condition (a communal value) for entering the contract and transforming private wills into a public will that is also general, leading Hartz and Nielsen (2015: 16) to conclude that 'what *justify* the civil state are thus arguments based on *freedom*. What defined the *form* of the civil state, however, is an argument based on *equality*.' Individuals recognise themselves, and are recognised by others, as mutual participants in collective activity. However, in conditions of high levels of inequality, Rousseau's approach can be used to make the case for equality (and a more equitable social contract) as a normative goal and to question the extent to which individuals are achieving ends that encourage and justify shared cooperation in society.

Bringing the debate up to date, Hutton (2015: 4) argues that 'even the notion of a social contract is in peril' and 'the last vestiges of an approach to organising society based on a social contract informed by a concept of justice have been shredded'. While I have some sympathy with his argument, on balance this kind of broadly social democratic approach has to be resisted. What constitutes justice and even social justice is open to debate and is not the property of social democrats and the political and academic left, more generally. By effectively dismissing a libertarian conception of justice too readily, Hutton misses a crucial point about what appeals to individuals in society across competing views of justice and where these sit in determining the social contract. So when Hutton (2015: 44) moves on to say that 'in its place there is an emergent system of discretionary poor relief imposed from on high, in which every claimant is defined not as a citizen exercising an entitlement because they have encountered one of life's many hazards, but as a dependent shirker or scrounger', he is, in my view, talking about part of the social contract, rather than something that has emerged in its place. This is an element of the welfare state that is either embraced, accepted, ignored or insufficiently challenged by a large proportion of society and, therefore, is part of the social contract. We need to take ownership of this as a feature of society and ask why it is acceptable as a social outcome. Is it, for example, because for these kinds of individuals their outcomes and experiences do not matter enough to sufficiently undermine the overall contract between individuals and the state?

Put simply, are some people inherently better and more deserving than other people? It is certainly part of human nature to make these kinds of judgements. But from what position? Bourdieu, for example, would argue that social, economic and cultural capital are accumulated over time. This occurs across social class, ethnicity, gender, families, sexualities and so on and has a profound implication for whether one's tastes, preferences and skills fit with certain fields. This is extremely complicated stuff to disaggregate when factoring in the influence of inequality of condition, not to mention taking into account implications of things like effort, and again the complex relationship between structure and agency in motivating one's effort. So, I prefer not to think in terms of whether people are deserving or not but I am in a very privileged position (as most academics are) to have the (paid) time to consider not thinking in this way! Clearly, the significance of individual prejudices, preferences and ideological beliefs is leading to sufficient support and/or acceptance of a social contract that is closely tied to the neoliberal political economy in England. All of this leads us to a far from promising starting point and puts me somewhat at odds with Rousseau's view of human nature. However, much has changed since he was writing, and the political economy has co-evolved with society, and these have influenced the collective psyche in quite profound ways.

The social contract is not in peril. It is clever and sneaky and hard to pin down. Depending on your point of view it may be a lot less democratic than originally conceived, but it is resilient and in some senses thriving and from a broadly left-wing perspective it is certainly rotten. The further left you go on the political spectrum the more it stinks and this is because, I argue, the answers lie to the left of the left-wing. They are closer to understanding the social contract than the modest social democracy that informs much of the well-intentioned social policy debate. Key to this, as Mitchell and Fazi (2017: 233) highlight, is the significance of neoliberal narratives for marking a shift to living in economies rather than societies, in which 'people and nature exist primarily to serve the economy' and the demise of a collective will is a casualty of this form of political economy. In this context, true justice is market justice, which is based on the idea that everyone is rewarded based on their contribution rather than needs (Streeck, 2016). Rejecting these kinds of assumptions rather than trying to engage with, mitigate and modify the market for social ends is an important starting point for a more equitable social contract.

A key purpose of this book is to identify and challenge the social contract in England. In the previous section I outlined key features of the nature and direction of the political economy and the implications of this for the trajectory of society. Here, a start has been made on framing the social contract but this requires much more depth and that will develop over the course of the book. For now it is useful to summarise key points about both how I am proposing the notion of the social contract (influenced primarily by Rousseau's framing of this) is used to understand society and how it might be applied:

- The notion of a social contract provides a lens through which we can question and test what position a person or people find themselves in, in a free society, and whether there is a mutually beneficial contract that exists between equals in society.

- If (as most mainstream political parties claim) we agree that we are all born equal, then Rousseau's social contract theory provides a basis for pursuing greater equality as a normative goal in society. It does so by:
  - emphasising the need to pursue general (as opposed to particular[9]) wills/interests that connect individuals to an interdependent and cooperative political community; and
  - creating a form of cognition, or 'we intentionality', arising from strengthened social ties across autonomous individuals – it is through our social ties that common interests can be identified and pursued.
- Equality is a necessary condition for freedom given the significance of egalitarian and non-exploitative human relations for achieving this.

Social contract theory, when used in this way, is both analytical and prescriptive. Clearly, we are some way from a social contract that articulates common interests in the way Rousseau conceived. By applying aspects of Rousseau's theory to debates about the political economy and social policy I hope to highlight the normative structures that tend towards individualistic and unequal interests and explore the implications of this for the challenges facing social policy in contemporary society (using England as the focus for the research).

Social policy

The motivation for writing this book partly stems from teaching third-year undergraduate and Master of Arts (MA) students a social policy module for a number of years. The module sits within an undergraduate sociology programme and an MA research methods programme, with students from a wide range of disciplines including history, politics, anthropology, education studies and geography also electing to take the module. This creates both a challenge and an opportunity. Taking the challenge first, social policy is wide-ranging and involves a great deal of complexity that, according to Alcock with May (2014), cuts across both an academic discipline and a series of actions taken within society. Consequently, the task is to introduce an academic discipline that is both broad (covering or touching on a broad range of aspects of social life) and includes a lot of depth to a group of students who are in either the final year of their degree or their first year of postgraduate study. They, therefore, need to demonstrate a depth of analysis, understanding and critical engagement to do justice to the complexity of the subject matter and which is appropriate to their level of study. In this respect, I have been pushed towards teaching social policy in a way that also deals with some longstanding frustration I have with the discipline when it is too narrowly defined. For example, Spicker (2014: xi) has argued that 'the study of social policy is often descriptive, or based in commentaries around specific government policies'. In short, debates about social policy can leave big questions about the nature and structure of society unaddressed. Too often, social problems are identified as issues to be addressed through social policy solutions, without due consideration to the wider political economy that influences both the nature and extent of these problems/outcomes *and* the social policy responses to these. By taking a broadly sociological (and a broadly materialist and, therefore, economic sociological) perspective, I am interested in, and have had the opportunity to teach, a module that explores where social policy sits in relation to society. In writing this book I hope to build on this opportunity and respond to calls for a debate about social policy challenging, rather than concurring, with conventional wisdom and providing more than consensual and technocratic solutions to social problems (Page, 2018).

Politicians, policy makers and the wider public do not often confront the difficult questions about what it would take, and mean, to live in a more equal and equitable society. For example, is it really credible to talk about social mobility as a key policy goal when little is done to challenge protective mechanisms around individualism and accumulated capital? Are policy responses, such as paying top-performing graduates more to work in schools in disadvantaged areas, but which do not also seek to radically redistribute wealth accumulated in places and households, likely to achieve greater social mobility? Why do we continue to invest in, and protect, the National Health Service (NHS) (primarily an 'illness/treatment service') to a much greater extent than we do public health and local government, when health inequalities are so prevalent in society? Is the function of social policy to improve and/or provide a degree of legitimacy for society when considered in these terms? Too often, social policy is 'tagged onto' the market, acting as a 'sticking plaster' for largely structural social problems, while doing little to challenge the social inequalities it concentrates on. By focusing on the influence of the political economy in shaping broader contextual changes to society (for example, various types of inequalities), the purpose of social policy will be scrutinised in terms of its scope to insulate individuals and groups from these changes. In this respect we can follow Streeck's (2016: 242) call to focus on the relationship between economy and society and employ the related discipline of sociology to 'restore the economy as a central subject of any theory of society worth its name'. By merging elements of social contract and complexity theory we can more fully integrate social policy into an understanding of the interrelationship between the political economy and society. For example, the Department of Health and Social Care and Department for Education (2017) *Transforming children and young people's mental health provision: A Green Paper* has sought to tackle health inequalities in this area through enhancing schools-based support while not taking into account the socioeconomic inequalities that are widely regarded to be a causal factor in the inequalities of outcome of mental health conditions. In so doing, the relationship between economy and society is undervalued. The role of the state to intervene in people's private economic interests through redistribution[10] to reduce inequalities[11] is considered to be too interventionist and beyond a legitimate role for the state, while at the same time social policy and the state can go to great lengths to intervene in the lives and behaviours of those experiencing problematic outcomes from living in society. The excessive assessment and monitoring of unemployed and/or disabled people when the labour market fails to deliver both employment and good-quality work, provides an illustrative example here. Employing social contract theory is an attempt to rebalance discourse about social policy and in so doing reframe debates around how much inequality is tolerated in society and where, and to what extent it is legitimate for the state to intervene on our behalf to address these.

Before we move on to consider some of the implications of choosing to understand social policy within a complexity frame of reference, it is necessary to spend a little time outlining how social policy is understood. It is important to stress that there is a lot of value in the conventional wisdom about social policies and that this can be highly complementary with the complex systems approach adopted here. Alcock with May (2014: 2) describe policy as 'actions taken within society to develop and deliver services for people in order to meet their needs for welfare and wellbeing'. Meanwhile, Spicker (2014: 5–7) makes four generalisations about this field of study:

- *Social policy is about welfare*, which in its widest sense is about wellbeing but more specifically about people who lack wellbeing and the problems and needs they have plus the services that provide for them.
- *Social policy is about policy*. The core things to understand about a policy are its origins, goals, process of implementation and results. It is also concerned with considering the elements in policy that are common to different issues.
- *Social policy is concerned with issues that are social*, that is, some kind of collective response to perceived social problems.
- *Social policy is an applied subject*. It is concerned with what should be done about social issues – with prescription as well as analysis. Knowledge not geared to practical effects is not much use.

Social policy stems from and cuts across a variety of: mechanisms (for example, legislation, guidance, reports, service delivery and so on); levels (for example, national, regional, local and neighbourhood); administrative boundaries (for example, local government, local enterprise partnerships, clinical commissioning groups and so on); and sectoral boundaries (public, private, voluntary and so on). Given the extent and diversity of these, the approach to understanding policy adopted here tends to focus more on policy areas (for example, childhood obesity) rather than on specific policies (for example, *Childhood obesity: A plan for action*, Department of Health and Social Care, 2016).

In discussing welfare, policy and social problems we need to cast our nets wide to consider the complex causal processes that we have begun to explore in the previous sections. In this respect I hope to develop a form of social policy analysis that responds to Page's (2018) call to build on the approach of scholars who invigorated the discipline between the late 1960s and early 1980s through considering social policy alongside its broader historic, economic, social, cultural and political context. It is worth reiterating that the onset of neoliberalism has fundamentally accelerated a process of loss allocation already identified by Titmuss (1968) during the 'golden age' of welfare *and* has simultaneously constrained the ability of social policy to respond to these at a practical level. Writing a little later but drawing on Titmuss' work, Adrian Sinfield (1978) argued that people had come to accept the social divisions of welfare as seen through the eyes of elites and experts; increasing the guilt of people in poverty while those not living in poverty see this (falsely) as their own achievements entitling them to a better standard of living. This is an important observation and a complicating factor in understanding the social contract and the role of social policy within it. In other words, the nature and composition of society (including social policy itself both shaping and reflecting this) are defined and perceived through a lens skewed towards those in more privileged positions. The role of social policy, then, must come under scrutiny alongside what Therborn (1980) describes as the materially situated character of ideologies and subjectivities and the role of organisational structures and material supports. Systems break down when what he describes as a matrix of affirmations and sanctions underpinning the given regime and ruling ideology break down. These occur when ideological, political and economic contradictions and situations of uneven development have emerged and disarticulated the previous system of affirmations and sanctions (Therborn, 1980). In this light, social policy has a crucial role in preventing these kinds of contradictions and limiting uneven development. A key question for us, and simply put, is: Is this a good thing for social policy to do? Is it more counterproductive than not? Does social policy have a key role in legitimising and securing a neoliberal social contract with its unequitable social outcomes? If so, social policy undoubtable has an important role in society relative to affirmations and sanctions, but when viewed in relation to more far-ranging debates about theories of distributional justice, the scope of social policy is more limited and too often 'tinkers around the edges'.

Burawoy's (2005) paper 'For public sociology', is instructive here. He categorises two types of knowledge (2005: 9–11):

- 'instrumental knowledge', comprising academic audiences in 'professional sociology' (consisting of methods, accumulated knowledge and conceptual frameworks) and 'policy sociology' (providing solutions to problems or legitimating solutions that have already been reached);
- 'reflexive knowledge', comprising extra-academic audiences in 'critical sociology' (which seeks to make professional sociology aware of its biases and silences) and 'public sociology' (a dialogic relationship between the sociologist and the public).

Clearly, each of these is relevant and significant for what will be discussed here. However, the balance is important. For example, Scambler (2011) wrote a commentary on a paper about policy and practice designed to tackle health inequalities that I was a co-author of, in which he argued that there is a tension between critical and policy sociology and that the differential distribution of health throughout a society is more a function of the characteristics of a society than of its healthcare system. Writing in Wistow et al (2015), I argued that we must seek to 'ride both of these horses' and that just because I agreed that inequalities in society are highly significant, it does not mean it is not important to make policy as effective as possible. Writing now I am less sure that this is a good idea or sensible strategy.

It is certainly true that social policy can make real and important differences to people's lives, from providing free childcare and social care to lessen the generally gendered burden of caring for young, chronically ill, disabled or older people, to improving young people's access to higher education through policies geared to widen participation, to name just a couple of examples. However, I keep returning to Marmot's work in the field of health inequalities (which, given the complex social and economic causal processes at work here – and something we will return to in Chapter 5 – it is unsurprising that this has much wider relevance and applicability to a range of social policy issues and outcomes) and his argument that we must deal not only with the causes of health inequalities but also with the causes of the causes. Taking the examples I have just provided, the focus is largely on causes as opposed to the causes of the causes. If it were on the latter we would be talking about things like a generous universal basic income and/or much better remuneration for people providing a variety of caring services; and about things such as regional economic policy that can radically rebalance regional and localised spatial economies to iron out the extreme disparities between places in the UK that correspond with educational outcomes. These are big claims to make on the way that society is organised, require serious resourcing and redistribution of resources, and crucially appear to lack sufficient support in society. However, they raise important questions about the status quo that could shake it up and offer a route to a better society as the dust begins to settle.

In my professional experience (as a local government officer, contract researcher and now lecturer) and through watching and reading debates in the mainstream media, I am concerned that focusing on the causes takes precedence and crowds out the causes of the causes, and that to varying degrees we pay only lip-service to the former, in any case. I am convinced that we need to radically rebalance the scales towards the latter. What I am less certain about is whether to follow strands of Marxism (for example, Ralph Miliband) whole-heartedly in understanding the role of social policy in relation to the social contract and the political economy and take this to its logical conclusion and view social policy and its main arena – the welfare state – as undermining class radicalism. This would mean fundamentally reassessing the role of social policy and considering its function in a social contract that is concerned with preserving social cohesion and legitimising the state, while at the same time leading to profoundly unequal and inequitable social outcomes. However, the potential to do considerable and irreversible damage to individuals and society as a whole by following the Marxist logic is real. So this was a big question for me in the run-up to writing this book and one that I am still struggling with as I near its conclusion.

Finally, it is necessary to provide a brief explanation of the geographical focus of the book, which is on England and is not intended to be at all parochial. However, and returning to our earlier discussion about complexity, it is very important to have a boundary around both social policy and the social contract in order to understand the relationship between the two and contextualise these appropriately. Much of the debate and discussion that follows relates to aspects of the global economy and society and to England's place in this, as a basis for looking outwards. In this sense, the English social contract sits within a broader and more heterogeneous context. But England is our 'entry point' (see Jessop, 2016) into understanding these. A key reason for this stems from devolution in the UK, which began in earnest with the Scotland Act 1998, the Government of Wales Act 1998 and the Northern Ireland Act 1998, which established three legislatures with powers previously held by Westminster. Further powers have been devolved since then, with the Scotland Act 2016 and the Wales Act 2017 being the most recent. Blakemore and Warwick-Booth (2013) highlight the significance of different historic relationships with England for the asymmetric devolution that has followed. We will explore these in more detail in Chapter 3 but, for now, it is important to recognise that a wide range of powers to make social policies (including on health and social services, education, housing and local government) have been devolved to all the nation states of the UK and some additional ones to each of the nations, with Scotland having most independence. These differences create a good deal of complexity and inconsistency across the policy frameworks and agendas in the UK as a whole and it is for this reason that the book focuses on England as the task of connecting social policy to the social contract becomes very complex to narrate. Of course, the UK also has a form of social contract that exists across its constituent parts and it should be recognised that the terms England and the UK are used somewhat interchangeably at times in the text. More generally, the theoretical framework developed here integrates elements of the social contract and complexity theory to explore the relationship and dynamics between the political economy and social policy across complex systems and has wider applicability to different contexts.

Structure of the book

As indicated earlier, what follows takes a particular approach to social policy analysis that sets out to challenge how we respond to social problems. Chapters 2 and 3 continue to contextualise the role of social policy within the social contract and the political economy. In complexity theory, the notion of a nexus, or system of systems, is used to conceptualise the interrelationship and interactions between complex systems at different scales and with different functions and organisational logics. The argument being developed here is that the political economy needs to be integrated into our understanding of the nexus more fully because it relates to the modes of production, to the types of social problems that emerge from this and to the capacity, role and nature of the state to respond to these in the social contract through the mechanisms of social policy. The political economy is, therefore, central to understanding the role of social policy in the nexus and should be treated as such. Only once we have developed an understanding of how this functions and how it relates to the kind of deal that exists between the state and individuals can we move on to consider the second-order issue of the nature, purpose, design and capacity of social policy within, and cutting across, complex systems. Chapter 2 provides an overview of the political economy in England. It develops a historical overview of developments in the post-war period and concentrates, in particular, on the growing individualism in society in the past 40 to 50 years. We explore implications for social policy development in a broadly neoliberal political economy and question what this reveals about the social contract in England. In Chapter 3, we broaden the discussion to consider the global economy, global social policy, Brexit and devolution. Here the argument about the significance of the political economy is contextualised through consideration of globalisation and the global economy. Through exploring global social policy, our focus is largely on England and the implications of global developments for social policy development and implementation. The chapter concludes with discussions about devolution and Brexit, considering connotations for the social contract and social policy development and interactions between these.

Chapter 4 grounds the consequences of the interrelationships and linkages within the nexus in place. First, we explore the highly centralised and London-centric nature of the political economy and social policy and the consequences of this for the social contract. The analysis then moves on to consider regional social and economic disparities in England and how the economic trajectories of place, in particular, impact on social policies and outcomes. The chapter concludes with a discussion about land and housing and how these have changed, and contributed to changing the social contract, over the past 40 years or so. In Chapter 5 we turn to health, which, it is argued (after Marmot), is both highly significant as a social outcome and a very good indicator of the nature of society, in general. The chapter is framed around health inequalities and how policy, the political economy and the social contract interact relative to these. In Chapter 6, the analysis moves on to consider social mobility and its privileged position in both the social contract and social policy rhetoric. We will examine the nature of mobility in society and the implications for who designs and benefits from social policy as well as from wider opportunities. Chapter 7 focuses on intergenerational aspects of the social contract. This is a significant feature of the kind of 'deal' people get out of society across the lifecycle. The argument developed from the previous chapters about the legitimacy of the political economy and social contract in producing mutually beneficial outcomes across society is continued here. The chapter concludes with a discussion about potential routes for change in the social contract and explores possible implications of the technological revolution in artificial and machine intelligence and automation for future developments. In the final chapter, Chapter 8, we will take stock of the preceding analysis and argument and make some recommendations for the development of a contemporary social contract that broadly aligns with the intentionality developed by Rousseau.

2

The political economy

Introduction

In this chapter we will explore the nature of the political economy in England (and the UK) and how it relates to the social contract and social policy. The conceptualisation of political economy adopted here follows the 19th-century tradition, which, to reiterate, Streeck (2016) describes as viewing capitalism as both an economy and a society, and that one needs to start from the point of society, as a set of social actions and institutions that cannot be separated from the economy. Put more strongly, society should be considered the first-order issue and the economy second and, therefore, the economy functions, or should function, to serve society. So it is important to link the political economy to how people experience living in society. Kristofferson, in his 1969 song *Sunday Mornin' Comin' Down*, captures a type of experience associated with a feeling of being alone and at odds with life, and society more generally. The alienation described in the song is associated with a lack of meaning, purpose and control over one's life that most people will have experienced at one time or another (albeit from unequal positions in the political economy and society) and, as such, provides a useful metaphor. Sunday morning is the beginning of the end of the weekend and can be a difficult time because the fun and (possible) excess of Friday night and Saturday are over (and maybe taking their toll). Our free time is drawing to an end as work starts up again the next day and this means re-entering a different form of society (and one we are not always willing and/or ready to engage with). Under capitalism the unequal economic relations between employer and employee, for many, are a key part of this dynamic (Sayer, 2016). As we will see in Chapter 5, our position in the labour market is often associated with the degree to which we can exert control over not only our working lives but also our (and our families') lives as a whole, which in turn is a key contributory factor in inequalities in health, whether that be in terms of quality or duration of life. The lower your position in the labour market, the poorer your quality of life is and the shorter it is, as a general rule.

The political economy presently functions and interacts with society in a very particular way, which influences waged labour and wider social processes through its drive towards securing economic efficiencies to maximise profit. As Massey (1980) argued, measures of efficiency were developed by and for the profit-seeking private sector, which has very different objectives, responsibilities and priorities from the public sector (Christophers, 2018). For Crouch (2011), this represents a key success of neoliberalism as it has made public service organisations (which have multiple goals extending beyond economic efficiency) behave like business corporations and be judged on a notion of efficiency linked to profit maximisation. The extension of the logic of (private-sector or market-based) efficiency to how we measure and value things such as public services is, therefore, a category error that frames and favours private interests over public or social ones. This is an example of the tension Streeck (2016) describes in democratic capitalism between a free play of market forces and social need, with the logic of the former winning out. The implications for the social contract are that capacity in public and social systems is too readily viewed as surplus or redundant. In short, the economy is geared towards profit maximisation and not to serve society. Given the demands and stress placed on human and social systems from living in a competitive and individualistic political economy and by association a society with wide inequalities of opportunity, experience and outcome, we might question whether we have the balance between economic and social priorities right. Compounding these trends is an attack on the public sector institutions and organisations (that are central to the delivery and design of social policies) supporting and responding to issues and problems generally found towards the bottom of the social distribution. From a neoliberal standpoint, these institutions are viewed as both inefficient and creating dependency.

Before considering the current nature of the political economy, the next section will explore what many in the centre-left consider to be the 'golden age' of post-war welfare state capitalism – a period in which the social is generally regarded to have, if not parity with the economic, then at least a high point in its prominence. In the subsequent section we explore neoliberalism as a form of political economy and then briefly outline the development of this in England. The following section explores the implications of the changing political economy for the governance and delivery of public services in England through discussions about New Public Management. The chapter then considers and applies Colin Crouch's (2000) notion of 'post-democracy' to debates about the political economy, the social contract and social policy, before concluding.

The 'golden age' of the post-war welfare state

The 'golden age' of welfare states took place in what Hobsbawm (cited in Byrne, 2019) calls the fortunate third quarter of the 20th century. During this period, post-war democracy derived legitimacy from intervening in markets and correcting their outcomes in the interests of citizens (Streeck, 2016). T.H. Marshall (1950) famously regarded the creation of the post-war welfare state as a culmination in the development of citizenship rights, which we might also regard as a high point towards meeting (although not fully achieving) an equality-preserving version of the social contract, along the lines Rousseau advocated for. Marshall described an expansion of citizenship rights from civil rights (property and freedom before the law) and political rights (association and political representation) in the 18th and 19th centuries to include social rights in the 20th century (Holmwood, 2000). Marshall (1950: 11) summarised social rights as embracing 'the whole range from the right to a modicum of economic welfare and security to the right to share to the full in the social heritage and to live the life of a civilized being according to the standards prevailing in the society'. Put simply, social rights make a strong claim for a degree of equality in society, without which people towards the bottom of society may be considered less than citizens because they do not have an equal right (or potentially corresponding responsibilities) to experience what society has to offer. Van Gunsteren (1978) argued that older theories of citizenship solved this problem by denying citizenship to those without a secure and independent economic position in societies. However, at the time Marshall was writing, political rights were well established in the UK, with the expectation that all people were citizens regardless of social class,[1] and this led to a demand for social rights, especially following the collective effort of fighting in the Second World War. In this respect, van Gunsteren (1978: 29) argues that Marshall highlighted that 'effective citizenship does not only require a political say and a legally protected status, but also a certain level of socio-economic security'. However, it is also important to recognise, as Byrne (2005) highlights, that this approach was tagged onto the market rather than the market being tagged onto a universalistic ideal of citizenship. This is an important distinction and a useful reminder that debates about welfare states are best framed as debates about welfare state capitalism and more critically that the balance between the economy and society was skewed towards the former, even during the 'golden age'.

Briggs (1961) defines welfare states as a state in which organised power is used (through politics and administration) to modify or 'change the play of' market forces in three directions, by:

- guaranteeing individuals and families a minimum income;
- meeting certain 'social contingencies' (for example, sickness, old age and unemployment) – in so doing it limits the extent of insecurity that can lead to individual and family crises; and
- offering a range of social services to citizens regardless of status or class.

The first two equate to a 'social service state' – communal resources used to abate poverty and assist those in distress, while the third objective goes beyond minimum standards to the equality of treatment and the aspirations of citizens.

Titmuss (1968) argued that in the UK the principle of universalism was embodied in key pillars of the welfare state, including through the Education Act 1944, the Family Allowance Act 1945, the National Health Service Act 1946 and the National Insurance Acts 1946 and 1949. These were all geared towards making publicly provided services available for the whole population, with the aim that accessing them would not result in any loss of status or self-respect, or a person being seen as a public burden (Titmuss, 1968: 42). In other words, by making these kinds of services a social right, people who accessed them had a degree of equality in both experience and status with those who could meet these needs by private market and/or family means. As we have already seen, but it bears repeating, Titmuss (1968: 133) considered these services as 'partial compensations for disservices, for social costs and insecurities' of a rapidly changing industrial–urban society. Taken together, Marshall and Titmuss made a major contribution in linking the welfare state, and by association social policy, to the trajectory of the economy and society and in theory, at least, there is a reasonably close alignment to the notion of an egalitarian social contract.

We will now turn to the wider political economy and the Fordist-Keynesian period, which the post-war welfare state both developed within and was also a key component of. Byrne and Ruane (2017: 16) describe the Keynesian mode of regulation as 'the complex of economic and social policy interventions' that was responsible for the post-war welfare state and for economic policy maintaining both full employment and smoothing cyclical recessionary trends to maintain overall aggregate demand. They continue to describe Fordism as both a form of mass production with a highly systemised division of labour via the assembly line and a form of labour and capital relation in which labour was paid sufficiently well to afford the products they were making. Similarly, Mitchell and Fazi (2017: 21) describe the Fordist-Keynesian period as 'marked by the heavy use of public spending to supplement private spending – and more generally by the systematic and pervasive involvement of the state in the economy – with the aim of maintaining full employment, on the basis of class compromise between labour and capital'. Jessop (2018) also argues that conditions included spreading the benefits of growth through infrastructural investment, collective bargaining, collective consumption and welfare state measures, extending to measures to compensate for uneven regional growth. State intervention was indispensable to Fordism (Mitchell and Fazi, 2017), with post-war democratic capitalism redistributing the proceeds of the market economy downwards through industrial relations and social policy, which provided rising living standards while stimulating economic growth to provide a sufficient level of aggregate demand (Streeck, 2016).

The Keynesian 'golden years' were generally fiscally sound and taxation was used to fund redistribution so that, between 1945 and the late 1970s, inequality was at its lowest ever (Byrne and Ruane, 2017). Crouch (2011) describes Keynesianism as 'a true social compromise' as it protected the capitalist economy from major shocks to confidence through arm's-length demand management, while the lives of working people were protected from the vagaries of the market, and the markets from more detailed intervention from governments. Similarly, Streek (2016) describes the post-war consensus in democratic capitalism as a historic compromise and attributes this to a uniquely powerful working class and uniquely weakened capitalist class, rather than skilful social engineering. However, Mitchell and Fazi (2017) cite Usmani (2017) to argue that many socialists convinced themselves that under Fordist-Keynesianism more had been done to shift the balance of class power and the relationship between states and markets, than was the reality. O'Connor's identification of two basic and often contradictory functions of the state is instructive here (see Byrne and Ruane, 2017: 18–20). First, O'Connor argued that the state had a crucial role in ensuring that social and economic arrangements are in place for capital accumulation to function for capitalists. Second, maintaining social harmony was a necessity for capital to be able to exploit workers and take surplus value from them; therefore, the state must return some of this value through taxation in the form of cash and services in kind (Byrne and Ruane, 2017). That these functions of the state co-evolved alongside the golden age of the welfare state is revealing and, for Srnicek and Williams (2016), reflects the social democratic adherence to capitalist growth in this period. Joan Robinson (as highlighted in Mitchell and Fazi, 2017) also described this period as being dominated by 'bastard Keynesianism'. Robinson argued that Keynes' revolutionary analysis was marginalised in the application of his theory, in order to make it more palatable, specifically in relation to his view that market economies when left to themselves may remain permanently depressed and not automatically self-correct in the case of high unemployment.

It is important to recognise that during this golden age there were real structural inequities, from the global to the household level, that enabled the system to function. Srnicek and Williams (2016) summarise these as an international hierarchy with an underdeveloped periphery, a national hierarchy of racism and sexism, and a family hierarchy of female subjugation, combining to make the conditions and pay of White male workers improve. Virdee (2019), for example, highlights the party political and state racism, alongside social closure from all social classes of the 400,000 migrants from the Indian sub-continent and Caribbean between 1948 and 1962. Furthermore, Srnicek and Williams (2016: 100) argue that the 'height of the social democratic era required the exclusion of women from the waged workforce' and, therefore, question 'whether full employment has ever been possible'.

While it is the case that there were huge imbalances in the employment rates of men and women, with 53% of women employed compared with 92% of men in 1971, there was large-scale employment of women in industrial work (especially clothing and textile factories), which led to the growth in household income and prosperity (Byrne, 2019). Nevertheless, Streeck (2016) is correct to point out that women not working was a sign of the economic success of a family, whereas now it is a social obligation and a condition for social self-respect and membership of the community, although Williams (1989: 132) has characterised this within the 'false universalism' of the welfare state that obscured social diversity behind a screen of an imagined community, 'built upon a white male, able-bodied, heterosexual norm'.

The oil crises (and price rises) of 1973 and 1978 are commonly regarded to have led to a crisis in the (bastardised) Keynesian consensus operating globally, which enabled a shift to neoliberal ideology, as the-then Labour government submitted to budgetary restraint and austerity mandated by the International Monetary Fund (IMF) (Harvey, 2005; Crouch, 2011). As we will see in the section on UK governments in the neoliberal era, later in this chapter, the architects of neoliberalism were ready to exploit this crisis. For now we need to note that, alongside the United States (US), the UK was particularly vulnerable to inflationary pressures due to the absence of a strong form of corporatism collectively negotiating wage rises in a coordinated manner (Crouch, 2011). Stagnant growth (or recession) and high levels of inflation, known as 'stagflation', ultimately led to a war on inflation through tight monetary policy, which increased unemployment to a level acceptable to capital, reducing the power of the working class and ending full employment (Srnicek and Williams, 2016). Mitchell and Fazi (2017) consider that rather than being imposed on a reluctant but powerless government, the IMF loan and the conditions for spending cuts and monetary restraint, reinforced a change in policy orientation in the Labour Party (in an internal battle between left and right) away from social welfare and full employment. Alongside these developments, deindustrialisation was beginning to take effect in England, which we will return to in Chapter 4, especially. It is important to recognise here, as Byrne (2019) argues, that there has been a massive decline of industrial employment as a consequence of both the relocation of manufacturing and major productivity increases in manufacturing, which have changed the economic base, with implications for the 'possibility space' in which social policy exists.

This period (albeit with important qualifications around the privileged position of England in the global economy, often at the expense of other nations, and with differential experiences related to gender, ethnicity and disability, for example) can rightly be regarded as a high point for an egalitarian form of the social contract. It is also tempting to view it as a 'blip' when viewed in historic context. As we will see, there are serious questions about how far equality can be embedded in the social contract. We will return to these issues in a discussion about neoliberal governments in the UK later in this chapter. Next, we will explore what emerged in place of the so-called 'golden age'.

Neoliberal influence

Crouch (2011), Sayer (2016), Srnicek and Williams (2016), Mitchell and Fazi (2017) and Davis (2018), to name a few, all maintain that neoliberalism has been the predominant form of ideology influencing England's (and the UK's) political economy over recent decades. The UK began to adopt and develop a form of neoliberal capitalism from the 1970s onwards that intersected with other significant processes across the economy and society, including post-industrialism (Byrne, 2019) and post-Fordism (Jessop, 2018). This trajectory has formed a cornerstone of the social contract in the UK for more than 40 years and has been remarkably resilient to internal and external threats, with the 2007/08 financial crisis being a particularly noteworthy example – although the Organisation for Economic Co-operation and Development (OECD) and the IMF have increasingly seen growing economic inequality as threatening the economic system (Crouch, 2020). It is my contention (not a particularly controversial one in the field of social policy) that neoliberalism is damaging society and simultaneously tying the hands of policy makers, practitioners and communities to respond to the social problems it creates, amplifies and distorts. It is difficult to describe neoliberalism as producing a mutually beneficial contract between equals in society but that does not seem to matter sufficiently for societies to change direction away from neoliberalism. As we will see, there are a range of powerful systemic factors rigging, and maintaining, the political economy in favour of this trajectory. However, much less discussed (certainly in the well-intentioned largely social democratic academic debates about social policy) is the continued appeal of neoliberalism to the public and national psyche. Here, then, I want to introduce a couple of strands of analysis that help us to understand the continued success and influence of neoliberalism over the UK's political economy and what this, in turn, reveals about how the social contract functions. First, we will explore some of the inherent contradictions and inconsistencies in the ideology. Second, we need to appreciate the appeal of competitive individualism (especially in an increasingly unequal society where, for example, much is known about the significance of where we start in life for where we end up, especially in terms of inequities) and to do so by turning to social psychology. Before considering these issues we need to introduce how neoliberalism is understood here.

As a concept and ideology, neoliberalism generates much debate in academia. Peck (2013) has expressed concern about imprecision and loose-handedness through a promiscuous application of the term, which is echoed in arguments for more definitional clarity (see, for example, Byrne, 2017) and claims (see, for example, Clarke, 2008) that neoliberalism has become so overused it should be retired as a concept. These are important debates, but we will not spend too much time on them here, first because, as we have already seen, a key feature of neo (that is, new) liberalism, highlighted by Christophers (2018), is the privatisation of public services and utilities, which has a good deal of significance for social policy given the implications for the changing role and capacity of the state and the social systems it interacts with. Second, the inconsistencies in, and flexible and opaque nature of, neoliberalism/s are themselves defining features of the concept and ideology. It is challenging, to say the least, to be precise in defining something that is so malleable, adaptable and, at times, contradictory. In short, neoliberalism is a form of capitalism and a trend in its development and some believe its endgame/stage, albeit from different sides of the political spectrum and, therefore, for different reasons. The influence of neoliberalism fluctuates, co-exists and co-evolves with other parts of the nexus over time, to varying degrees, and is an economic model that exerts significant influence over the system of systems.

Neoliberalism is rooted in the classic liberalism of Austrian School economists such as Ludwig von Mises and Friedrich Hayek, who viewed any form of government intervention that disturbed the natural functioning of the market as both likely to fail and an assault on human freedom (Srnicek and Williams, 2016). In this respect, key instruments of the welfare state were, and have continued to be, seen as placing constraints on the central state's marketisation project (Crouch, 2011). Hayek's (2014 [1959]) argument, that through claiming exclusive rights in certain fields the development of post-war welfare state activities was an exercise of coercive power that was both inefficient and a threat to freedom,[2] has exerted considerable influence. Neoliberalism, therefore, emphasises free-market policies, including the privatisation of state enterprises, trade liberalisation, the deregulation of the financial sector and fiscal retrenchment (Mitchell and Fazi, 2017), and does so according to Jessop (2015: 169) based on promoting the 'fictitious commodification of land, labour power, money, and knowledge by subjecting them to market logic'. As Peck et al (2009: 51) argue, 'neoliberal ideology rests upon a starkly utopian vision of market rule, rooted in an idealized conception of competitive individualism and a deep antipathy to forms of social and institutional solidarity'. In short, a key feature of neoliberalism is its antagonism towards the state fulfilling social goals, which are viewed as best left to the market. In fact, the argument is that as long as markets are 'near-perfect' then the outcome of individuals' selfish behaviour will be consistent with overall welfare (Crouch, 2011). However, as Crouch argues (and we explore in more detail in the section on post-democracy later in this chapter), markets are far from perfect and the term is generally used (especially among the political right) to refer to corporations and their selective approach to gaining favourable access to markets. Srnicek and Williams (2016) provide a useful summary about neoliberalism functioning as a political project that both fosters hostility to the state and has sought to take control of the state and repurpose it, for example through creating and sustaining 'natural' markets, which includes defending property rights, enforcing contracts, repressing dissent and maintaining price stability at all costs. Peck's (2003) distinction between neoliberalism's tendency to both 'roll back' and 'roll out' the state sums this up well. The former relates to both the privatisation of, and a reduction in, public services in order to create more space for private capital, while the latter is concerned with the use of state apparatus to embed and extend neoliberalism in the economy and society.

The notions of *freedom* and *efficiency* are very significant in neoliberalism and both have particular, yet highly contestable, meanings that have become part of the 'common sense' through the continued influence of the ideology over the political economy. We will return to freedom later in the discussion. For now, let us focus on efficiency, which sounds like a good idea, right? For example, being efficient in our work might mean that we get to go home on time and/or not have to work when we have gone home and finished our household chores (which, in turn, we also want to be efficient at so that we can get down to some leisure time). However, who is ever fully efficient at work or in tidying up, cooking, cleaning and so on? As human and social beings we are not, which is why at the start of the chapter I introduced the notion of efficiency and the weekend as something that builds (economically) redundant capacity into our lives. We need spare time and spare capacity to build some slack into our lives because we cannot be fully efficient at all times. If we do not have spare capacity then these kinds of tasks become increasingly pressured and stressful, potentially undermining our ability to perform them well. As we have already seen, neoliberalism is highly preoccupied with economic efficiency and, critically, from a narrowly defined economic perspective that also exerts considerable influence over systems geared towards the delivery of social policies. As Christophers (2018) argues, the logic of efficiency through markets attacks and undermines other forms of use value. It is in this respect that Mitchell and Fazi (2017: 239) highlight that unemployment, growing income and wealth inequality, increasing poverty and declining standards of basic public services can exist in neoliberal conceptions of efficiency, 'despite the overall well-being of citizens being compromised by the behaviour of the capitalist sector and the policy responses of government'.

The use of a particular conception of economic efficiency has formed part of a wider attack on social rights, which in neoliberal narratives are themselves viewed as limiting individual rights and freedom. It is important to get back to basics here and as Sayer (2016: 342) simply states, 'contrary to neoliberalism, economies are supposed to serve societies'. However, that is not currently the case. Instead, Mitchell and Fazi (2017) highlight Joe Earle's notion of 'econocracy' to point out that we are much closer to living in a society in which its logic and political goals are defined in terms of their effects on the economy. Returning to the example of spare capacity, or in engineering terms redundancy, is illustrative when applied to human and social systems. In general terms, redundancy is a good thing and in engineering is often necessary. For example, the highly inefficient steam engine was central to the development of industrial capitalism and relied on building up steam pressure in order to have sufficiently high output to power industrial machines and steam locomotives. When these machines are worked hard (that is, using a lot of power/energy), boiler pressure can build up to dangerous levels that would lead the boiler to explode without the addition of a safety valve, which releases, or lets off, steam close to the boiler's maximum safe pressure. In the case of steam locomotives, in particular, the demands for power fluctuate greatly depending on gradients and unexpected speed restrictions, meaning that redundant capacity is both necessary and inevitable given the need for high power output and fluctuating and somewhat unpredictable demands on the use of this. This would be highly dangerous without a safety valve (the steam engine would essentially be a large bomb) but also involves wasting a lot of energy. The argument I am developing here is that we need a societal safety valve – something that will enable us as children and adults alike to 'let off steam' (to, in economic terms, waste capacity) and function as human beings. Instead, Crouch (2016: 134) argues that 'the individuals for whom the market caters are not whole human beings, but abstractions of us'. By abstracting us the market reduces our complexity as human beings and even more so in terms of complex social relations. The inbuilt logic of the market does not recognise use value outside of economic relations and, therefore, seeks to remove redundancies across the nexus that viewed through a social lens are in fact important and necessary conditions of a mutually beneficial and equality-preserving social contract.

Mitchell and Fazi (2017) argue that, in an econocracy, politicians and policy makers can (mis)represent unpopular political decisions as neutral and technical, separate from political and class interests. The coalition government's austerity programme provides a prime example that we explore in more depth in the next section. However, this is a much longer-standing trajectory that, over the past 40 years or so, has led to a narrowly and ideologically defined economic understanding, and organisation, of social relations to predominate (see, for example, Dean, 2010; Sayer, 2016; Mason, 2019). As a consequence, social rights and the role of the welfare state in protecting these have come under attack. We might view these as a form of redundancy or spare capacity built into complex systems that act as a form of societal safety valve. As these decline in significance we would do well to keep an eye on the pressure building up across the nexus and the implications for social systems, in particular. In reality, as Crouch (2011), stresses neoliberalism has been selective in calls for shrinking the state, which despite decades of neoliberal dominance, has resulted in considerable government activity remaining in areas such as public education, pensions, health and social care and the regulation of monopoly utilities. Consequently, key fields or pillars of social policy remain intact in a system in which the political economy is apparently antagonistic to state intervention. Byrne and Ruane (2017) turn to O'Connor, who highlights how large amounts of tax-funded state expenditure goes towards maintaining the social order for capitalism, with some going towards capital accumulation and some subsidising capitalist corporations and covering their costs. Byrne and Ruane (2017) argue that we should see taxation as playing a large role in resolving capitalism's internal/inherent contradictions. Once we do so we should also question how taxation is being used to resolve these contradictions and in whose interests. This is about how *the pie is being sliced up* across revenue earned through taxation. It is important to recognise that neoliberal theory is concerned with limiting the size of the pie as well as having a strong say over how it is shared out. Whether this is the basis of a mutually beneficial contract is highly debatable and is a primary concern for much of the discussion that follows. Put simply, we need to question whether the amount and allocation of public expenditure is equitable in the sense that it will strengthen human ties through egalitarian human relations. This seems incredibly significant at the time of writing, given the economic and social impact of the ongoing COVID-19 outbreak. For example, Blakeley (2020) argues that massive state investment and intervention is currently possible and going largely unquestioned by politicians and economists so as to forestall political and economic transformation. In this respect, capitalism (as influenced by neoliberalism) also appears to be very resilient – first, because of its inherent (and I would argue intentional) contradictions and inconsistencies and, second, due to the appeal of capitalism and a neoliberal form of this across relatively large sections of society. We will conclude this section by looking at these in turn.

Contradictions and inconsistencies in neoliberalism

The influence of multinational corporations and global finance are key contributors to the inconsistencies in neoliberalism (see, for example, Blakeley, 2020; Crouch, 2011, 2020). As Blakeley (2020) argues, when markets are dominated by a few large firms, states become ever-more dependent on them for revenue and these businesses take a greater interest in regulation and tax policy. This is extremely well illustrated through the origins of the 2007/08 financial crash, where banks and associated financial organisations played a key role in reducing corporation tax and higher rates of income tax and crucially in deregulating the banking and financial sectors (Crouch, 2011; Sayer, 2016; Streeck, 2016; Mitchell and Fazi, 2017). We will explore this more later in this chapter and again in Chapter 3, but the bailout of banks supports the view that they were deemed too big to fail and too central to the nexus to be allowed to be fully exposed to the cleansing effects of market economics. Blakeley (2020) argues that both the 2007/08 financial crisis and the response to the COVID-19 crisis in 2020 demonstrate demands for government intervention and the increasing dependence of capital on the state, in order to save capitalism from itself. She concludes that 'the risks of running an investment-grade business have been socialised, while the gains have remained private' (Blakeley, 2020: xiv). Whether this is a continuation of the inconsistencies of neoliberalism or a new form of capitalism is open to debate but as Crouch (2011: viii) suggests, 'actually existing' neoliberalism is nowhere nearly as devoted to free markets as is claimed in 'ideologically pure' neoliberalism and is, instead, devoted to (and seeks to conceal) the influence of giant corporations over both politics and the market.

In this respect, Mitchell and Fazi (2017: 175) summarise 'mainstream economics' as being built 'on a sequence of interrelated lies and myths that have no connection to reality, but reinforce the view that a self-regulating private market with minimal government interference will deliver maximum wealth for all'. The reality is very different. Sayer (2016) and Streeck (2016) both provide very good accounts of how the current system is not working in terms of growth and, especially, how the stagnating growth is distributed increasingly unequally across society. Furthermore, in *Reckless opportunists*, Davis (2018) makes the case that neoliberalism may have become destructive to the establishment given that the contradictions in neoliberalism lead to the crippling of national institutions that markets and large corporations require to function. He argues that 'elites require a rule of law, security, a transport infrastructure, an able workforce and social stability to function. But neoliberalism promotes an ever-smaller state, a poorer, less able employee pool, and nods through corporate and super-rich tax evasion on an industrial scale' (Davis, 2018: 21). Christophers (2018) highlights the inconsistent logic that is applied to the public and private sectors in which the guiding conviction of the public sector as 'bad' and 'wasteful' has reached the heart of government. For example, the Cabinet Office (2013) report, *State of the estate in 2012*, was critical of the civil state for having vacant (surplus) land, despite the private sector owning more vacant land and the public sector decreasing its share at a faster rate than the private sector (Christophers, 2018). Christophers (2018) concludes that this is an example of the multi-component logic espoused by Whitehall in neoliberal Britain, in which the state is both part of the problem (through, in this case, its role in the planning system) and part of the answer as it owns surplus developable land.

The ongoing appeal of neoliberalism

We have already seen that there are persistently high levels of inequality in England and the UK and there is a wide range of literature that makes the case for greater socioeconomic equality as a prerequisite for a more equitable society (see, for example, Dorling, 2013; Schrecker and Bambra, 2015; Calder, 2016; Reay, 2017; Friedman and Laurison, 2019; Marmot et al, 2020a). Why, then, is there not more demand for an equitable distribution of resources across society and/or demand for a radical change in direction in the political economy? In understanding these developments, Castellani (2018: 128) frames 'our complex social psychologies' as being driven by top-down societal desires and bottom-up id-based drives, concluding that 'our psyches are formed as much by societal drives as they are by instinctual drives'. The co-evolution of the social contract and political economy (through the continued influence of neoliberalism as a particular form of capitalism) has been increasingly successful in capturing and appealing to our id-based drives and, therefore, in controlling/influencing societal drives. On the one hand, the crisis in Keynesianism provided an opportunity for a neoliberal infrastructure (what Hayek described as the 'second-hand dealers in ideas', think tanks, journalists, academics, broadcasters, writers and teachers) to respond to and exploit (Srnicek and Williams, 2016). On the other hand, capitalism is an inherently competitive system and it both taps into an important element of human nature and, as Berardi (2019) argues, has a force of its own through the process of extending capitalism across the system and containing and constraining forms of life within it. This would not be possible without at least some appetite for competitive individualism. We can see this in the mass appeal of competitive sport in terms of both participation (both in the flesh and online through video games) and viewing (either in the flesh or through streaming services), which provide examples of the fascination with (and motivational force of) enjoyment taken in and from competition, which in turn has been monetised to a very high degree, for example in the case of (male) football.

A significant shift in attitudes away from a collectivist political culture took place in the mid to late 1970s, to one in which high taxes, welfare benefits and strong trade unions supporting income equality were increasingly being viewed as holding the country and individuals back (Fevre, 2016). These were the conditions in which a neoliberal ethos of competitive self-improvement (including of one's marketable human capital) has flourished

(Streeck, 2016). Fevre (2016) highlights the influence of Herbert Spencer's philosophy over what became American individualism and later had global influence. In particular, the notion of the 'demoralising effects of government' shielding people from their extravagances, preventing self-reliance (Spencer was thought to coin the term 'survival of the fittest') while interfering with individual rights was highly significant (Fevre, 2016). In other words, government is seen to not only stifle our freedom (that is, individual rights) but also hold us back from becoming independent human beings and fulfilling our potential. The subsequent work of Charles Murray (1984, 1990, 1994) around the notion of 'dependency' would become highly influential over political discourse and social policy on both sides of the Atlantic and complemented the individualism in neoliberal economics. As Dean (2010) argues, Murray's work was also associated with Hobbes' moral-authoritarianism, in which the social order is seen as depending on the moral obedience to rules. Murray (1990) sought to move away from considering people at the margins of society (the 'underclass') as 'victims' and instead reintroduce 'blame' for their own exclusion from society's protective norms (see Dean, 2010). In England the notion of a 'safety net' to catch those falling through the gaps in society came under attack and too high a safety net was considered to be causing dependence on the state and, therefore, people had to be allowed to fall further in order to foster a sense of competitive individualism. In this respect, neoliberal narratives of lives in 'under-governed' societies can be glorified as living in liberty, pursuing idiosyncratic preferences freely and without constraint from institutions (Streeck, 2016).

The centrality of consumption to capitalism has been discussed by scholars as diverse as Marcuse (capitalist society implants 'false need in people'), Veblen (on the 'conspicuous consumption' of rich people setting fashions and standards for people in poverty to aspire to but not achieve) and Galbraith (on 'the affluent society' and the role of the advertising industry in generating new needs not everyone could satisfy) (see Dean, 2010). Having 'spare' money to spend on individual goods and services has been a key feature of the appeal and the coercion of capitalism, especially when the collective pooling of individual income and wealth is framed as creating and rewarding dependency. As a consequence, Yamamura (2017) argues that the majority of people in developed economies live in a world of 'too much stuff', in which unprecedented amounts of goods and services are increasingly seen as 'necessary luxuries'. In turn, Han (2017: 36) describes the development of neoliberal 'psychopolitics', which:

> Instead of administering 'bitter medicine', it enlists Liking. It flatters the psyche instead of shaking it and paralysing it with shocks. Neoliberal psychopolitics seduces the soul; it pre-empts it in lieu of

opposing it. It carefully protocols desires, needs and wishes instead of 'depatterning' them. By means of calculated prognoses, it anticipates actions – and acts ahead of them instead of cancelling them out. Neoliberal psychopolitics is SmartPolitics: it seeks to please and fulfil, not to repress.

In this respect, neoliberalism is tapping into something in our collective psyche. Given that the system is based primarily on competition and exploitation, these are the avenues people will use to pursue their instinctual drive to happiness (the 'pleasure principle') (Castellani, 2018). The necessity to continually develop new desires among a population whose needs have been met impacts on social relations, which become redefined as relations of consumption and status increasingly linked to one's status as a consumer in society (Streeck, 2016).

Streeck (2016) argues that capitalist development and markets, in particular, are deeply interwoven into how people organise their way of life and in line with cultural assumptions about what is natural and normal. Similarly, Berardi (2019: 170) considers that in the social field 'the capitalist semiotizer has force' (essentially this is a process of capitalism extending across the system), containing and constraining forms of life within it, which do not have sufficient force to crack the container. It is instructive to return here to Therborn's (1980) book, *The ideology of power and the power of ideology*, and his development of three modes of ideological interpellation. His argument is that ideologies function by telling subjects, relating subjects to and making subjects recognise: *what exists* (and its corollary, what does not exist); *what is good* (and what is bad); and *what is possible* (and what is impossible). Neoliberalism has been successful in this respect and influences the path dependency and, therefore, trajectory and 'possibility space' of systems through the power of ideology. The 2007/ 08 financial crisis is an instructive example here as alternatives to the neoliberal social contract lacked sufficient purchase to seem either possible or good, and ultimately, therefore, to exist. At the time of writing, the current COVID-19 crisis (given the consequences across society and the economy and the need for significant injections of public monies) will lead to far bigger challenges to the position of neoliberalism in the nexus. However, we should not underestimate the appeal of the status quo, which has been persistent because enough people are happy, satisfied, disengaged, insufficiently motivated or lacking the resources to radically change the direction of society. For these reasons, changing the nature of the social contract is very difficult and, in fact, is a part of the social contract! As Castellani (2018: 235) argues, 'people do not like to change until the pain of changing is worse than the pain of remaining the same; and even then, they do not want to change'.

UK governments in the neoliberal era

Thatcherism

Margaret Thatcher's election in 1979 as Prime Minister was the 'starter gun' for the spread of neoliberalism in England and the UK and a template for later neoliberal victories (Fevre, 2016: 172). Crouch (2011) frames the victory of neoliberalism as a historic defeat of the political centre-left and a victory for the right and its preference for strong, wealthy and powerful individuals over collective interests. Berardi (2019: 115) highlights Thatcherism's debt to Hobbes, Darwin and Hayek in inscribing 'competition into the soul of social life and the cult of the individual as an economic warrior'. Fevre (2016) identifies three critiques of the Labour Party outlined in the 1979 Conservative Manifesto:

- the politics of envy had discouraged the creation of wealth and weakened the economy;
- enlarging the state had diminished the role of the individual and crippled enterprise; and
- giving trade unions privilege without responsibility had provided a minority with the power to abuse individual liberties.

Taken together, shifting public attitudes and the crisis in Keynesian economics contributed to what Streeck (2016) describes as a new form of received wisdom emerging during the 1980s and 1990s in which the state was seen as dictating to people what they were supposed to need whereas private markets catered for what people really wanted, as individuals. The Thatcher governments tapped into this and fed its growth through developing a narrative concerned with supporting 'wealth creators' and 'self-made people' to justify deregulation, freeing up the City of London and privatisation.

Under Thatcher, Britain became the undisputed trailblazer of privatisation. She stated in her memoirs that privatisation must be at the 'centre of any programme of reclaiming territory for freedom' (Christophers, 2018: 322). Her Chancellor Nigel Lawson (BBC, 2019) described privatisation as 'the single most successful innovation of the Thatcher governments'. Through 'selling off the family silver', the Thatcher governments created a home-owning and shareholding democracy that was built through the sale of state-owned industries and housing to the public. During Thatcher's period in office, her government sold 40 state-owned businesses (employing 600,000 people) but by far the largest privatisation was of council homes, with an estimated £22 billion worth of sales (Broughton, 2019). This period marked the start of a massive shift of capacity from the state into private hands, which co-evolved with growing inequalities in society. As we shall see in Chapter 4, there was a strong spatial element to these interacting processes, operating at different scales. For example, the deregulation of the financial sector based in London and the attack on, and lack of support for, the country's industrial base led to growing regional (see, for example, Martin, 2015; Beatty and Forthergill, 2016a, 2016b, 2018), local and neighbourhood (see Lupton and Power, 2004) social and economic disparities, while the capacity of the state to respond to these inequalities was rolled back, along with its role (Newman, 2014). When questioned in a television interview with Robin Day about the divisions her policies were creating, Thatcher responded by claiming that opening up private market-based opportunities to all provided the public with something in common (BBC, 2019). While there was sufficient popular support for the management of the political economy to ensure three Thatcher-led Conservative Party election victories, and a fourth term under John Major, there is no doubt that this period was divisive. During this time the political economy began to align more strongly with individual and particular wills. As Hutton (2015: 239) concludes, this would have lasting consequences: 'the simultaneous deregulation of the labour and financial markets, with no thought for equity, justice or the complexity of the relationship between society, work and business, was to be a major contributory cause of the financial crisis and all that followed from it'.

New Labour

New Labour came to power in 1997 under the leadership of Tony Blair, with a landslide victory in the general election and a parliamentary majority of 179 seats. After four consecutive election defeats, New Labour embraced Thatcher's approach to the aspirational working class, with Blair arguing in his 1996 conference speech that many better-off working-class people voted for the Conservatives because Labour was preventing them from getting on in life (Broughton, 2019). Peter Mandelson famously declared (in his speech to Silicon Valley Executives in October 1999) that the Party was 'intensely relaxed about people getting filthy rich as long as they pay their taxes'. As Sayer (2016) argues, the qualification about paying tax was soon forgotten, with New Labour similarly obsequious to the rich as the Conservatives, as, for example, taxing more than 50% for high earners was seen as a politics of envy and penalising 'wealth creators'. In this respect, Marmot (2015) concludes that political parties of both the centre-right and left between 1979 and 2010 moved to no longer viewing inequality as a problem, or certainly not to the extent that equality should be prioritised over individualism (Fevre, 2016). As Sayer (2016) highlights, Blair went so far as to state that he was not concerned about the gap between the rich and poor in the 2001 election campaign, and by 'ducking questions of economic justice', Blair failed to acknowledge how the rich had used 'advantage' to monopolise opportunities. These are really significant aspects of New Labour's legacy over the political economy, with the failure to challenge the 'top' of society making it both harder to close gaps in inequalities around social outcomes while further embedding the notion that big gaps between winners and losers in society are a natural part of the social contract. Indeed, Lupton et al (2013) conclude that, although New Labour increased overall public expenditure by 20% to modernise public services to bring them up to European standards, there was a long way to go in terms of creating a more equal society as overall income inequality and relative poverty rates remained high by international standards.

New Labour's focus on becoming electable led to it amending and watering down 'Clause IV' of the Labour Party constitution from a symbolic commitment to common ownership of industry to:

> The Labour Party is a democratic socialist party. It believes that by the strength of our common endeavour we achieve more than we achieve alone, so as to create for each of us the means to realise our true potential and for all of us a community in which power, wealth and opportunity are in the hands of the many, not the few, where the rights we enjoy reflect the duties we owe, and where we live together, freely, in a spirit of solidarity, tolerance and respect.

At best, this can be portrayed as an articulation of social democratic values through Third Way politics, which Blair himself described as a commitment to a centre-left form of social justice that rejects Old Left and New Right conceptions of the state. Crouch (2011) summarises Third Way parties as being influenced by neoliberalism to see more possibility in state intervention to improve the operation of the market, rather than replace it. Indeed, it is debatable whether the Third Way was anything more than a 'flanking and supporting mechanism to maintain the momentum of neoliberal regime shifts' (Jessop, 2018: 1731). For example, Byrne and Ruane (2017) argue that New Labour did not develop a coherent programme to challenge the influence of capital in shaping post-industrial society. The introduction of place-based approaches to regeneration such as the New Deal for Communities and the Neighbourhood Renewal Unit are examples of Third Way state intervention, providing much-needed resources to 'left-behind' places, but did little to level the playing field for these types of places through addressing structural imbalances in the political economy. In this respect, Telford and Wistow (2020) highlight the Labour Party's failure to respond to deindustrialisation and represent regional and working-class interests. Byrne and Ruane (2017: 50) summarise this period as one in which 'New Labour had no coherent industrial policy to speak of, massively neglected its own electoral heartlands in former coalfield and heavy industrial areas, and continued the process of deindustrialisation reinforced by active policy and passive neglect which had characterised the Thatcher years'.

New Labour took its electoral base for granted not only in terms of place (something we return to in Chapters 3 and 4) but also in terms of its origins in the labour movement and its relationship with trade unions. It did not challenge the political right's campaign to link crises of capitalism to union power (Srnicek and Williams, 2016) and Blair went so far as to promise that British law would become the most restrictive for unions in the Western world (Schrecker and Bambra, 2015). Srnicek and Williams (2016) conclude that this was part of the re-engineering of public opinion around a broadly neoliberal agenda of individual freedom and negative solidarity.

These examples suggest that New Labour was nowhere near radical enough in seeking to change the trajectory of the political economy. Given the significance of the political economy in shaping the 'possibility space' and 'attractor state' of the nexus, there are considerable implications for the nature and extent of the social problems that occurred across the nexus. For example, in their review of social policy under New Labour, Lupton et al (2013: 61) highlighted that, despite high levels of public spending, large socioeconomic gaps remained on most indicators, and argued that 'another conclusion is that socio-economic inequalities in outcomes are hard to shift, in the context of persistent high inequality – that there are limits to what social policies can achieve in the absence of economic change'. Ultimately, the 2016 referendum on the UK's membership of the European Union (EU) (see Telford and Wistow, 2020) and the 2019 general election are, in part, related to New Labour's failure to alter the trajectory of the political economy and the impact of post-industrialism and neoliberalism, in particular, on its heartlands.

The coalition government and austerity

The 2010 general election resulted in a coalition government between the Conservative and Liberal Democrat Parties. From the outset, their central priority was outlined in the Coalition Agreement (Cabinet Office, 2010): 'the deficit reduction programme takes precedence over any of the other measures in this agreement'. We will consider the consequences of austerity throughout the book and in Chapter 3 we explore the origins and implication of the financial crisis causing much of this austerity more fully. It is important to state here, though, that while the financial crisis had its origins in the banking sector, the consequences for the public sector have been profound. In total, £500 billion was spent on bailing out the banks in the UK (Mason, 2019). In normal times this kind of injection of public money into the economy would be unthinkable, but as several commentators

(Crouch, 2011; Sayer, 2016; Jessop, 2018) have pointed out, the financial sector was deemed too big to fail (despite criticism by these, and many other, authors about the extent to which the financial sector contributes as a productive, as opposed to extracting, part of the economy). Nevertheless, the bailout and subsequent austerity programme are illustrative of the centrality of a financial, market-based form of neoliberal capitalism in the English political economy. Jessop (2018: 1731) summarises the response to the crisis as follows: '[T]oxic assets and losses were socialised at the expense of households, the public debt and industrial capital. Financial crisis was translated discursively and practically into public debt and fiscal crises and intensified neoliberal vilification of state spending, with further calls for austerity measures.' Streeck (2016) demonstrates how the financial crisis and the response to it are part of a longer trajectory of neoliberalism, in which the market-correcting capacity of democracy and collective organisations such as trade unions and political parties has continuously diminished, leaving the contradictions of democratic capitalism to be negotiated between states and investment banks. Despite being key players in the most serious economic crisis for 80 years, the City of London seems to have deepened its grip on power, leading Sayer (2016: 235) to state that, 'absurdly, the UK Coalition government claims that the crisis is the product of excessive state spending ... aided by a compliant press and a feeble, craven opposition, has set up the public sector as scapegoat for the crisis'. While agreeing that Ed Miliband's big mistake as Leader of the Labour Party between 2010 and 2015 was to not argue against austerity, Chakrabortty (2019) also points out that he was, nevertheless, constructed as 'Red Ed' and as the biggest threat to the establishment by the media and civil society institutions. These institutions play a crucial role 'as arbiters of what is politically permissible', which did not include Miliband's very modest form of social democracy (Chakrabortty, 2019).

Edminston (2018: 3–4) argues that, 'rather than a withdrawal of the state from the provision of public goods and services, welfare austerity can be understood as an enhanced and accelerated reorientation of the UK welfare state towards neoliberal productive ends'. Hutton (2015) points out that over the past 300 years, national debt has been much higher than it was following the financial crisis and considers austerity to be ideologically driven as other options existed to respond to the financial crisis, including increasing taxation on property, business, inherited estates, the rich and overall income tax. That these were not considered flies in the face of research from even the IMF, which explored credit crunches in 107 countries between 1980 and 2012 and concluded that growth constrained by bank lending and monetary policy is insufficient and public spending cuts should be avoided as much as possible (Hutton, 2015). Instead, Streeck (2016: 124) describes a move towards a 'consolidation state', in which 'commercial market obligations take precedence over its political citizenship obligations, where citizens lack access to political or ideological resources with which to contest this'. One result in England has been a significant reduction in state capacity. Between 2010–11 and 2014–15, total public spending was cut by 3.0% in real terms, with departmental spending, which includes the administration and delivery of public services, planned to be cut by 10.2% over this period (IFS, 2015). The brunt of the impact was felt by those either employed by or dependent on state services (Porter, 2013). Indeed Cribb et al (2015) have found that the public sector workforce is now smaller than at any point over the past 40 years. As Crouch (2011) argues, not only were the banks protected from their folly but also other sectors were not similarly protected and the public sector was required to take massive cuts in resources. The National Audit Office (NAO, 2018a) calculated that there was a 49.1% real-terms reduction in government funding for local authorities between 2010–11 and 2017–18, hitting cities and deprived areas the hardest. At the same time, Taylor-Gooby (2016) highlights that the net effect of changes through post-2010 tax reform has been to shift revenue-raising away from the better off and businesses towards those with lower incomes.

Writing in April 2019, the United Nations (UN) Special Rapporteur on extreme poverty and human rights reported that in the fifth largest economy, 14 million people (a fifth of the population) live in poverty and it concluded (UN, 2019: 1):

> The bottom line is that much of the glue that has held British society together since the Second World War has been deliberately removed and replaced with a harsh and uncaring ethos. A booming economy, high unemployment and a budget surplus have not reversed austerity, a policy pursued more as an ideological than an economic agenda.

As Byrne (2019) concludes, post-2008 we have had 'socialism for the rich' in the form of state support for banks, bankers and holders of real wealth, with austerity for the rest of us. There is an important role for social sciences to play in identifying these issues, but as we will discuss more fully in Chapter 7, the turn towards a postmodern focus on discourse, intersectionality and identity politics has contributed to a loss of focus on the role of the economy relative to society. As Streeck (2016: 242 and 246) argues, 'sociology must restore the economy as a central subject of any theory of society worth its name ... [and] must be able to impress on the public consciousness that the present crisis is not an accident'. For Hutton (2015), the Conservatives exploited the banking crisis to cut public spending and that has 'raised fundamental questions about the state's capacity to deliver public good, justice and equity'. Even while acknowledging the imperfections of the electoral system in the UK, the results of the 2015, 2017 and 2019 general elections in the UK suggest a lack of resistance to austerity and raise serious questions about the possibility of developing a social contract that will seek to redress some of the social and economic inequalities in society. Nevertheless, applying both the analytical and the prescriptive forms of social contract theory, outlined in Chapter 1, to identify and question the positions people find themselves in, in a society such as this, draws our attention to the economy and to Streeck's call for action.

New Public Management and governance

New Public Management (NPM) is a logical corollary of neoliberalism and has been a key vehicle for extending key aspects of the latter into the public and state spheres. Fevre (2016: 183) argues that 'it is rarely pointed out that one of the defining policies of neoliberalism, NPM, was also concerned with the individualisation of employment relations in that last bastion of unionism, the public sector'. Rhodes (1997: 48–9) usefully distinguishes between two aspects of NPM:

- *managerialism* – the introduction of private management techniques to the public sector through explicit standards and performance measures, value for money, and managing by results; and
- *new institutional economics* – the introduction of incentive structures (market competition) into public service provision.

According to Rhodes this led to the transformation of the public sector, which now involves less *government* and more *governance*. We will return to governance later, after unpacking the two aspects of NPM in a little more detail.

Davis (2018) highlights that through the introduction of NPM, from 1979 onwards, private sector management techniques, including the use of targets and audits, were extended into the public sector in the UK. The intensification of managerialism included the introduction of systems geared towards performance appraisal and efficiency rather than policy (Bevir et al, 2003) and, as Crouch (2011) points out, a shift away from seeking to improve performance by strengthening professional commitment and values. The use of performance targets feeding into league tables enabled comparison between organisations in the hope that this would lead to increased efficiency (Fevre, 2016) and acted as a means of transferring the ideas and rhetoric of politicians into meaningful action and as an evaluation tool to judge performance and claim success (Davis, 2018). However, Bevan and Hood (2006) highlight the challenge of taking something relatively small that is supposedly characteristic of the domain under evaluation and using that as a basis to judge and prioritise performance of a wider system. It is in this respect that Davis (2018: 101) argues the 'target-driven tails began wagging the dog' to the extent that, for example, whether someone is seen in Accident and Emergency (A&E) within four hours matters more than the result and quality of the treatment they get. Targets, then, are an example of Campbell's Law (Campbell, 1979: 85), that is, 'the more any quantitative social indicator is used for social decision making, the more subject it will be to corruption pressures and the more apt it will be to distort and corrupt the social processes it is intended to monitor'. A further factor here is that elites are often part of the negotiation and construction of auditable targets and, therefore, get to be the game player as well as setting the rules of the game – and often pick the referee too (Davis, 2018).

The origins of the 'new institutional economics' that Rhodes describes can be traced at least as far back as the 19th century and the ideas of Herbert Spencer, in particular. Fevre (2016: 119) summarises Spencer's view of society as being 'far too complex for the state to be able to pull policy levers and affect behaviour in the way it desired' but businesses, which he considered had no such desire to affect behaviour, were fulfilling their functions within a market and in so doing could not help but produce order. While we may agree (and it is in fact a core argument being developed in this book) that society is complex and hard to affect with 'policy levers' alone, the notion that businesses are not trying to influence or affect behaviours is no more credible now than when Spencer was writing. However, this does not make his argument any less significant or influential. What we have here, is an apparently reasonably popular line of argument against state intervention in societies and people's lives, in favour of private and market-based solutions – which are constructed as much less problematic and intrusive and are, therefore, much less likely to be construed as negatively interventionist. In this respect, Fevre (2016) links NPM to Spencer's idea that corruption and laziness flourish when the antiseptic of free competition is absent. This kind of extension of market rationality has been used to privatise state activities (Jessop, 2015) through the use of quasi-markets, disaggregating public bureaucracies into agencies that deal with each other on a user pay basis, and of the contracting out of services to foster competition and cost-cutting (Bevir et al, 2003). Thus, the core aims of neoliberalism are also the core principles of NPM (Jessop, 2015) and the contracting out of services and the use of markets have been justified in order to deliver efficiencies and used for state retrenchment since the early 1980s. For example, the civil service is half the size it was when Thatcher came to power, despite a population increase of 18% (Davis, 2018). In Davis' (2018: 35) words:

> [T]he departments of health, education, transport, work and pensions, culture and media, and the home office have all worked hard to make themselves redundant. A third of government expenditure on public

services is now spent through opaque private providers. It's no longer clear if the new regime still offers much accountability or makes the machinery of government work for the benefit of the nation.

Here we can see, as Hill and Hupe (2014) argue, that the government retrenchment of the 1980s and 1990s was at least in part enabled through the introduction of NPM, the introduction of business methods to government and the privatisation and contracting out of services, in particular. In short, NPM cuts across neoliberalism, both 'rolling back' and 'rolling out' the state.

These developments led to a shift away from Keynesian public administration (top-down structures and processes involving direct state involvement in public services provision) to the introduction of market-based models of service provision by independent agencies (under NPM), which Osborne (2006) has argued has resulted in New Public Governance. Governance has been described as states *steering rather than rowing* (Osborne and Gaebler, 1992) and as an increasingly complex set of institutions and actors, drawn from within, but also beyond government (Stoker, 1998). Debates about governance are, therefore, often formed in response to the growing plurality of providers of services, the potential fragmentation in service delivery resulting from this and the need to include individuals and communities in these arrangements. Governance also exists at different levels, with Verkerk et al (2015) describing this as an overarching complex and hierarchical system consisting of actors interacting in subsystems at multiple levels. They argue that these are *hierarchical*, as agents at higher levels (the global political economy and national governments) have the power to influence room for manoeuvre for agents at lower levels (local government and service providers). They are also based on *mutual interdependence*; and include *autonomous processes* with their own dynamics. These developments have created a system that is very complex in terms of the numbers of actors in the system, the lines of communication and the allocation of responsibilities.

The shift from the state rowing to the state steering is critical to understanding English social policy and the welfare state and has implications for the configuration of service delivery and local state capacity to respond to social problems (which we will return to in Chapter 4, in relation to the spatial configuration of social policies and outcomes). Jessop (2016: 56–7) argues that 'to talk of state managers, let alone of the state itself, exercising power masks a complex set of social relations that extend well beyond the state system and its distinctive capabilities'. For example, quasi-markets have produced greater diversity of service delivery, which introduces new and more varied types of self-organisation into the system. The growing plurality of providers of public services increases the complexity of service delivery and reduces the capacity of the state at different levels (especially at the national and local levels, given the ongoing relative weakness of the regional level in

England) to respond to social problems. The coalition government's *Open public services* White Paper (HM Government, 2011) provides a significant intensification of this trend through making it clear that for services that are amenable the default position is to switch from direct provision by the state, to the state commissioning services provided by a 'range of diverse providers', in the private and voluntary sectors.

Streeck (2016) argues that the privatisation of formerly public services limits the material base for the legitimacy of states. Put simply, by shrinking a state's capacity it has less resource to demonstrate its legitimacy to fulfil what might be considered vital functions, for example the provision of social care. What is considered to be vital can change over time and there is a strong case that through privatisation and contracting out (organised around economic efficiency) we are losing the social dimension of care, a trend that has been intensified under austerity (see Burns et al, 2016). At the time Burns et al (2016) were writing, 74% of local authorities commissioned 15-minute homecare visits and the authors highlighted how these were organised as procedural tasks (on a similar model to fast-food service delivery) and, therefore, poorly aligned with the complex social relations that correspond to service user needs. Given that social care covers support and care for some of the most vulnerable people in society and was an early casualty of neoliberal reforms of the public sector in England, it provides an important example of what happens when social goals are subsumed within a model of service delivery driven by an economic conception of efficiency. The coronavirus has once again highlighted the crisis in social care in England (which is discussed further in Chapter 3) but this is a longstanding issue and something we appear willing to live with at a societal level, at least. More generally, the contracting out of services also represents a well-established trajectory in terms of how the political economy interacts with social policy. Streeck (2016) is right to highlight the limitations this places on the legitimacy of states and it is hard not to conclude that this has been embedded into the social contract through successive governments in sway of neoliberal politics and economics.

NPM, and closely associated processes, have exerted a strong influence over the design and functioning of social policy in England through its influence over the systems delivering services and with significant consequences for the recipients of these. For example, Kirton and Guilaume (2019) describe the partial privatisation of the Probation Service as ideologically and politically motivated, rather than evidence-based, with *The Guardian* (Doward, 2019) reporting a 50% increase in serious crimes committed by people on parole since the reforms. For now, we will conclude this section by focusing on an illustrative example: medical assessments of disabled people claiming personal independence payments (PIPs). These assessments were contracted out (or outsourced) to two large private companies: Atos and Capita (being paid

£507 million between them to conduct assessments between 2013 and 2016 by the Department for Work and Pensions [DWP]). In its second report on PIPs, the Work and Pensions Committee (2018) provided extensive detail about the high levels of stress these assessments cause for some of the more vulnerable people in society. In its response to the Work and Pensions Committee review of PIPs in 2017, Disability Rights UK drew on responses from members and organisations to highlight a number of systemic problems, including the following:

- Assessors lack adequate expertise to conduct the assessments.
- Assessments are often too short to fully understand the complexities of people's conditions.
- Additional evidence (for example, from medical professionals who have both expertise and deeper relational understanding of people's circumstances) is not fully considered, alongside or as part of the assessment.
- There are frequent reports of assessors using information selectively, or misrepresenting information, to outright lying about people's conditions.

It is hard not to conclude that these issues are symptomatic of the development of social policy in an economy that is not functioning to serve society.

Disability Rights UK is far from alone in highlighting these issues. For example, *Private Eye* has frequently covered this issue, drawing attention to system-wide trends such as reporting that in 2018, 72% of cases (more than 60,000 people) won their appeal at a benefits tribunal (*Private Eye*, 23 August 2019, issue 1503), while also focusing on the human consequences of this. In issue 1,500 on 12 July 2019, *Private Eye* concentrated on the experiences of Ella Peel, who suffers complex and serious ill-health, including chronic kidney disease and pulmonary fibrosis, and applied for a PIP as the latter worsened. The DWP upheld the Atos assessment that Ella claimed had 14 serious errors, including simple and easily correctable mistakes such as recording she could walk 200 metres, when in fact she could only walk 20 metres. She took her case to the benefits appeals tribunal and waited 20 months for her hearing, which she won after the DWP failed to attend and produce the documents requested by the tribunal judge. The DWP was considering whether to comply despite the judge ruling that her pay had to be backdated immediately (*Private Eye*, 2019, issue 1,500). This serves as an example of the influence of neoliberalism in terms both of the growing conditionality in the benefits system and of the contracting out of services to private sector organisations that have an operating logic skewed towards profit, rather than social value.

Writing in 1980, Doreen Massey, through her critique of creeping marketisation of the UK public estate in the 1970s, had already identified the significance of the trajectory described here, which was the assumption that (in this case) land, even when publicly owned, can only ever have one type of value: market value (Massey, 1980). She argued that the state should be allowed to function as a public owner rather than having to ape private sector approaches and values. As Christophers (2018: 141) states, 'public ownership must be allowed to mean something truly different from private ownership for it to have any real worth or significance'. Unfortunately, NPM has played an important role in changing values and approaches in the public sector that mirror changes in society. The way that medical assessments for disability payments are conducted is one of many examples of how these changes can impact on individuals and society at large. To my mind this should not be viewed as part of a 'broken social contract'. To do so is to let society off the hook. Instead, Goran Therborn's (1980) work on ideology and power provides a useful lens to view the persistence of the social contract through. He rightly draws attention to the impressive stability of the political regimes of advanced capitalist countries, arguing that 'such consent may not involve a widespread sense of representation among the ruled, but it need not be based on massive fear. It could instead be rooted in resignation, deference and accommodation' (Therborn, 1980: 108–9). These are, he asserts, probably more important components of consensus than representation. The social contract should be viewed in this way too. It is highly complex, fragmented and even 'murky'. But despite (and also because) of this it is clear to me, at least, that the 'we' intentionality stemming from Rousseau's conception of the social contract is not sufficiently strong in contemporary English society to overcome the dominant logic of neoliberal capitalism. As Christophers, Massey and Streeck, to name a few, argue, this is not an appropriate logic model for public service delivery, nor for understanding and evaluating the value of these types of services. With the example of disabled claimants we can see that their interests (which should be paramount in the delivery of the PIP assessment service) are eclipsed by other priorities, influenced by a profit motive.

Post-democracy

The trajectory of the social contract and the political economy towards neoliberalism and away from social rights has responded to, and fed, drivers towards competitive individualism in society. These changes have occurred in, and been rubber-stamped by, democracy. However, much of the argument in this chapter has implications for the nature of that democracy and how it functions in the nexus in a post-democratic state.[3] In describing a shift to 'post-democracy', Crouch (2000) highlighted that public electoral debate had become tightly controlled around a small range of issues and despite the existence of a range of democratic practices; politics and government were 'increasingly slipping back into the control of privileged elites', overwhelmingly representing business interests, making egalitarian causes ever-more impotent. Post-democracy, therefore, encapsulates the tight control exerted by neoliberalism over the nexus and the significance of this for the nature and direction of the social contract. For example, Jessop (2020) identifies the neoliberal project's ongoing attempts to create demanding consumers aware of their choices and rights as well as actions to increase market mechanisms. This contributes towards a position in which citizens are increasingly valued as economic actors via the market, with accountability skewing towards this. In turn, this logic cuts across the nexus (to varying degrees), with wider implications for the legitimacy of the state as an arm of democracy within the social contract. For example, Streeck (2016) highlights implications from the extension of this logic to political decisions, which he argues cannot just be consumed but need to be produced through collective action involving the complex processes of examining and aggregating wills. Citizenship is, therefore, much less comfortable than consumerism and introducing the latter into public life undermines the former because we less readily accept decisions we do not agree with and that go contrary to our individual interests (Streeck, 2016). Furthermore, the reduction of the capacity of the public sector to respond to social problems and needs (through, for example, the impact of discourses about economic efficiency and dependency culture) run alongside heightened expectations of citizens as consumers of public services and social policies, which combine to reduce the legitimacy of the state, public services and democracy.

The outsourcing of public services provides an example of how neoliberalism and post-democracy intersect. Outsourcing services is often presented as a way of moving these from a state monopoly to the realm of customer choice, but the contract is between the public authority and the contractor and, therefore, the market only really exists at the discrete point in time when the contracts are up for tender (Crouch, 2020). Crouch (2020) highlights the dependence of the British state on the small number of corporations dominating outsourcing markets in the UK, whose expertise is in securing contracts and not on the wide range of fields they conduct their activities in. These are part of a culture in England (centred on the City of London) that focuses on: short-term performance and value-extraction (see Hutton, 2015); 'value skimming' and rentier capitalism[4] (see Sayer, 2016); and 'reckless opportunism' among elites (see Davis, 2018). These are key (world-beating) areas of strength in the UK but are areas in which actual service delivery is secondary and often left wanting. For example, the National Audit Office (NAO, 2020a) has reported on the use of extreme urgency regulation 32(2)(c) for contracts under the 2015 Public Contracts Regulations for COVID-19-related contracts issued by the UK government. It concluded that concerns about bias, transparency, conflicts of interest and risks to public money have arisen through the use of regulation 32(2) (NAO, 2020a). Christophers (2020) provides a recent example of outsourcing to supply personal protective equipment (PPE) during the COVID-19 pandemic that appears to tick all these boxes: a £252 million contract to supply 50 million face masks to a company owned by an adviser to International Trade Secretary, Liz Truss, that had no previous experience in this area and ultimately provided face masks that were unusable. This is just one of many examples where the post-democratic tendencies of outsourcing have been intensified through the COVID-19 crisis. More broadly, these sit very comfortably within what Christophers (2020) describes as 'unimaginably rentier-friendly' policies developed in Britain since the 1970s, with government playing a key role creating and allocating assets such as North Sea oil and the privatisation 'bonanza' of the 1980s and 1990s. A further consequence of this has been highlighted by the Intelligence and Security Committee of Parliament's (2020) report on Russia, which concluded that the introduction of the investor visa scheme has made the UK and London, in particular, especially attractive to Russian oligarchs. The report is generally concerned with the security implications of these ties, but it also demonstrates how money has been invested to secure patronage and influence over a wide sphere of the British establishment.

Post-democracy turns our attention to the links within the establishment and how politics and business interests have become closely aligned. Neoliberalism (through leading to a major increase in material inequalities and legitimising the use of wealth for political influence) has exacerbated a major unresolved problem in liberal democracy: the tension between the equality of citizens' votes and inequalities in economic power (Crouch, 2020). The sense of abandonment among sections of the working class in post-industrial areas, which found expression in the Brexit vote (see Telford and Wistow, 2020), provides a prominent example of these tensions coming to a head. In this respect, Byrne (2019) emphasises Thompson's (1981) notion of Experience I (the current reality of social relations), which he argues is increasingly contradicting Experience II (the ideological gloss of the dominant culture) in the current crisis and longer-standing harsh reality of post-industrial capitalism. The hope, then, is that material circumstances (and the medium- to long-term aftermath of the COVID-19 pandemic may be significant in this respect) will shed a harsh light on what Crouch (2020: ix) describes as follows: '[T]he real energy of the political system had passed into the hands of small elites of politicians and the corporate rich, who increasingly ensured politics responded to the wishes of the latter.' We, as a society, should not accept that this is in our best interests or represents a good deal for the majority.

Conclusion

In this chapter we have covered a lot of ground fairly quickly. In so doing I have provided a brief history about how the political economy has developed in England, and the wider UK, and highlighted some of the ways it interacts with social policy. The political economy has a powerful position within the nexus (the system of systems) that in complexity theory is viewed as constituting the make-up and interactions between social, political, economic, cultural and institutional domains cutting across complex systems. As such, there is a strong relationship between the political economy and the nature of the social contract. Both inform and influence one another but the argument being developed here is that this does not occur from an equal footing. In fact, the trajectory outlined here suggests that the turn to neoliberalism has seen a growing influence of the economy over society. As we will see, this has a considerable impact on the nature and extent of social problems and outcomes, while also influencing the capacity and type of social policies designed to respond to these.

There are signs, at the time of writing, that a space for a new way of doing things is emerging through the crisis cutting across the nexus, resulting from COVID-19 – the high death rate and toll in the UK and England (prior to a successful vaccine rollout), alongside the economic slowdown and concerns about the knock-on effects of restrictions on social, cultural and economic life on mental and physical health, jobs and income, educational attainment and child wellbeing, to name a few examples. It is too soon to say whether societies will revert to type when the dust settles. However, state intervention through economic support packages demonstrates the possibility for a renewed role for the state and social policy. What was considered impossible in terms of state intervention (albeit selectively) by mainstream economics is once again necessary, therefore we might consider whether in 'normal times' state intervention is necessary in other areas of economic life that have equally profound, but less immediate, impacts on society. In this light, questioning the efficacy of the political economy seems prudent – as Yamamura (2017) argues, given that the fiscal policy of reducing taxes and stimulating investment, aimed at increasing the money supply, has led not only to low post-1980 growth rates, stagnant real wages, frequent recessions and high unemployment but also to much less investment than necessary to meet social needs. The political economy is failing to deliver on a range of social and economic measures, which suggests the need to weaken the hold of the selective application of neoliberalism over the nexus. However, untangling the web of influence it exerts across complex systems is no easy task and would require widespread support from a range of stakeholders, including sustained popular support.

3

Globalisation and devolution

Introduction

Globalisation and devolution create twin pressures on the notion of an English social contract. The former draws our attention to a range of processes that extend beyond the boundary and direct control of nation states, and the latter to powers, organisations and identities at a smaller scale of analysis, which are significant given the spatial disparities in social outcomes at the regional and local levels. The next chapter focuses in more detail on the spatial implications for social policy at the regional and local levels. In this chapter we concentrate largely on global and national systems and consider the local in relation to devolution. Byrne's (2005: 105) conceptualisation of cases in the complexity frame is useful here as it encourages us to view cases as 'complex systems which are nested in, have nested within them, and intersect with other complex systems'. As Byrne (2005) argues, these levels have implications for each other through the ways they intersect and constitute one another. The analysis being developed here is a little more hierarchical than Byrne suggests, and it is important, therefore, to return to the significance of agency in path-dependent but not path-determined complex systems as a counterbalance. After all, Marx (1852), who is often (although many would argue unfairly) characterised as an economic determinist, said that 'men make their own history, but they do not make it as they please; they do not make it under self-selected circumstances, but under circumstances existing already, given and transmitted from the past'.

The next section of this chapter picks up the focus on the political economy from the previous chapter and sets it more explicitly within discussions about the global economy. We then turn to a discussion about global social policy. Here the focus is on how the global simultaneously creates social problems that cut across national boundaries and also influences the types of response that social policies can make in terms of, for example, resourcing, design and implementation. The following section briefly explores debates and developments in relation to devolution in the UK, across the nation states and within England. We then turn our attention to England and the UK's relationship with the EU. Here we consider direct and indirect impacts of the EU and Brexit on social policy, alongside more general reflections about what England's relationship to the EU tells us about the social contract. The chapter then concludes.

Global economy

In this section we return to the political economy and how this functions at a global level. The unilateral termination of the Bretton Woods Agreement by US President Nixon in 1971 marked a significant step change in the functioning of the global economy. The agreement was put in place in 1944 and restricted the movement of international capital, which enabled governments to establish social contracts with businesses and workers (Sayer, 2016). The termination of the agreement weakened the potential (and in many cases desire) of national governments to pursue a redistributive social contract. Credit creation was liberalised and capital became much more mobile, empowering rentiers/investors to pursue the best returns across the world (Sayer, 2016). We return to these trends when discussing the 'race to the bottom' later in the chapter. For now, Jessop (2020) illustrates how capital has properties that favour 'ecological dominance' through a profit-oriented and market-mediated economic regime, which imprints its logic on other systems' operations more than any of these can impose their logics on that system. We should, though, recognise that these systems are self-organising and co-evolving and, therefore, one system is not unilaterally imposing its logic or will on others (Jessop, 2020, citing Morin, 1981). Nonetheless, globalisation fundamentally strengthened the hand of capital due to the enhanced opportunities of exit resulting from the reorganisation of production across borders (Schrecker, 2014, citing Hirschman, 1970). The expansion of credit supply led to states, corporations and later private households all becoming increasingly 'leveraged' with higher indebtedness across the board and to growing power for global finance given its control over credit (Streeck, 2016). At the same time, the World Bank, the IMF and the World Trade Organization provided a global infrastructure for strong neoliberal economic policies and, from the 1980s onwards, sought to impose these conditions on countries in receipt of their loans (Artaraz and Hill, 2016). Hemerijck (2016: vi) summarises the changing dynamics of the global economy as follows: 'Since the 1980s, ever-increasing world market interdependency, created by the liberalisation of international finance, the rise of emerging economies, and the concurrent process of deindustrialisation in advanced economies, undermined the weight and efficacy of domestic institutions of socioeconomic policy making.'

Alongside these developments, the agency inherent within the growing individualism in societies co-evolved. For example, Yamamura (2017) highlights the continued growth of consumerism into a world of 'necessary luxuries', which he argues has been fuelled by pro-investment policies based on supply-side economics geared towards making government ever smaller. The result is that many of us (particularly in the West) live as though our unrestrained desires can be met while those at the wrong end of inequalities often face economic or ecological ruin (Castellani, 2018). Crouch (2011) describes this as having the function of creating aggregate demand in the economy as a form of 'privatised Keynesianism', with private household debt fuelling this. More fundamentally, Sayer (2016) argues that luxury spending by the rich distorts economies through trumping the basic needs of people on lower incomes through, for example, diverting workers from providing goods and services for ordinary people to producing luxury goods for the rich. In this respect, Castellani (2018) stresses how socially constructed notions of economic greed and motivation (which take the form of competing individuals and groups seeking happiness, often at the expense of others) are promoted and legally sanctioned through the world capitalist system. Cope (2019) also highlights the ongoing transfer of wealth from the poorest to the richest nations as a result of the inequalities between nations in the global economy, asymmetric trade and investment treaties, pressure to adopt free-market policies and the extreme exploitation of workers in the global south. These relate to the path dependency of economic history and the interdependencies of global systems, which Sayer (2016) argues goes back centuries to include the consequences of colonial domination on the unequal exchanges and the considerable inequalities between the forces of production in supplying the West today.

Debt has grown in systemic significance in the global economy from an individual (for example, through conspicuous consumption and privatised Keynesianism) to global level (for example, compound interest of indebted nations). Berardi (2019) argues that this has contributed to transforming money from a measure of value to a tool for blackmail and psychic and social subjugation. This has ramifications across complex systems but is felt most strongly in terms of global inequalities. World Bank data from 2018 demonstrates that 68 of the world's poorest countries had accumulated $457 billion in public debt and many spend more on debt relief payments than on public spending in health, education and social protection (Oxfam, 2021). From the early 1990s onwards, the IMF has influenced capitalist democracies to reduce indebtedness through public spending cuts (Streeck, 2016). In recent years, there has been a softening of approach (see, for example, Crouch 2020), although it is also important to recognise that indebted nations increasingly owe money to private banks and financial institutions rather than multilateral institutions such as the IMF (Oxfam, 2021). Neoliberal ideologues frame government and household deficit as intrinsically reckless but ignore a key difference between the two as households use currency and sovereign governments issue them (Mitchell and Fazi, 2017). National governments have been somewhat complicit in enabling and embracing the economic orthodoxy that government deficit should be viewed in the same way as those of households. In this respect, rather than just responding to globalisation, nation states have played a key role in advancing it, even at the expense of reducing space for policy development (Schrecker, 2014). Consequently, there is more room for manoeuvre than can appear to be the case should states (and their publics) be willing to use it – at least in the very wealthy capitalist countries as many national governments have chosen to embrace neoliberal economic orthodoxy.

Regardless of the argument, both Streeck (2016) and Crouch (2020) are correct to highlight that a consequence has been that the global economy has moved the governance of the political economy beyond the reach of national politics and democracy. Mason (2019) characterises this as neoliberalism designing an economic system but not a geopolitical system to contain it, which according to Streeck (2016: 24) has led to states being 'located in markets, rather than markets in states'. As Streeck (2016) argues, global financialisation has a claim over public policy (given its control over credit), with the consequence of social policy being redefined as public provision for private competitiveness, recommodifying labour and focusing on educational and occupational achievement rather than social citizenship. Those on the ideological right argue that unions and minimum wage laws disrupt the operation of the free market and throw the system off course (Blakeley, 2020). Mitchell and Fazi (2017), Jessop (2018), Blakeley (2020) and Crouch (2020), for example, all highlight that global competition has led to a 'race to the bottom' in which countries seek to attract transnational corporations and free-floating capital, through lowering corporation tax, deregulating financial and labour markets, and cutting back on welfare state spending. A further aspect of these trends is that competition between places at different geographical scales takes precedence over inter-regional and social cohesion (Jessop, 2018). The nature of the global economy is, then, highly significant for the national, regional and local systems that are nested within it and the features described here act to constrain the 'possibility space' for social policy development. More fundamentally, the global economy limits the type of contract that can be negotiated between citizens and their governments within a broadly neoliberal space. The massive investment of public money relative to the COVID-19 pandemic and the 2007/08 financial crisis are both exceptions that prove the rule. They demonstrate the strength of the global financial system across these systems and the self-preserving tactics that maintain these while simultaneously contradicting (and being sufficiently powerful to be able to contradict) the logic they have applied to social and public systems.

The 2007/08 financial crisis provides an example of the interconnections across global financial capitalism and the far-reaching consequences of this for national and local political, social and economic systems. The crisis began in the sub-prime mortgage market and 'metastasised' into global financial and debt systems (Fox Gotham, 2009). Essentially, there was a huge loss of confidence in the financial system due to the widely accumulated debt dispersed across it. The global financial system is part of a complex global economy stretching within and spanning across societies via a network of relationships between large institutions (both public and private) through to individuals and public authorities across multiple jurisdictions (Oatley, 2019). The deregulation of banks and financial institutions across these networks was designed to remove the chains from enterprise and led to spiralling rises in asset prices in secondary markets and successive upward repricing of financial assets that were repetitively bought and sold (Crouch, 2020).[1] As Lefebvre (2003) argues, investment in the secondary circuit of capital led to speculation becoming the principal source of surplus value. The process of securitisation illustrates this well as relatively illiquid assets such as housing are transformed into liquid and interest-bearing securities for resale in global markets (Fox Gotham, 2009). As a result, the global economy increasingly relied on private debt for speculative investment, which became increasingly opaque across a complex and vast array of financial transactions based on derivatives, that is, financial markets derived from other forms of assets. Deregulation encouraged this kind of trading and not only contributed to the crisis but, given its role in wealth creation, has also produced widespread problems for democracy as firms have become too big to fail (Crouch, 2020). As Sayer (2016) makes clear, the crisis was a result not just of malignant growth in the financial sector but also of interactions between these and the 'real economy' (that is, the parts of the economy producing and distributing goods and services). The financial crisis of 2007/ 08 led to states absorbing the bad debt created by the private sector through financial deregulation (Streeck, 2016). As we have seen through the UK's approach to austerity, a large deficit was then viewed as bad by a neoliberal government, but in reality, it provided an opportunity to cut welfare spending and public investment and to sell off public assets, which provide income (economic rent) for private companies (Sayer, 2016). Streeck (2016) describes this as a process of 'fiscal consolidation' in which states devote themselves to reassuring financial markets that debt obligations are sacrosanct. Furthermore, Blakeley (2020), like many others (for example, Crouch 2011; Sayer, 2016; Christophers, 2018), questions how governments could afford to bail out banks and the financial sector (which had behaved so irresponsibly) but not provide free childcare, higher education, housing and healthcare. Ultimately, the crisis led to reduced living standards, an increased sense of insecurity, long-term damage to public services and inferior labour market conditions (Crouch, 2020). In short, the financial crisis provided a clear illustration of the ecological dominance of capital over global political, economic and social systems.

As we saw in the previous chapter, an inconsistent and selective application of its internal logic are inherent features of the neoliberal political economy and the massive investment of public money in response to the financial crisis provides a particularly salient example of these tendencies. The crisis was an opportunity to reconsider the role of capital in the global economy but it has been remarkably resilient (for a fuller discussion see, for example, Crouch, 2011; Sayer, 2016; Streeck, 2016). However, more recently the OECD, the IMF and the World Bank are increasingly acknowledging the limitations of neoliberalism and are changing their approach to inequality and redistributive taxation (Crouch, 2020). For example, the OECD (2019) has highlighted growing questioning of the economic benefits of economic globalisation among increasingly 'squeezed middle classes' in OECD countries. It demonstrates the 'dismal' income growth of the middle classes over the past 30 years not keeping pace with the costs of living, which alongside educational and health outcomes that relate to socioeconomic inequalities are undermining public trust in policy and institutions (OECD, 2019). Calls for fairer taxation systems are growing among multilateral organisations (OECD, 2019; IMF, 2021). In response to the COVID-19 pandemic, the IMF (2021) has gone as far as to express concern about rising polarisation, erosion of trust in government and social unrest, and is calling for increased taxes on the wealthy to provide everyone with a 'fair shot'. In short, the legitimacy of the global economy appears to be under threat and the established order is sufficiently worried to be considering a change in direction. The global consultancy firm McKinsey & Company has highlighted the need for a renewed focus on how economic risks are shared in societies with deep social and economic divisions and calls for a more interventionist role for governments in responding to these (Madgavkar et al, 2020). The extent to which these developments will lead to a lasting change in the direction of the global economy remains to be seen.

Global social policy

Artaraz and Hill (2016) highlight the significance of transnational companies over global policy given that more than half of the world's biggest economies are corporations rather than countries. They emphasise that global trade and investment has impacted on welfare through, for example, unemployment in deindustrialising countries and a 'race to the bottom' through governments reducing workers' rights, health and safety, pay and environmental standards in order to attract investment. Alongside this, the project of 'society' takes on a life of its own at a global level through, on the one hand, greater interconnectivity and, on the other, open conflict and profound disagreement over the extent to which we should embrace shared systemic struggles (Castellani, 2018). These create a challenging context and dynamics that Jessop (2020) argues the inherently pluralistic forms of global social governance provided through, for example, the UN (for example, UNESCO and UNICEF), the World Health Organization

(WHO) and the International Labour Office (ILO) struggle to coordinate across different scales and social fields (Jessop, 2020). The inherent complexity of the global and its non-linear dynamics and complex causal feedback across multiple scales of space and time mean that we lack a cognitive map of the socioeconomic system (Srnicek and Williams, 2016). Instead, Srnicek and Williams (2016) argue, there is a tendency to reduce complexity to a human scale, which is out of step with the actual mechanisms of power. In short, the global is highly complex and, as we saw in the previous section, there are powerful path dependencies skewed towards the neoliberal political economy that exert influence over social systems.

Climate change provides an example of a global problem that social policy is increasingly responding to (IPCC, 2014, 2021; Lancet Commissions, 2015). In England, policy has focused both on measures to reduce carbon emissions (for example, a Clean Air Strategy, a Green New Deal and plans for carbon neutrality) and on adapting to, and mitigating against, a changing climate. We will focus on the latter type of policy here through the example of extreme weather events, such as heatwaves, coldwaves and flooding, which are projected to become more frequent as a result of a changing climate (Oven et al, 2012). Successive climate change risk assessments (Department for Environment, Food and Rural Affairs, 2012; HM Government 2017) have identified health and social care services as being susceptible to extreme weather events. These events have caused serious disruption to, and increased demand on, service delivery, especially for 'vulnerable' populations in recent years (see Department for Environment, Food and Rural Affairs, 2014; Public Health England, 2015, 2016, 2018). There is a UK-wide duty, under the Civil Contingencies Act 2004, to warn and inform the public before, during and after an emergency (including extreme weather events). In England, the responsibility for extreme weather event preparedness planning in relation to health risks rested with Public Health England (for cold weather and heatwaves) and with the Environment Agency for flooding. Public Health England was an executive agency of the Department of Health and Social Care (Public Health England was replaced by UK Health Security Agency and Office for Health Improvement and Disparities on 1st April 2021) and published heatwave and cold weather plans (see, for example, PHE, 2018: 4), which set out to 'prepare for, alert people to, and prevent, the major avoidable effects on health during periods of severe heat in England'. This type of planning is expected to reduce some of the adverse health effects of extreme weather events (see, for example, Boyson et al, 2014; Huang et al, 2011; PHE, 2018) and offers guidance about a variety of actions to carry out to prepare for, and respond to, extreme weather events across a wide range of end users in local governance systems.

Despite the development of robust national plans with sound implementation advice, Wistow et al (2017) found that organisations can be reluctant to engage in, and take ownership of, this agenda at a local level and it can be difficult to identify where it 'best fits' within these systems. Senior adult social care managers questioned the capacity of frontline workers to embed preparedness planning in their working practices, given both resource constraints and the 'hundreds of agendas' that have some relevance for practitioners, arguing that they should be reactive rather than anticipatory (Wistow et al, 2017). Previous research (Abrahamson and Raine, 2009; Boyson et al, 2014) into the Heatwave Plan in England also found it to be a low priority among frontline staff and managers, which acted as a barrier to full policy implementation. However, both Public Health England (PHE, 2016, 2018) and the Lancet Commissions (2015) emphasise the need for advance preparedness planning as part of 'routine business'. For example, the Lancet Commissions' (2015: 20) review of the international literature argues that 'effective adaptation requires institutional collaboration across levels, integrated approaches, appropriate long-term funding, and institutions flexible enough to cope with changing circumstances and surprise'. However, in the context of public sector cuts and fragmentation to service delivery it is, perhaps, overly optimistic to expect a 'gold standard' of implementation for extreme weather event policy (Wistow et al, 2017). Capacity to respond to this agenda has been limited by the public sector workforce being at its lowest level for 40 years (Cribb et al, 2015) and a 29% reduction in local government real-term spending power between 2010–11 and 2019–20 (NAO, 2021). Burchardt et al (2020) cite Skills for Care (2020) workforce estimates to highlight that about one third of independent sector care workers were on the minimum wage in March 2019 (compared with one in six, three years earlier). A similar proportion of both local authority and independent sector social care workers were on zero-hours contracts and staff turnover in 2018/19 was 32%. The Social Care Institute for Excellence (SCIE) (2020) reports a growing concern about low morale, burnout and anxiety in the sector. In a society that has, in general terms, embraced the global 'race to the bottom', the social care workforce has certainly experienced its share of the consequences.

In the study by Wistow et al (2017), senior adult social care managers noted a shift to local authority staff 'carrying out assessments and providing support' but no longer having 'continuous engagement with vulnerable people', which now falls to providers and was a consequence of the Community Care Act 1991, implemented from 1993. Most recently the Care Act 2014 sets out that local authorities are responsible for commissioning care, mostly from independent providers (NAO, 2021). There are now 14,800 registered providers of care across 25,800 locations in England (NAO, 2021). There are two important consequences of this that both occur within the logic of contracting out services to secure economic efficiencies and thereby remove 'redundant' capacity from social care systems. First, as Crouch

(2020) argues, the contracting out of services leads to public authorities losing the knowledge and expertise that is needed to run these services, with implications for state capacity not only to deliver services but also to hold those running them to account. Second, partnership working crossing institutional boundaries faces difficulties in mutually coordinating across distinctive logics (Jessop, 2020). All of these trends led Wistow et al (2017) to conclude that local policy seeking to embed emergency preparedness planning was being developed in a context that was sub-optimal for developing the resilience of these systems to emergency events.

The COVID-19 crisis represents another example of a global problem with national and local social policy ramifications. At the global level the Independent Panel on Pandemic Preparedness and Response (2021) concluded that preparedness for the COVID-19 pandemic was inconsistent and underfunded, that there were weak links at every point in the chain and the WHO was under-powered. Globally there has been a lack of capacity and mechanisms to coordinate responses to the pandemic effectively. Here, though, I want to continue the example of emergency and preparedness planning and focus on what the events of the early stages of the pandemic demonstrate about local health and social care systems, from the 'entry point' (after Jessop, 2016) of social care homes in England, in particular. Exercise Cygnus took place between 18 and 20 October 2016 and was delivered by Public Health England on behalf of the Department of Health (the Department of Health became the Department of Health and Social Care in January 2018) and was designed to assess the UK's preparedness and response to a pandemic influenza outbreak (PHE, 2017). Across the nexus, 950 people took part in the exercise, which highlighted the complexity of response required across multi-agency working for pandemic influenza planning and the need for a central repository of information and overview of response (PHE, 2017). At the time of the exercise there was: evidence of silo planning between and within organisations; no overview of the pandemic response and procedures; and variable understanding of response arrangements (PHE, 2017). The exercise also drew attention to the limited understanding of, and therefore assumptions about, how the public would react to a pandemic. Finally, the review also identified the demand for services outstripping the capacity of local responders, including social care and the NHS. In particular, local responders were concerned about the expectations on the social care system to provide the level of support needed if the NHS implemented its plans to move patients from hospitals to social care facilities (PHE, 2017).

Between 17 March and 15 April 2020, approximately 25,000 people were discharged, untested for COVID-19, from hospitals into care homes, which is particularly concerning given the knowledge about the high levels of vulnerability of this population to the virus (Amnesty International, 2020).

In total, 18,500 residents of care homes died from COVID-19 between 2 March and 12 June 2020 (40% of total deaths) and there were a further 28,000 excess deaths in this period, which is 46% higher than the annual average (Amnesty International, 2020). These figures reveal not only the exceptional vulnerability of the 400,000 residents of care homes (Amnesty International, 2020) but also something about the nature of the social contract and the position of adult social care (and of the generally older people it serves) within the complex systems cutting across social policy and the political economy. The mantra from the government to 'protect the NHS' stemmed from concerns about the capacity of hospitals to respond to demand but is also revealing about system priorities. Indeed, the absence of an equivalent concern for social care within the system appears to have contributed to some devastating consequences. SCIE (2020) has reported that those working in social care felt it was not a priority and support for funding was insufficient and slow to arrive. Years of underfunding had left the sector without the equipment and estates necessary to manage the crisis and contain the spread (SCIE, 2020). Amnesty International (2020: 6) concludes that some government decisions were 'heedless' and others were 'inexplicable' and ultimately 'exponentially increasing the risk of transmission to the very population most at risk of severe death and illness from disease. With no access to testing, severe shortages of PPE, insufficient staff, and limited guidance, care homes were overwhelmed.' Meanwhile SCIE (2020) emphasised the size, fragmentation and complexity of the social care sector as posing practical and logistical challenges in coordinating responses. More generally, the British Medical Association (BMA) has concluded that:

> the fragmentation of the health system and subsequent underinvestment in the NHS and public health services in England, as well as a longer-term trend towards increasing outsourcing of NHS support activities, have been significant factors in limiting the Westminster government's ability to mount a coordinated response during the public health emergency. (BMA, 2020: 1)

Similarly, Vizard et al (2021) highlight the erosion of the healthcare system's resilience in the past ten years, with capacity in both health and social care services to cope with increases in demand through adverse health shocks being of particular concern.

The COVID-19 crisis and extreme weather events draw attention to the capacity of local governance systems to respond to global social policy problems. The global political economy's turn towards neoliberalism has both reduced the capacity and enhanced the complexities of health and social care systems to respond to these. Rather than freeing up individual agency (as those advocating for neoliberal reforms of the state argue), individual behaviours are increasingly constrained as a function of both the nature and the capacity of health and social care systems in England. These systems sit within a multi-scalar and tangled system that is more complex than any state, political or social entity can understand and its evolution lies beyond the control of a state or its society (Jessop, 2020). The complexities of multi-sector governance systems highlight the significance of interrelationships between different types of infrastructures (social, organisational, economic, physical and technical), which should be viewed as a 'nexus' ('system of systems') or 'resource network' (Curtis et al, 2018). The best option in these circumstances is to recognise that many policy agendas and priorities overlap (for example, ageing, social isolation, cold/hot homes and place-based planning) and that emergency planning that responds to global policy problems such as the COVID-19 pandemic and extreme weather events can be integrated alongside these, rather than creating a separate policy workstream. Making this a reality (that is, embedding resilience) across the governance systems as presently configured, after 40 years of neoliberal reform driven by the logic of securing economic efficiency, is no doubt an uphill struggle and an example of contextual conditions making the task of social policy (in this case, emergency and preparedness planning policy) that much harder.

Devolution

Devolution relates to the delegation of powers from a sovereign state to the sub-national level and is geared towards providing mechanisms to respond to local needs closer to the level they are expressed or felt. As highlighted in Chapter 1, the devolution settlement that started in earnest after the election of the 1997 New Labour government has led to the establishment of legislatures in Scotland, Wales and Northern Ireland, which took on powers previously held by Westminster. There are now distinct trajectories of social policy development in each of these countries that has led to the focus of the book being on England within the UK, as opposed to the UK as a whole. In this section we shall briefly explore devolution within the UK and then move on to consider devolution within England. It is important to recognise that this has taken place within a growing sense of fatalism and anxiety about Britishness, following the abandonment of the empire and relative economic decline from the 1950s onwards (Gamble, 2003) and the economic dislocation resulting from the rapid shift to a post-industrial economy in the 1980s and 1990s (Kenny, 2015).

Scotland has the most advanced form of devolved government in the UK, with control of nearly half its spending, including on health, education and policing, and the power to amend income tax and a wide range of legislative responsibilities (Hutton, 2015). It is also the part of the UK most likely to leave the union, with 45% voting for independence in the 2014 Scottish referendum. Since the 2016 referendum on EU membership (in which 62% of the Scottish electorate voted to remain), polling on independence has overwhelmingly reported a majority wanting to leave the UK. The UK-wide social contract is, therefore, most under threat in Scotland and the powers to control large areas of social policy have not sated the appetite for greater national control of its affairs. The demand in Wales and Northern Ireland is less extensive (albeit with very strong historic claims for a united Ireland). Nevertheless, after exiting the EU the Westminster-led union is more under threat than at any point in living memory. The actions of the UK government in replacing and reinterpreting arrangements between the devolved nations and the EU have played a significant role here, with all devolved government being critical (to varying degrees) of the handling of the process of exiting the EU. For example, the Scottish Government (2021) highlights an increasing disregard for the Sewell Convention (a constitutional rule based on the notion that the UK Parliament should not legislate over devolved affairs or adjust devolved competencies without the consent of the Scottish Parliament). In particular, it raises strong concerns about the implication of the UK Single Market Act 2020, for a loss of powers in relation to, for example, spending replacement funding for the EU's Structural Funds, and over powers to regulate food products in line with its obesity policy (Scottish Government, 2021). More generally, the possibility of independence for any of these nations focuses attention on the make-up of the English, as opposed to UK, social contract. In this respect, the devolved nations have historically played a role in tipping the balance of power away from the natural party of government in the UK, the Conservative Party, although mainly in terms of reducing the size of the majority for the government in general elections. England is more Conservative than the UK as a whole and during my lifetime (which coincides with the shift to neoliberalism) there have been 11 general elections and in only two of these (1997 and 2001) have the Conservative Party not had the highest proportion of votes in England (Cracknell and Pilling, 2021)[2]. Given the Conservative Party's emphasis on individual responsibility and maintaining the social order as it is currently configured, developing an English consensus for a radically redistributive social contract is, therefore, more challenging than doing so for the UK as a whole. Instead, Kenny (2015) highlights the influence of Roger Scrutton's critique of the liberal political elite's contempt for English heritage and his characterisation of England at the mercy of globalisation, immigration and Europeanisation. As Kenny (2015) argues, this has been influential over the Conservative Party, not least through responding to the emergence of the United Kingdom Independence Party (UKIP).

The UK and England are highly centralised as a political economy and in terms of social policy development. We will explore the over-centralisation of economic, social, political and administrative systems and the implications for geographic disparities in the social contract in the next chapter. For now, Jessop's (2020) argument that top-down command places excessive demands on prior centralised knowledge and accurate anticipation of likely interactions with other systems is salient to discussions about devolution in England. Until 2012, regions provided an administrative tier for social (through Government Offices) and economic (through regional development agencies) policy organisation in England. Although these lacked direct democratic accountabilities and, compared with other nations, did not provide strong regional development strategies in England (Martin, 2010; Crisp et al, 2019; UK2070 Commission, 2020), they did include some devolution of powers and provided a linking governance mechanism between central and local states. In their place, local enterprise partnerships have emerged and provide sub-regional governance in city-regions. Some city-regions such as London, in particular, and Greater Manchester have more devolved powers than others in what has become a somewhat piecemeal approach to devolution at the sub-regional level. Despite variable capacity within, and demand placed on, the welfare state at regional, local and neighbourhood levels (Warren and Wistow, 2017) and the lack of strategic regional governance being a barrier to economic growth (UK2070 Commission, 2020), it is striking that there is not more demand for devolved articulations of the social contract in England. In this respect, Hutton (2015) is right to emphasise that the lack of trust in government appears to correspond with a lack of demand for constitutional reform. It is, though, worth noting that the COVID-19 pandemic has led to enhanced calls for localism with 'metro mayors', in particular, enhancing their standing. The limitations and/or failures in the centralised system to respond to the diversity of interactions in complex systems have become more visible during the crisis, which may provide the impetus for growing demands for greater regional and local autonomy.

Turning to local government, in the post-war welfare state a significant role was established for local authorities in planning, place-shaping and the delivery of education, housing and social services (Newman, 2014). Councils were largely 'sovereign' in terms of service delivery responsibilities and local democratic legitimacy (Barnett et al, 2021), although it is important to recognise that this did not lead to socialism through municipal collective action, not least because utilities such as water and electricity and services such as health were nationalised (Newman, 2014). However, Leach et al (2018) argue that over the past 40 years, there has been a profound shift in the balance of power away from local and towards central government. The onset of neoliberalism and NPM (described in the previous chapter) took a large toll on local government through the introduction of mechanisms such as compulsory competitive tendering for services previously delivered by local government and, in particular, in social care. As we shall see in

Chapter 4, local government's role in housing development and provision is much reduced through the Right to Buy Scheme and the transfer of remaining housing stock to housing associations. Similarly, since the Thatcher years, education has increasingly moved away from local authority control. From above, central government exerted more control through the national curriculum and central attainment tests and, from below, schools were devolved more powers to manage themselves through head teachers and governing bodies (Alcock with May, 2014). These developments were tied to the notion of choice and competition within local education as a means to improve standards across the board and, therefore, reflect the philosophy of the broader political economy in social policy development. By the time I was working in local government in the early 2000s it was clear that the local level of government was struggling to assert its authority within local governance systems that had become highly complex and fragmented. This contributed to reduced democratic accountability within these systems and by association has led to a decline in the legitimacy of the local state. As Barnett et al (2021) demonstrate, responsibilities have been 'hollowed out' to the extent that councils are now one provider among many and face difficulty maintaining strategic oversight on key services. The growing complexity in governing and governance stems from, and is intensified by, the increased diversity of partners involved in service provision in neoliberal governance systems, generating new non-linear dynamics and fragmentation resulting from increased plurality of self-organising actors. These are 'path dependent' as the strategic selectivities of the local (in particular) state are structurally inscribed within the neoliberal redrawing of boundaries between state and non-state actors that have reduced the authority of the state, while shaping the opportunities for reorganising specific structures and strategies (Jessop, 2015). In short, neoliberal government policy has reduced its own service delivery capacity to a minimum, while preferring to contract out organisational activities (Hill and Hupe, 2014).

These trends weaken transparency, accountability and democracy at the local level, which undermines the potential for the local state to pursue common interests and strengthen social ties at this level. Devolving more power could enable local government to make a fuller contribution to the social contract but, as Tomaney (2016) highlights, implementing devolution during austerity leads to decisions about cuts to services and, without limitations, to competition between places. Localities are embedded in national and global systems (Byrne, 2019b) and their histories and path dependencies determine how favourably aligned they are with these and, therefore, the extent to which socioeconomic conditions such as labour markets and levels of deprivation shape, influence and affect those charged with the implementation and delivery of policy at different levels within welfare states (Warren and Wistow, 2017). Gray and Barford (2018) argue that austerity has changed the relationship between the central and local state, increasing territorial injustice and inequity, with citizens' access to public services becoming increasingly dependent on the local tax base, leading to poorer places providing fewer public services and having less basic infrastructure. Jones (2019) argues that in this context the localisation of welfare is a national state project, as aspects of social policy have been transferred from (collective) public to (individual) private spheres, which takes place in localities. In the early days of the coalition government there was a focus on the 'Big Society' as a form of localism. The Coalition Agreement (Cabinet Office, 2010) outlined three core components: empowering communities, opening up public services and promoting social action. The agenda was criticised for paying very little attention to the types of power inequalities generated around social and economic inequalities in society (see, for example, ACEVO, 2011; Dorling, 2011; Corbett and Walker, 2013). This type of approach is consistent with Nozick's (1974) view that social justice cannot be achieved through essentially redistributive means and is, therefore, contrary to Rousseau's concern with equality. As Grimshaw and Rubery (2012) argued at the time, austerity and the Big Society led to a departure from nationally implemented minimum standards. The approach to localism took place alongside the coalition government's 'northern powerhouse' agenda and the current Conservative government's 'levelling up' agenda, both of which are vague and ad hoc in their approach to systematically levelling the playing field. In contrast, Crisp et al (2019) propose an alternative approach to central–local funding, allocated relative to need and economic disparities in place. This chimes with Marmot's (2015) focus on proportionate universalism, and would provide a basis for ending austerity and rebuilding the economy and society relative to spatial inequalities after the COVID-19 crisis. Indeed, the UK2070 Commission (2020) has argued for a £375 billion 25-year fund to provide the resources to 'level up' and that this should take place together with the necessary fiscal and strategic powers for devolution. In so doing, a meaningful role would be provided to local government that would help revitalise the local arm of democracy to identify, respond to and build common interests, and strengthen social ties from the local level up.

England and the EU

This book has been written over a period in which the UK struggled to exit the EU. Brexit became both a national obsession and something that far exceeded a large proportion of the population's interest. The vote and subsequent fallout from this represent a rare occurrence in which the justification for the state through the consent of individuals has come under significant and prolonged attention. Indeed, Jessop (2017, 2018) considers

Brexit to be a symptom of the ongoing crisis of the British state and society and highlights the significance of the polarisation of wealth and income, alongside uneven spatial development of parts of the economy through variable integration into internationalised financial capital. Similarly, Telford and Wistow's (2020: 553) research on Teesside draws attention to 'how leave voters rooted their decision in a localised experience of neoliberalism's slow-motion social dislocation linked to the deindustrialisation of the area and the failure of political parties, particularly the Labour Party, to speak for regional or working-class interests'. In this respect, we can see how large-scale systemic problems occur in local communities but should not be reduced to this level of analysis, as doing so denies the interconnected nature of the social world (Srnicek and Williams, 2016).

Before we consider Brexit and the nature of the social contract, we will briefly consider the implications of leaving the EU on social policy and wider social and economic prospects. Artaraz and Hill (2016) argue that the EU stands out as an international body given its aspirations to make *supranational* policy and the consequences of a single (labour) market for social rights across boundaries. The *acquis communautaire* effectively provide an accumulation of social policies that have to be adopted by new member states and lead to cross-national cooperation extending beyond trade relations into labour conditions, health, safety, environmental standards and cultural and scientific activities (Crouch, 2020). However, Artaraz and Hill (2016) argue that despite the 1992 Maastricht and 2000 Lisbon treaties, the focus of the EU remains principally on employment rights and the social policy areas of health, social security, education and so on remain largely national policy concerns. In short, England and the UK had a large degree of discretion over social policy as a member of the EU. The process of Brexit has, in itself, been time-consuming and distracting, which has extended beyond public debate into the functioning of government and social policy design and delivery. For example, in the short term, at least £4.4 billion was spent by government departments on preparations to exit the EU between June 2016 and January 2020, with a peak of 22,000 staff at any one time taking part in this (NAO, 2020b). Stewart et al (2019) also emphasise the impact of Brexit on the capacity to develop policy as ministerial and Civil Service time has been taken up elsewhere, highlighting the problematic rollout of Universal Credit as a prime example of policy development and implementation that has suffered as a consequence of this. In the longer term, likely reductions in the number of EU migrants will have much greater consequences in terms of lost contributions in service delivery and taxation than potential gains from reduced demands placed on services and costs of benefits (Stewart et al, 2019). More generally, Stewart et al (2019) argue that the evidence points to lower economic growth under all Brexit scenarios, which will lower living standards and lead to less money for public services.

There are, nonetheless, good reasons to question the legitimacy of a social contract that includes membership of the EU, not least in terms of the 'democratic deficit' associated with a large bureaucracy, weak parliament and the influence of the European Commission and the European Central Bank (ECB) over member states. More specifically, the nature of the EU's political economy has seen convergence towards a neoliberal financialised capitalism and one-size-fits-all monetary regime (Streeck, 2016). Varoufakis (2017) highlights the limited room for manoeuvre this has created through the impact of the 'Troika' of the European Commission, the ECB and the IMF over the Greek (and wider European) debt crises, which emerged from the global financial crisis of 2007/08. A series of strict austerity measures was imposed on Greece and other (largely southern) EU member states, emphasising the relative power of global and supranational economic interests over national and local social interests. Crouch (2020) highlights the post-democratic tendencies of the EU in its alignment in the Troika and, specifically, in relation to presenting the Italian parliament with the choice of an unelected technocratic government under Monti's leadership, between 2011 and 2013, or receiving no help out of the crisis. Streeck (2016: 162) too considers the EU to be post-democratic and also focuses on the ECB withholding liquidity from states refusing to 'follow its precepts as to their public finances, the size and composition of their public sectors, and even the structure of their wage-setting systems'. The UK, of course, remained outside of the European Monetary Union (EMU) and, therefore, avoided the ECB's direct influence over social policy. However, through the austerity programme of the coalition and Conservative governments there has been a good deal of policy alignment through national government decisions (which, it is again worth noting, as a demonstration of the make-up of the social contract, were democratically ratified in the 2010, 2015, 2017 and 2019 general elections). More generally, while Brexit allows for more state intervention in the economy, enabling, for example, the nationalisation of railways and targeted industrial subsidies, the UK had a history of being less willing to intervene in these areas than other member states while it was a member of the EU (Stewart et al, 2019). Streeck's (2016) overarching criticism of the EU is that extending democracy to the scale of markets has not worked as European integration alongside globalisation and financialisation have weakened the former and strengthened the latter. In these circumstances, Streeck (2016) argues that markets need to be brought back to the scale of democracy and, as we have seen in the earlier section on the global economy, Mitchell and Fazi (2017) emphasise the untapped potential power of sovereign-currency-issuing governments.

Brexit was a positional issue concerned with values, personal conviction and identity (Hay, 2020). In this respect, the political leadership (for example, Boris Johnson, Nigel Farage, Jacob Rees-Mogg, Michael Gove and Steve Baker) of those playing an active role in the campaigns to leave the EU is striking and (at the time of writing) has strengthened the right-wing, conservative and neoliberal hold over the social contract and the trajectory of society (albeit with the complicating factor of the response to the COVID-19 pandemic thrown into the mix). Given the wider sense of loss and resignation motivating working-class voters in places such as Teesside and the opportunity the EU referendum provided to vote for genuine change (Telford and Wistow, 2020), opposing Brexit has placed the political left and the moderate social democratic side of this, in particular, in a very difficult position. The uncertainty and ambiguity over the terms on which the UK would leave the EU further complicated the politics of Brexit and was the basis of much heated debate among the political and media establishment. However, the 2019 general election result decisively supported Boris Johnson's central commitment to 'get Brexit done' as leader of the Conservative Party. The extent to which this represents a new cleavage in the social contract or a continuation of the drift away from the Labour Party since the historic high point of the 1997 general election is open to debate. It does, however, strongly reaffirm the position of the Conservative Party as the default party of government in England and the UK.

More fundamentally, the global nature of social problems (for example, climate change, global pandemics and refugee crises) requires some form of cooperation and metagovernance to respond to them effectively. The fact is that the UK (and to a greater extent English) public did not consider, on balance, that the EU was the correct mechanism to respond to them; were not sufficiently interested in or motivated about the problems to want to join a global response; or, as Telford and Wistow (2020) argue, took a unique opportunity to voice their dissatisfaction with the dominant social, cultural and political hegemon in contemporary England; or there was a combination of these factors at play. Brexit can, therefore, be interpreted, at least in part, as a 'complex social psychological' reaction to globalisation and global civil society and to the social commitments and responsibilities required through greater interdependence (Castellani, 2018). The disconnect between politicians and the public (and working classes in particular) found expression in the Brexit vote, which raises significant questions about how centrist and left-leaning politicians can regain trust. As Telford and Wistow (2020) argue, a good starting point is to demonstrate that they are more than self-interested and are willing to challenge, rather than preserve, the status quo. In this respect, Brexit may well be viewed historically as a firm underlining of the trajectory of the social contract in England towards individualism, or as the beginning of a wake-up call to the political left to organise around and sell a more optimistic vision of collectivism, redistribution and equality.

Conclusion

In this chapter we have explored the significance of the global economy for social policy developments. There is debate about the extent to which Western capitalist democracies have been complicit in the development of this but less debate about the consequences. For example, Jessop (2020) claims that ultimately the internationalisation of the economy has undermined the faith in nation-states' capacity to govern the 'unstructured complexity' of the economy, which poses coordination problems relative to inter-scalar and inter-systemic dependencies. A contractual perspective questions 'the deal' citizens receive across these systems and scales and spotlights the role of global economic institutions and processes here. There are growing concerns about the legitimacy of the global economy to deliver. For example, the OECD (2019) describes a situation in which opportunities for social mobility are declining, automation is likely to enhance labour market uncertainty and prospects for children to experience the same living standards as their parents are declining, which are combining to create a growing perception that the current socioeconomic system is unfair. Streeck (2016) demonstrates that long-term trends in the global economy include declining rates of growth in the OECD, rising indebtedness and growing economic inequality, alongside cuts in public investment, which strangles government policy discretion and delegitimises social policies. These are a reflection of the social contract developing across the most privileged societies and for the increasingly constrained 'possibility space' for social policy to interact with and shape the social contract. Throughout this chapter the significance of the nature of the global economy has been highlighted as providing a form of 'ecological dominance' (after Jessop, 2020) over multi-scalar complex systems. We have seen how the global 'race to the bottom' has left health and social care systems fragmented and without sufficient capacity to fully embed resilience. This is not so much an issue of policy design but of the capacity and nature of systems to integrate and implement policy agendas, which are not routinely part of 'core business'.

The notion of devolution raises questions about the highly centralised nature of the social contract in England and the weakening of the local state and democracy through successive neoliberal reforms. Greater devolution of powers and resources, taking into account disparities in need and local economies, could provide a strong platform to enhance the responsiveness and accountability of the state to its citizens. As we shall see, in subsequent chapters, the current system produces, and responds to, inequalities in social outcomes in ways that should raise fundamental questions about the way things are run. Where this issue seems to have come to a head was around the vote to leave the EU and the fact that it represented genuine change in the way things are done. However, despite its faults the EU is not the primary target we should have in our sights. Instead, Jessop's (2020) argument about the ecological dominance of capital provides the basis to focus our attention on the complex interactions and causal processes embedded across policy systems and the social contract. The legitimacy of global capital is left much more wanting in this respect, given its influence over these systems, compared with the EU. Global capital is obviously much more diffuse, despite the existence of global institutions (including the EU) that tend to work towards enhancing the position of economic over social relations through broadly neoliberal economic policy. A more tangible focus for our attention is what Castellani (2018: 217) describes as the 'revolting elite' of the world's economic top 20%, which are disproportionately spatially concentrated in the richer economies and are seeking to pull away from the rest of the working and lower-income masses. These distributional, positional and relational issues are central to debates about the role of social policy to develop equitable outcomes in systems geared towards competition but rigged in favour of those who have secured the benefits of hierarchical status.

4

Place: uneven geographies and spatial inequalities

Introduction

Place plays a significant role in influencing the lives of individuals across society and is an important factor for exploring and understanding the social contract and the extent to which this can be considered to be mutually beneficial from a geographical standpoint. As Martin (2015: 245) demonstrates, significant spatial variations have implications not just in terms of inequalities but also for equity:

> [I]ndividuals should not be seriously and systematically socially disadvantaged with respect to job opportunities, housing conditions, health, access to public services and the like, simply by virtue of living in one region than another. We know that areas which persistently suffer from low wages, inferior employment opportunities and job insecurity tend to have lower rates of educational attainment, higher rates of child poverty, ill health and crime, and lower life expectancy, than areas with high incomes and more favourable labour markets, and that such conditions can become self-reproducing over time.

There is a large body of research highlighting the interrelationship between globalisation, neoliberalism and deindustrialisation for growing spatial inequalities and imbalances in England (see, for example, Massey, 1991; Martin, 2010; Beatty and Fothergill, 2016b, 2017; Byrne and Ruane, 2017). As we will see, the political economy, and the influence of neoliberalism over this, has failed to ensure an equitable distribution of opportunities and outcomes within the social contract that is profoundly spatial in nature. The uneven regional and local socioeconomic trajectories of places (see Martin, 2010) have a particular characteristic in England, with implications for the size and nature of the tasks facing social policy. Massey (1991) suggests that national structural changes involve geographical restructuring, leading to different parts of the country experiencing highly contrasting trajectories of change. In exploring these trajectories, we will return to the nature of the English political economy and consider this in relation to the spatial distribution of power, wealth, resources, infrastructure and social outcomes in the country. Particular focus will be paid to the privileged position of London within the political economy and the influence it exerts over both social policy (including design, bureaucracy and decision making) and the social contract. The next section explores the economic and social disparities that exist in England and the following section considers these from a regional perspective.[1] The subsequent section focuses on land and housing as two spatial policy systems that have a particular role in embedding inequality and individualism in the social contract. The chapter then concludes.

London, the cause of and solution to all our problems

Since the mid-19th century, there has been a longstanding spatial imbalance in the national political economy, with London dominating (albeit fluctuating to a greater or lesser extent) the map of relative prosperity in England (Martin, 2015). In this section we will explore the influence of London over this trajectory as a systemic feature of the social contract and the complex systems that cut across it. As Martin (2015) demonstrates, policy interventions to rebalance the spatial economy, such as the Barlow Commission of 1940, made the case for deliberate government intervention to redistribute economic activity away from London and had a major influence on post-war regional policy, coinciding with a decline in the regional economic imbalance between London and the rest of the country. Since then, regional imbalances have grown again (as measured by GDP) and Martin (2015) concludes that these are greater now than at any time in the UK's modern industrial history. Furthermore, the UK is the most regionally unequal country in the developed world (Raikes, 2020) and the most centralised major developed economy (UK2070 Commission, 2020). London's metropolitan population of 14,187,146 in 2017 is larger than the combined population of the eight other metropolitan areas in England with populations of more than a million (Eurostat figures from 2018). In England there has been an obsession with economic growth concentrated around agglomeration (effectively spatial imbalance) (Martin, 2015) and it is not surprising, therefore, that London and the South East of England (home to a third of England's population) has accounted for almost half (47%) of the country's increase in jobs in the past decade (Raikes, 2020). In short, the sheer size of London would be a factor in the regional spatial disparities we explore in more detail in the next section but this is far from the full story of its influence over the political economy and the social contract.

London's power as an international finance centre includes the ability to reinvent itself (Hall and Wojcik, 2021). Jessop (2018), for example, highlights both the City of London's deep historic roots as the leading international finance centre and its changing nature with domestic banks and financial institutions ceding primacy to international finance. London is one of the three world financial centres that are supported by specialist accountants and lawyers, making it one of the easiest places in the world to do takeovers, trade shares and buy and sell property (Davis, 2018). Indeed, London's financial services infrastructure and property market are key attractions for overseas oligarchs. For example, the Intelligence and Security Committee of Parliament's (2020: para 50) report on Russia highlights both the 'ideal mechanisms by which illicit finance could be recycled' through the London 'laundromat' and how money has been 'invested in extending patronage and building influence across a wide sphere of the British establishment'. The City of London broadcasts its role in the British economy, highlighting that there are 360,000 banking jobs, £31 billion in direct tax revenue and a £60 billion financial trade surplus (Shaxson, 2018). However, Sayer (2016: 226) argues that the financial sector has damaged the economy through encouraging the switch from investment in productive use to speculation and rent-seeking, while being 'highly active in helping clients to avoid tax; in so doing it has taken fat commissions for reducing the state's income'. Despite its privileged position, the financial sector accounted for just 6.5% of employment and provided 6.8% of government tax receipts compared with manufacturing's 13.4% (Sayer, 2016). Baker et al (2019) estimate that £4,500 billion of lost growth occurred between 1995 and 2015 in the UK due to a reliance on finance. They describe this as a 'finance curse', arguing that the economy would have performed better if we had less finance and if finance was focused on supporting the economy rather than being used to extract wealth. Instead, economic and government policy has benefited the producer and rentier interests located in London and the South East (Jessop, 2018).

To illustrate London's contribution to wealth extraction in the UK's political economy, Shaxson (2018) provides the example of Strathclyde Police Training and Recruitment Centre, built by Beatty Balfour in 2002 under a Private Finance Initiative (PFI). He does so by quoting Boris Johnson, when he was Mayor of London in 2012, stating that 'a pound spent in Croydon is of far more value to the country from a strict utilitarian calculus than a pound spent in Strathclyde'. In this example, the training centre cost between £17 million and £18 million to build but the flow of payments to the PFI consortium will add up to £112 million between 2001 and 2026, through a 'complex pipework' of money flowing from police budgets in Scotland through international financialised pipelines into the City and South East and offshore (Shaxson, 2018). Shaxson (2018), therefore, concludes that Johnson had it exactly back to front and cites this as an example of Massey's description of the 'colonial relationship' between parts of London and the rest of the country. Hodge and Greve (2018) describe PFIs as long-term complex contracts that act as a governing regime, which Jessop (2020) frames within market competition as a mode of governance that is both lacking in transparency and accountability and tends to subordinate social activities to the logic of profit-oriented and market-mediated competition. In the UK, PFI projects had an estimated total capital value of about £60 billion in

2017 but taxpayers will ultimately spend more than £300 billion on these, with approximately £240 billion of public money being extracted through the London-focused financialised pipeline (Shaxson, 2018). London, which hosts many of the powerful interests in the political economy, therefore plays a significant role in the extraction of public money to private interests. In effect, capacity is being removed from the system that might otherwise be used to tackle regional economic and social disparities through investment in, for example, infrastructure, jobs, the environment and services.

There was a time when the UK had a regional banking system and stock markets, and local authorities raised the bulk of their finances locally, but now all three are controlled from London (Martin, 2015). Only 3% of revenues are collected sub-nationally in the UK and 35% of expenditure is allocated to this level, in comparison with 33% and 60%, respectively, across the OECD (OECD, 2017). The UK2070 Commission (2020) argues that centrally defined decisions have the tendency to be place-blind and, in England, are dependent on eroded local capacity. As Martin (2015: 261) concludes, 'state spending and the national policy-making apparatus are London-based and London-centric'. The Treasury provides a good example of an overly powerful and centralised body (Hutton, 2015). For example, Crisp et al (2019) highlight how the design and use of Treasury assessment criteria for transport infrastructure spend pinpoint time savings as the basis for investment. They argue that this is geared to reducing congestion for the highly paid workers in and around London rather than tilting 'infrastructure spending towards where it unlocks new opportunities for development' (Crisp et al, 2019: 24). The inward focus of politicians, the media and the Civil Service on London and the 'Westminster village', in particular, is a feature of a system in which, for example, Tony Blair and David Cameron, as Prime Ministers, came to spend more time with big funders, media moguls and campaign experts in the 'exclusive parts of the Westminster village' than with their own MPs and supporters (Davis, 2018: 31). Research by the Centre for Cities suggests that the feeling among cities and regions outside London is that their conditions and needs are not taken into account in the highly London-centric national politics and policy making (Wilcox et al, 2014). However, whether there is sufficient demand for a radical shift towards stronger local or regional articulations of the social contract in England is debatable. As we will see in the next section, there is certainly a strong basis for regions and localities to question the efficacy and equity of the outcomes of the highly centralised configuration of the social contract as it functions currently.

I do not want to give the impression that living in London guarantees a good deal out of society. Concern about inequalities and the circumstances of people living in poverty has been a prominent feature of public life in London since at least the 19th century and patterns of poverty have persisted through the years, despite a multitude of social and regeneration programmes (Travers et al, 2016). Rapid increases in house prices are a new driver of inequality in London, especially in inner London, further inflating wealth disparities, pushing private renters into poverty and suburbanising poverty (Travers et al, 2016). Between 2016–17 and 2018–19, London had both the highest poverty rate (28.2%) and the highest proportion of households in the top 10% of the income distribution (15.7%), after household costs (AHC), as a region (Agrawal and Phillips, 2020). However, the flip-side of this is that between 2006–08 and 2016–18, mean household and financial wealth in London increased by 150% compared with an average of 50% for Great Britain, and mean household wealth in London was £560,000, compared with £278,000 for Great Britain, in 2016–18 (Agrawal and Phillips, 2020). Indeed, the cost of housing is both a measure of the wealth held in London and the costs of living in the capital. It acts as a barrier to moving to London, especially for people from poorer social economic backgrounds, to access the labour market opportunities concentrated there (see, for example, Friedman and Laurison, 2019; SMC, 2019). As Davis (2018) argues, those who are most able to take advantage of global networks are those who gain most and Friedman and Laurison (2019) equate the ability to move to the capital to the privileged sorting into higher-paying occupations and larger firms. London is much less deprived than the rest of England as measured by the Index of Multiple Deprivation (IMD) and there has been a reduction (between 2015 and 2019) in the proportion of neighbourhoods that are highly deprived in London (MHCLG, 2019). The number of neighbourhoods – measured in terms of Lower Layer Super Output Areas (LSOAs) – in London among the most deprived 5% in England is just eight out of a total of 4,835 LSOAs (or 0.2% of London's LSOAs), which only increases by a further 2% (an additional 99 LSOAs) in England's most deprived 10% of neighbourhoods.

One factor in the reduction of deprivation is that London is a significant site of state-led gentrification of council estates whereby poorer people and affordable housing have been displaced for affluent newcomers and profit-seeking (Lees, 2014; Broughton, 2019). For example, Balfour Tower (a Grade II listed block of flats) was sold into private ownership by Tower Hamlets Council at a time when 23,500 people were on the social housing waiting list and 1,500 people were officially homeless in the borough (Broughton, 2019). By decanting the residents from the flats, Broughton (2019: 234) argues that this provides 'an example of council housing seemingly judged too good for poorer local citizens for whom it was originally built'. Similarly, Christophers (2018) highlights the evictions of tenants in Sweets Way (a former council housing estate) in the London Borough of Barnet as an example of Smithian economic rentierism and Polanyian social dystopia, with private owners exploiting land for profit rather than sustaining the communities depending on it. The owners (a private equity firm called Terra

Firma) received much public criticism but as Christophers (2018: 312) points out, once the property was acquired from (and sold by) government, the eviction of 'low value tenants' was entirely predictable; 'it is the economically "rational" use of a resource whose commodification is socially irrational'. As Christophers (2018) concludes, we should criticise the system and that takes more than criticising market actors for behaving as market actors. In other words, this example is symptomatic of the wider-system failure to prioritise social rights over individual (economic) rights. The selective application of free-market economics in a competitive but highly unequal playing field provides those people and places with greater resources and power with a competitive advantage over those lacking similar resources.

The UK2070 Commission (2020: 22) quotes the Prime Minister, Boris Johnson, as saying: '[W]e no longer accept that your life chance ... should depend on which part of the country you grow up in.' However, the power and centrality of London within the social contract, as a global city and key node in global financial (neoliberal) capitalism, *and* its dominant position across national, political, administrative (and to a lesser extent) cultural systems, need to be addressed in order to achieve the Prime Minister's aim. In short, systems are rigged or geared towards London's needs because of its position within the nexus. Jenkins (2019) goes so far as to state that 'an iron law of modern British government says that whatever London wants, London gets'. It may be better to think of this not as an 'iron law' but rather as a principle, tendency and/or bias cutting across different systems geared towards 'whatever London wants, London gets', which, in turn, creates feedback into the types of social problems that emerge across the country and has influence over the design and capacity of policy responses to these. As Martin (2015) concludes, it would be:

'stretching credulity' to suggest that the concentration of finance, corporate and political power and institutions in London had no role in the growth or persistence in the spatial economic imbalance between the north and south of the country. These recursive circular and cumulative forces have themselves become institutionalised and embedded in a national political economy that is spatially concentrated in and controlled from London and help to explain regional differences in the UK.

It is to these regional differences that we turn, in the next section.

Regional disparities

We have seen that London provides the location for one of the most centralised national political and economic systems in the OECD and is central to the New Economic Geography (NEG) that has shaped regional economic policy in recent decades (see, for example, Martin, 2015; Crisp et al, 2019). It is also the recipient of vast sums of public expenditures on infrastructure, transport, education, health services and major cultural institutions, therefore, to argue, as some do, that the economic activity in London is 'market driven' is quite misleading (Martin, 2015). As Jessop (2018) asserts, the combined impact of macroeconomic policies, microeconomic measures and government investment projects favouring London and the South East have regional implications, particularly when the decline and closure of traditional industries have not been replaced with new sectors and where public services have been cut. Some regions were structured around the regional differentiation of dominant industries (for example, Clydeside and ships and heavy engineering, the North East and export coal, iron and steel, ships and heavy engineering), which exposed them to changes in the UK economy and the new international divisions of labour in the global economy (Massey, 1979: 235). As Massey (1979: 235) states, 'sectoral decline brought regional decline'. Indeed, Agrawal and Phillips (2020) highlight that many places are still living with the legacy of deindustrialisation and the large increase in inequalities that took place in the last quarter of the 20th century. This is central to the path dependency of place in England and for the complex systems that are located within the regions and the localities situated in these. Just over a decade into the neoliberal 'phase shift' in the political economy and society, Massey (1991: 268) concluded that 'among the significant changes under way in British society, some of the most important ones were geographical. There was a spatial restructuring as an integral part of the social and economic. The economies of the big manufacturing cities went into severe decline. The bases of heavy-industry regions were undermined.'

Employment in manufacturing industries in the UK reduced from 8.9 million jobs in 1966 to just 2.9 million 50 years later, destroying the economic base of many communities (Beatty and Fothergill, 2016b). As Warren et al (2021) state, the world's first industrial society is now a post-industrial society, and although the UK is an extreme, it stands as an example of a global process and of the economic, social and cultural impact of deindustrialisation. In very general terms, 'laissez-faire' has enabled the City to thrive in a deregulated and international environment but failed to respond to the challenge of deindustrialisation (Jessop, 2018). Schrecker and Bambra (2015: 46–7) highlight the extent to which this has been prioritised through quoting Norman Lamont (then Chancellor of the Exchequer) as stating in 1991: 'rising unemployment and the recession have been the price that we have had to pay to get inflation down. This price is well worth paying'; and Eddie George (then Governor of the Bank of England) as saying in 1998: 'northern unemployment is an acceptable price to pay for curbing southern inflation'. New Labour developed a stronger focus on regions and regeneration but did not go far enough to reverse the trajectory of the previous 20 years. In fact, Martin (2010) demonstrates that regional inequalities in GDP per head grew during its time in office and Byrne and Ruane (2017) highlight the failure of 'left parties' to address the 'absolutely recursive' causal processes of deindustrialisation, which weakened the organised working class and, thereby, weakened their social and political base. The 2019 general election result and the Conservatives' breakthrough in the 'red wall' of traditional Labour-voting constituencies provide a strong recent example of this tendency.

As we have seen in the previous section, England is one of the most centralised and regionally unequal countries in comparably developed economies. In their review of the health of the nation, Marmot et al (2020a) provide an overview of the range of regional, local and neighbourhood inequalities between 2010 and 2020. Regional inequalities in this period included: inequalities in wealth increased, with London and the south of England increasing their share of national wealth compared with the north of England; average household wealth was 2.6 times higher in South East England than in the North East; and from 2010, London became the richest region in northern Europe but over the period of the review the UK also contained six of the ten poorest regions, making the UK Europe's most geographically unequal economy (Marmot et al, 2020a). Raikes et al (2019) also highlight that the UK has the highest regional inequality in terms of productivity and disposable income of any OECD country. At a lower level of spatial aggregation, Marmot et al (2020a) draw attention to:

- progress around child development in readiness for school but, despite this, a clear graded relationship with socioeconomic inequalities and area deprivation;
- these inequalities tending to increase by deprivation decile through primary and into secondary schools; and
- much higher rates of violent crime associated with higher area deprivation – for example in 2016/17, 26.2 people experienced violent crime per 1,000 people in the most deprived areas compared with 15.3 per 1,000 people in the least deprived areas.

We will explore the spatial nature of health inequalities in the next chapter but, for now, Raikes et al (2019) conclude that the UK is one of the most regionally unequal countries in terms of age-adjusted mortality in the OECD, while Marmot et al (2020a: 49) state that 'the shifts in funding away from more deprived areas, low-income families and the North over the past decade have significant implications for health inequalities and for inequalities in a range of other outcomes throughout life'.

The UK2070 Commission (2020) sums up regional policy as 70 years of policies that have either directly or indirectly sought to ensure minimum standards of living across income and work, education, health and housing, but without addressing the deep-rooted systemic issues dividing the regions and nations of the UK. In other words, there is a well-established trajectory of dealing with the symptoms rather than the causes of regional disparities in England. In this respect, Byrne and Ruane (2017) draw attention to two important features of the tax and benefit regime that have developed since the 1970s (and been intensified in recent years): first, the (gradual at first) introduction of tax credits to subsidise low wages in a flexible labour market; and second, the conditionality around benefits for those not actively seeking to work on a full-time basis. They conclude that 'the benefits regimes govern the lives of the precariously employed to a degree far beyond that which prevailed in the era of Keynesian regulation' (Byrne and Ruane, 2017: 29). The reliance on these types of benefits to compensate for the failure of the labour market and political economy to provide adequate standards of living has become a key feature of the post-industrial social contract in England and has a profoundly spatial character. Beatty and Fothergill (2016b: 2) sum this up well by arguing that:

> The Treasury has misdiagnosed high welfare spending as the result of inadequate work incentives and has too often blamed individuals for their own predicament, whereas in fact a large part of the bill is rooted in job destruction extending back decades. The welfare reforms implemented since 2010, and strengthened since the 2015 general election, hit the poorest places hardest. In effect, communities in older industrial Britain are being meted out punishment in the form of welfare cuts for the destruction wrought to their industrial base.

Beatty and Fothergill's (2016a, 2016b, 2017, 2018) research has identified how welfare reform impacted unequally across the country, with older industrial areas, less prosperous seaside towns and some London boroughs being hit hardest, and other parts of London and southern England escaping lightly. This corroborates the trend identified by Pearce (2013) during the early stage of austerity, and later supported by Gray and Barford (2018) and Marmot et al (2020a, 2020b), that in general the areas most in need and with the highest levels of deprivation have been hit hardest by austerity measures.

Table 4.1 provides an aggregate of the spend per head in pounds for each of the English regions between 2013–14 and 2018–19, for the four nations of the UK and for the UK as a whole. Over this period, London received the highest total public expenditure on services per head at an average of £10,131, with the North East and the North West of England the only other areas receiving an above-England average spend per head. What the

Table 4.1: Average public expenditure per head between 2013–14 and 2018–19 (£)

	General public services	Public order and safety	Economic affairs	Environment protection	Housing and community amenities	Health	Recreation, culture and religion	Education	Social protection	Total expenditure on services
North East	86	476	615	122	168	2,297	108	1,328	4,489	9,689
North West	77	450	614	376	102	2,256	103	1,262	4,254	9,492
Yorkshire and the Humber	69	420	589	121	144	2,065	105	1,315	4,005	8,835
East Midlands	86	376	516	108	120	1,890	87	1,256	3,862	8,302
West Midlands	86	397	572	107	120	2,134	89	1,315	4,029	8,848
East	98	345	608	159	109	1,887	81	1,250	3,695	8,214
London	91	662	1,097	127	243	2,626	143	1,518	3,624	10,131
South East	106	338	612	130	108	1,893	88	1,215	3,594	8,085
South West	92	339	560	162	95	1,957	85	1,163	4,035	8,488
England	89	429	669	163	136	2,122	100	1,297	3,842	8,897
Scotland	211	489	1,118	234	323	2,276	201	1,490	4,260	10,602
Wales	166	425	805	210	223	2,192	165	1,339	4,608	10,134
Northern Ireland	213	678	886	141	403	2,234	259	1,460	4,833	11,107
UK	106	441	719	170	163	2,141	116	1,320	3,983	9,158

Source: Author's calculations from HM Treasury (2019)

table starkly illustrates is a real difference in the type of spending across the regions. For example, the spending on economic affairs in London was nearly double that of any other region in England. Here we see how a political economy centred on London uses state spending to continue to embed and support the functioning of capital in the capital, as the central hub of the nexus. At the same time, the powerful financial institutions and organisations overwhelmingly based there and which rely on publicly funded infrastructure to protect and enhance their privileged position in the global and national economy are generally (but selectively) antagonistic towards state intervention in market economies. Titmuss' notion of welfare as a partial compensation for the allocation of disbenefits or social costs provides a useful framing for a geographical understanding of how the state, political economy and social contract interact across complex systems. The high spending on social protection, in particular, in the regions of England that relied most on industry (the North East, the North West, Yorkshire and the Humber, and the West Midlands) and in the South West provides an example of how the system is geared towards meeting these social costs. It does so in a wider context in which the fortunes of the less well-off have declined dramatically (UN Special Rapporteur, 2019), where spending on economic development (per head) in less prosperous regions should be much higher in order to rebalance the economy (see, for example, Beatty and Fothergill, 2016a; Crisp et al, 2019; UK2070 Commission, 2020), and where action needs to be taken to improve the coherence, powers and fairness in England's sub-national governance (Hunter, 2017; Raikes and Giovannini, 2019; Raikes et al, 2019).

High Speed 2 (HS2) provides an example of the approach to economic development in England. It is a planned high-speed rail line linking London to the West Midlands, in phase one, and then to Leeds and Manchester in the second phase. While the line does link into the existing high-speed network, it does not improve the network north of Leeds or Manchester. Tomaney and Marques (2013) argue that it has commonly been referred to by government as contributing to a 'rebalancing' of the economy and helping to bridge the north–south divide. The HS2 website (in 2021) goes as far as to state: 'HS2 is the most important economic regeneration project in decades. It will act as a catalyst for growth and help level-up the country, boosting growth in the Midlands and North.' There are serious doubts about whether it will do this. The project was originally expected to cost £37.5 billion and is now expected to cost at least £78.4 billion.[2] This is a major investment of public money, especially at a time of austerity and regressive per-capita spending in the more deprived areas with the greatest need (Harris et al, 2019). Questions about whether this is the best, or even a good, use of public money have persisted throughout the project development, but despite spiralling costs it remains live. We might interpret HS2 as an example of the wider trend towards what Crisp et al (2019) describe as a longstanding and almost ideological faith in the benefits of 'agglomeration' and 'trickle down' resulting from this. First, Tomaney and Marques (2013) argue that the evidence base is at best ambiguous and at worst negative in terms of the potential of HS2 to rebalance regional economies. Second, Tomaney and Marques (2013) also highlight that the theoretical and empirical evidence base suggests that intra-urban and interregional transport systems may provide more benefits. In short, we do not need another link to London as a priority. As Raikes (2019) argues, the transport network in the north of England has let down its people and economy for decades, across five major cities, 265 towns and about 1,000 villages and, therefore, requires significant investment. Instead, transport investment in London is 2.6 times higher per head than in the north and two times higher than for England as a whole (Raikes, 2018).

More generally, the coalition government launched the 'northern powerhouse' agenda (HM Treasury, 2016: 5) as a 'vision for joining up the North's great towns, cities and counties'. The strategy document (HM Treasury, 2016) was very thin and short on detail, it did not clearly define the 'north' and does very little to bring the north up to the pace of London and the South East, let alone close these gaps. Under Boris Johnson's leadership, the Conservatives have moved to talking about 'levelling up' the country. At the time of writing, this agenda is still vague but does, at least, appear to be more ambitious. The UK2070 Commission (2020) has argued that the success of the levelling-up agenda must be measured against performance indicators for outcomes and not activities, in order to secure long-term thinking. It is also calling for a £375 billion 25-year 'New Deal' recovery strategy to create a resilient and connected economy as part of the response to the COVID-19 pandemic, while arguing that this be used to empower local leaders to take action through a full devolution settlement. The UK2070 Commission (2020: 6) states that we need a genuine transfer of fiscal and political powers as 'our extreme centralisation inhibits national economic growth and productivity, erodes the capacity for local action and for innovation and flexibility'. Crisp et al (2019) emphasise that local and regional development requires:

- infrastructure;
- business investment and enterprise, encouraged by public financial support where necessary;
- a skilled workforce;
- a supportive business environment;
- a growing national economy; and
- exchange and interests rates that encourage trade and investment.

Crisp et al (2019) propose creating a National Investment Bank to provide long-term support for business and technological innovation, and funding proportionately less prosperous economies. They recommend a £250 billion fund to be spent over 10 years and, based on Gross Value Added (GVA) per head, calculate that the proportionate allocation of funding per head (with the UK = 100) to the less prosperous regions of England should be: North East 129; Yorkshire and the Humber 116; West Midlands 113; East Midlands 111; North West 109; South West 102; East 99; South East 84; and London 54. This kind of approach takes into account the longstanding trajectory and path dependencies of regional disparities in the UK. It could also provide the basis for an overarching rationale for regional economic development that is based on proportionality and redistribution, in order to address the allocation of disbenefits relative to progress.

Land and housing

Having discussed a key organisational (and spatially significant) node in the nexus of English policy systems and the regional disparities that in part flow from this, we will now explore the organisation of space in relation to land and housing. For the former I will draw on Christophers' (2018) book, *The new enclosure: The appropriation of public land in neoliberal Britain*, and for the latter on Broughton's (2019) *Municipal dreams: The rise and fall of council housing*. These books provide excellent critical overviews of the trajectories of two spatial policy systems, within the broader political economy and social contract.

Land

In 2017, the ONS published details of UK net worth by type for 2016. More than half (£5 trillion) of the total UK net worth is land, a further £3.5 trillion is made up of buildings on land and just £1.26 trillion (or 13%) is comprised of other forms of wealth (Christophers, 2018). Therefore, as Christophers (2018) concludes, there is not too much of value, proportionately, in the UK aside from land and property. Land ownership is highly material to capitalist and social and economic development, with, for example, *accumulated capital* in land being passed down over generations, across individual families (Christophers, 2018). The implications for social policy are clear, given that land is an important mechanism for locking wealth and advantage into families, which in turn, intersect with debates about equality of opportunity relative to equality of condition and the wide range of social outcomes arising from the extent of inequalities in these. The ownership of land also has significance for our day-to-day lives, or lived experience. Land matters as it provides a foundation for people's lives – through, for example, shelter, work, mobility, play and protest – and, therefore, who owns land matters too as they have the ability to determine how it is accessed, used, and by whom (Christophers, 2018). These issues are fundamental to the social contract and can be illustrated through two important tendencies and trajectories in the ownership of land that are relevant to social policy: rent and privatisation.

Land by its nature is a largely finite commodity as it cannot be easily produced and, therefore, tends to be owned by a minority, with landowners charging rent for the use of their land (Sayer, 2016). As Sayer (2016: 50) explains, 'a person who derives unearned income from ownership of existing assets or resources is known in political economy as a *rentier*'. In the late nineteenth and early twentieth century Veblen considered economic rent to be the excess price over the real productive cost for access to natural resources, bank credit and other basic needs and, therefore, is unearned income. As Sayer (2016) highlights, during the infancy of modern taxation, Adam Smith, Thomas Paine and John Stuart Mill thought it obvious that unearned income for rent should be the first thing to tax, whereas modern governments would rather tax earned income than unearned income. That this is essentially ingrained within the social contract shows just how embedded self-interest and *freedom from* intervention (from a position of high and growing inequalities) have become in England. Christophers (2018) argues a land tax would make the British land market more efficient (because landowners would have less of an incentive to hold onto and not use land, while its value grows) and secure gains for society of increases in land valuation. Sayer (2016) makes the case for increased state ownership of land as, in theory, the unearned income derived from this would go to the state and be distributed via democratic means, or if privately owned the rent could be taxed. The argument of both Christophers (2018) and Sayer (2016) is for a more direct role for the state in representing public interests and challenging property rights in order to protect and support those currently being exploited and ripped off by those using property to extract rent. This is an example of why the nature of the political economy is a first-order issue relative to social policy. Redistributive policy that would both reduce damaging inequalities in wealth and help to change the direction of the political economy and social contract would also make the job of social policy in areas such as affordable housing, social mobility and health inequalities, for example, much more responsive to policy interventions through tackling underlying inequalities. As Sayer (2016) concludes, we need not only to tax the rich and redistribute wealth but also to cut back on their unearned income, which means stopping private owners from extracting rent.

For Christophers (2018), the privatisation of public land, which he considers nothing short of a project concentrated primarily at Whitehall to shrink Britain's public estate, has helped turn Britain into a rentier capitalist economy and contributed to widespread social dislocation. He (2018), alongside Fevre (2016) and Sayer (2016) all draw attention to Adam Smith's (1776) argument in the *Wealth of nations* that increased private ownership of land leads to the increased significance of renting as a distorting economic phenomenon.[3] Meanwhile advocates of land privatisation (across right-of-centre media, think tanks, politicians and neoliberal academics) argue that it delivers houses, jobs and growth, and they contrast this with the planning system and state bureaucracy, which they say are not capable of providing enough land for the private sector to do its job (Christophers, 2018). As we have seen in Chapter 2, the advocates of privatisation have been very successful in employing this narrative, with nearly half of public land privatised in the 1980s alone. However, Christophers (2018) concludes that the private sector does not lack land, land that is suitable for development or planning permission to develop land, given that about a half of all planning permissions in England remained unimplemented between 2006 and 2014. Instead, land hoarding by the private sector takes place in order to 'drip feed' homes into the market to maximise sale price and keep supply below demand so developers can make money through market speculation (see, Lund, 2016; Christophers, 2018). Nevertheless, Barnett et al (2021) argue that, since 2010, planning has been viewed as a regulatory burden by government and that policy and legislation have weakened local government controls over development. Land banking or hoarding, therefore, not only is a distorting economic phenomenon but also has consequences across the nexus as, for example, the capacity of the local state to use land for social and public purposes is reduced and the cost of land relative to the cost of housing continues to grow at a time when affordable housing is a significant issue for many in society. As Christophers (2018) argues, we cannot expect socially and economically beneficial outcomes to result from releasing land to the private sector; instead, this process has led to the people of England being distanced – economically, socially and politically (just as they were in the 18th and 19th centuries) – from the land they inhabit.

As we saw in the previous chapter, the secondary circuit of capital accumulation (that is, capitalised investment in land, real estate, housing and the built environment) grew in significance from the 1980s onwards (Fox Gotham, 2009). Byrne (2019) argues that this has been expressed through planning decisions in the form of industrial destruction and the transfer of these sites for residential and commercial uses and then the transfer of social housing away from direct democratic local authority control. A key act, and one of the first, by the 1979 Thatcher government was to terminate the use of Redundant Lands and Accommodation, which provided local authorities with the first opportunity to develop this land prior to the private sector having an opportunity to purchase it (Christophers, 2018). Not only is this significant in terms of curtailing local government's (and by association local democracy's) role in place-shaping, it also signals part of the shift in the logic of the system towards economic notions of efficiency and profit at the expense of public and social goals. Furthermore, Lund (2016) points out that land ownership in the UK is obscure and highlights that the 2014 Lyons Committee argued that the lack of transparency and data about ownership, options and transactions were holding back the operation of the land market. Christophers (2018) states that this goes against the Hayekian notion of the market as an information processor. Not only is this an example of the inconsistencies in the application of neoliberal market economics but also it has further ramifications for the effective governance of the system. For example, Christophers (2018) cites the Government Office for Science's (2010: 27) *Foresight land use futures project: Final report*, as concluding that 'much urban land is now managed by a range of quasi-public, private or market-led management and delivery mechanisms. These sit alongside the local authority planning mechanisms, and, are not easily coordinated.'

The development of 'green belts' provides a further example of the dynamics of land politics. Successive governments (especially Conservative ones) have sought to contain, or 'fence in', urban expansion through the designation of 'green belts' around urban areas (Lund, 2016). In 1955, the process of designating green belts started leading to high-density accommodation in inner cities and an escalation in land prices (Lund, 2016). Between 1979 and 1997, green belts more than doubled in size as the result of Conservative government policy (Lund, 2016). However, in England only about 10% of land is built on (which includes green spaces such as gardens, allotments, parks and sports pitches) (Christophers, 2018). Christophers (2018), therefore, argues that this puts the notion of the public sector not freeing up surplus land in the cities into context and highlights the effectiveness of the green (countryside) lobby in (over)emphasising the threat to green space.

Housing

Turning now to housing and we will focus on changes to council and social housing relative to the ideological shift that has taken place in the social contract. We return to housing and wealth in Chapters 6 and 7 in relation to social mobility and the generational contract. After the Second World War, both Labour and the Conservatives entered into a 'numbers game' over progress in housebuilding (Lund, 2016). Broughton (2019) identifies ideological differences between the parties as, broadly speaking, Labour saw council housing serving a cross-section of society, whereas the Conservatives saw it as housing for people in poverty. The Labour government's Housing (Homeless Persons) Act 1977 marked a turning point towards 'residualisation' in housing policy. Broughton (2019) highlights that through placing a statutory duty on local authorities to rehouse vulnerable groups with priority needs, the unintended consequence was to increasingly reserve council housing for the least well-off in society, as, at best, a social service for people in need and, at worst, as housing of last resort. More recently, Slater (2018) highlights the influence of a 2010 report by free-market think tank Policy Exchange called *Making housing affordable* (Policy Exchange, 2010) over the coalition government's housing policy. The report contends that social housing makes tenants unhappy, poor, unemployed and welfare dependent, which Slater (2018) argues is a reversal of the causation established in the academic literature, that is, that poverty and need lead to people seeking social housing. As Broughton (2019: 288) states, despite making a huge contribution towards meeting housing needs and providing nearly all those who lived in them secure and decent homes, 'the form and nature of council housing has been unfairly blamed for problems entrenched in our unequal society and exacerbated by the politics which reflect it'. Furthermore, council housing has come under threat due to the general political allegiance of its occupants. For example, Minton (2019) cites Stone's (2016) account of Nick Clegg (Liberal Democrat leader and Deputy Prime Minister in the 2010–15 coalition government) describing how plans for more social housing were blocked by senior Conservatives because 'they just create Labour voters'. Slater (2018), Broughton (2019) and Minton (2019) all argue that council housing was (and still is) intentionally stigmatised as 'ghettos of deprivation' and 'sink estates' in order to undermine the place of social housing within spatial social policy.

Lund (2016) highlights that, between 1951 and 1979, on average 324,000 new houses were constructed per year, with 48% of these in the social sector, which he argues demonstrates that the public sector can deliver when it is willing to use the levers of the national and local state. Consequently, when Thatcher came to power there was not a shortage or crisis in housing and council housing catered for about a third of the population, the majority of whom were in work (Minton, 2019). However, by the late 1970s, council housing was increasingly seen as limiting choice and personal consumption, shielding tenants from the discipline and ambition of the market and, therefore, impeding the efficient and beneficial operation of the market (Broughton, 2019). In this respect, council housing was associated with the wrong kind of accountability for the times, that is, to democratically elected local government and tenant associations, rather than to the market (Broughton, 2019). The right to buy council housing (which had existed in various forms prior to this) was massively accelerated in this context. Under the Housing Act 1980, council tenants who had rented their property for at least three years were given the 'right to buy' their home, with the Environment Secretary given the means to intervene against councils resisting sales (Broughton, 2019). Although the right to buy had been used by Conservative councils as far back as the 1920s (Broughton, 2019), the

1980 Act was decisive in making this an individual right to buy one's home, rather than an obligation for local authorities to sell to their tenants (Lund, 2016). Discounts of between 33% and 50% (depending on the length of the tenancy) and up to £50,000 were applied to the purchase price, enabling Thatcher's ideal of a property-owning democracy (Broughton, 2019). In 1978–79, 79,160 new council homes were started, but by 1996–97 it was just 400; 1.8 million council homes were sold by 1997; and council housing reduced from 31% of the total stock to about a fifth (Broughton, 2019). Owner occupation increased from 55% of households in 1980 to 67% in 1997, central government subsidy to council house maintenance construction fell by over 40% over the course of the 1980s and homelessness rose from 76,342 people to 178,867 in the same period (Broughton, 2019).

The right to buy was designed to transfer wealth to the less well-off and was popular and arguably the most important privatisation of the past 40 years (Minton, 2019). The policy represents an ideological shift in the social contract and is an example of where social policy can be very successful when it aligns with, as opposed to seeking to counter the flow of, the direction of the political economy. Broughton (2019: 171–2) argues that the right to buy marked a shift from 'society, [which] through its agent the state, had the duty to ensure all its citizens were decently housed … [to] the case of the now ascendant New Right *against* council housing [which] was in some respects equally simple: that it offended the efficient and beneficial operations of the free market'. These changes corresponded with, and reinforced, the growing individualism in society and reduced the role and capacity of the local state in the collective provision of social housing. In this context, there remain good examples of state activity, with Broughton (2019) highlighting the Decent Homes Programme as something New Labour should take credit for as it brought about 1.4 million homes up to a decent standard at the cost of £22 billion, improving the lives of millions of people. However, the near halving of public land ownership (60% of this coming from the local government estate), often at below market value, and the right to buy (explicitly below market value) represent state-led policies (Christophers, 2018) that have made a significant contribution towards the trajectory of the social contract. The shortage of housing and increasing costs of this (which we explore in Chapter 7) are consequences of the actions of the state in interaction with the political economy and individual preferences for wealth creation centred on housing markets. As Christophers (2018) argues, Whitehall could introduce measures to require housebuilding to take place within a specified time period as a condition of sale of public land and introduce a scheme to compensate public bodies for selling under market value. That it does not is a further example of the selective use of levers and legislation at the disposal of the neoliberal state.

Buy-to-let mortgages were introduced in 1996 and accelerated the sales of former council housing to the extent that about 40% of council homes sold under the right to buy in England were being rented out privately by 2016 (Minton, 2019). Byrne (2019) identifies that privately rented housing is typically rented at twice the rent charged by social housing and Minton (2019) highlights that they are three times the rent of social housing in London, on average. The increase in rented housing costs contributed to a near doubling of the housing benefit bill between 2005 and 2016 (Minton, 2019) and across Britain housing benefit costs are estimated to be £1,000 higher per year for the private rented sector than for social housing (Christophers, 2018). Nearly one million working households were in receipt of housing benefits in 2017 and 3.2 million working households (around a quarter of households containing a worker) in 2015–16 were in receipt of some form of cash assistance on a means-tested basis (Byrne, 2019). As Marmot et al (2020a) argue, increasing costs of private renting have led not only to increased arrears for renters (about a fifth of people who are reliant on benefits fall into arrears, with Universal Credit slow to respond to changing circumstances and when people lose work) but also to record incomes for private landlords, fuelled by a growing number of private renters receiving Housing Benefit. Christophers (2018) cites an *Observer* article from 2014, which claims that 20 times as much is spent through the state subsidising buy-to-let private landlords through housing benefits as the state spends on affordable housing. Again, this is an example of the role of the welfare state (after Titmuss) as a partial compensation for the costs some people bear for the progress of others. That neoliberalism is so complicit in this is all the more damning when we consider what the subsidised market produces. The private rental sector has grown at a remarkable rate in recent years but the product falls far short of expectations as one in three properties are considered 'non-decent' on official measures and one in six are physically unsafe (Citizens Advice, 2015). Citizens Advice (2015) argues that private renters pay more for these homes than those in other tenures and estimates that in 2012 £5.6 billion was paid to private landlords for unsafe homes, of which £1.3 billion was paid by the state in the form of Housing Benefit.

Marmot et al (2020a) demonstrate that the number of households living in temporary accommodation increased by 74% between 2010 and 2019 and the number of people sleeping rough almost tripled between 2010 and 2017. Minority ethnic households are disproportionately likely to face homelessness and new migrant groups are overwhelmingly concentrated in private rented housing and, therefore, face vulnerability to housing precarity (Shankley and Finney, 2020). As we have seen earlier in this chapter, housing and place are very important for the kinds of conditions we live in and for the opportunities that exist within these. Social outcomes have a strong relationship with place, from the national through to the neighbourhood level, and housing is a key mechanism for locating people in place relative to inequality of condition, opportunity and outcomes. We will explore these issues both explicitly and implicitly throughout Chapters 5 to 7, across health and health inequalities, social mobility and the intergenerational contract. For now, we can conclude by making the claim that the housing market and social policy are failing to deliver optimal outcomes for large sections of society. The significance of housing and how this interacts with organisational, social and cultural factors to create a degree of path dependency in terms of the wider conditions and opportunities people experience can be illustrated through consideration of ethnicity. Shankley and Finney (2020: 149) argue that 'ethnic inequalities in housing stem from the particular settlement experiences of postwar migrants to the UK in terms of the location and housing access afforded to them'. In this respect, Broughton (2019) highlights the institutional racism in council housing allocation to people from minority ethnic backgrounds. This is an example of the wider British nationalism underpinned by a shared allegiance to 'whiteness' held by the British state, employers and workers (Virdee, 2019). Bonilla-Silva's (1997: 469) concept of 'racialised social systems' draws attention to the ways 'in which economic, political, social and ideological levels are partially structured by the placement of actors in racial categories or races'. The allocation of housing can be seen as central to what Bonilla-Silva (1997) describes as the inferior position and life chances of people from minority ethnic groups. In short, place in interaction with racialised social systems limits opportunities open to people in the social order. While neighbourhoods have become more mixed in recent years, with segregation across minority ethnic groups decreasing (Shankley et al, 2020), there are, nevertheless, stark and persistent inequalities in housing, and changes to the housing landscape in recent decades have exacerbated the disadvantages faced by many minority ethnic groups (Shankley and Finney, 2020). The Race Audit 2017 (Cabinet Office, 2017) reported that Black and Asian households are most likely to be poor and in persistent poverty and that Black, Pakistani and Bangladeshi people are most likely to live in areas of deprivation. About one in ten Black, Pakistani, Bangladeshi and mixed background people are unemployed compared with one in twenty-five White British people (Cabinet Office, 2017).

Conclusion

The UK's (and England's) uneven geographical development is a 'cumulative consequence' of choices and events that set places on different paths of development and of regions' and cities' relationship to the differentiating processes that have transformed the economy over time (Martin, 2015). The nature of the political economy plays an important role in shaping the trajectories of spatial development. Since the 1980s there has been a greater shift to the City of London as the heart of establishment power in which neoliberalism and self-interest have been the dominant driving principles (Davis, 2018). As Crisp et al (2019: 9) conclude, 'the changing structure of the UK economy has concentrated businesses and jobs in some parts of the country but destroyed the economic base of others'. At the same time, NEG has exerted considerable influence over policy makers, through the view that spatial agglomeration is a 'natural' market-driven process, and that spatial imbalance is an 'equilibrium outcome' (Martin, 2015). The argument being developed throughout this book is that neoliberalism exerts ecological dominance but it does so selectively. We have seen in this chapter that the logic of NEG has overridden that of neoliberalism at times and does so generally when it favours, or protects, the interests of financial capitalism concentrated in London. In this respect the co-evolution of neoliberalism and NEG is embedded in the spatial social contract through the concentration of wealth and power in the nexus in London. However, this logic is applied selectively in neoliberalism across economic sectors, which is significant for the nature of spatial imbalances in England. On the one hand, the logic of limited state intervention in market economics is clear through, for example, the deregulation of the City of London and the extremely limited response of successive governments to processes of deindustrialisation. On the other hand, the use of vast sums of public money to bail out the banking and financial sectors and the higher investment of public money per head to enhance economic affairs in the capital are highly inconsistent with the logic that any form of state intervention disturbs the natural functioning of the market. This inconsistency leads to significant inequities in the spatial foundation of the social contract, which as we have seen produces an uneven landscape for social outcomes and social policy development and response.

There are further inconsistencies and selectivities of neoliberalism that operate at a much more micro level of spatial analysis but are no less significant for this. First, the privatisation of 'surplus' public land and the notion of a home-owning democracy align with a reduced role for the state and individuals being freed up to pursue their goals through the market. However, we have also seen that there is a substantial role for the state in subsidising housing costs produced via the market through benefits, while the private sector is seemingly immune from the pressures to sell off surplus land from which it derives unearned income. Christophers (2018) summarises this very well by arguing that discourse about surplus is both political and performative as it shapes political-economic futures. In Jessop's (2015) terms, 'path dependent' strategic selectivities of the local (in particular) state are structurally inscribed within the neoliberal redrawing of boundaries between state and non-state actors that have reduced the authority of the state, while shaping the opportunities for reorganising specific structures and strategies. We have seen that the Barlow Commission led to regional economic policy that reduced regional spatial imbalances. The state and social policy can, therefore, play an important role in spatial policy but much has changed since the Barlow Commission and, as we have seen in this chapter and those preceding it, the capacity and nature of the state are not what they were and need considerable investment and powers at regional, local and neighbourhood levels to begin to respond effectively to inequalities and needs at different levels of aggregation. At the same time as the disinvestment in public services and infrastructure, the notions of individual responsibility and choice have grown. Blackman (2006) argues that the more unequal a society, the greater the impact of choice and that area effects are both a cause and an outcome of these individual strategies. In the next two chapters we will deal with individual choice and responsibility in the highly unequal but apparently universalistic policy systems of health and health inequalities and social mobility.

Health and health inequalities

Introduction

In this chapter we will focus on the relationship between health, health inequalities and society. Michael Marmot's work (for example, Marmot, 2010, 2015; Marmot et al, 2020a) makes an excellent case for viewing health inequalities as *the* most significant health problem in societies while arguing that we need to better understand the societies and environments people live in, in order to understand the distribution of health outcomes. The complex relationships between the social contract, the political economy and the types and resourcing of policy responses are, therefore, highly significant in understanding health outcomes. They raise questions such as: What is an appropriate balance between individual and social responsibility for health? Should a contract exist between citizens and the state around the duration and quality of life experienced by all? And what is a legitimate focus for state intervention and, critical to discussions about policy, in what areas and to what extent? However, despite the success of Marmot's work in developing a powerful contemporary perspective on the social determinants of health, there are concerns about how policy and research continue to neglect key causal factors that produce the social and economic inequalities in which health inequalities are reproduced (see, for example, Scambler and Scambler, 2015; Wistow et al, 2015; Lynch, 2017; Schrecker, 2017, 2021; Harvey, 2021). Scambler (2018: xxvi) provides a response to this inattention, arguing:

> If individual behaviour is not socially determined, and it most certainly is not, it is undoubtedly socially structured and filtered through the properties of global, national, regional and local cultures. Individuals and individual behaviour, in other words, cannot be explained without reference to the societies which they inhabit, reproduce and, far more rarely, elaborate and even transform. The social is intimately related to who gets sick when, why and with what consequences.

This kind of understanding chimes with the notion of the social contract as an analytical device for framing the position people find themselves in, in a free society. It also pushes us to think about the structure in which people interact with society and social policies and, crucially, the role of the political economy in shaping these complex systems and the consequences this has for the distribution of health outcomes. The concepts of health and health inequalities, then, are critical to understanding the contract between the state and the population it serves. Our chances of living a long and healthy life seem to be fairly fundamental to being free (given the alternatives are premature death and being encumbered to various degrees by illness, disease and disability). The evidence base points to the need for a variety of interventions on behalf of citizens to equalise people's chances of having a long and healthy life; essentially protecting parts of society from the systematic (and systemic) impact of the political economy in producing and reproducing inequalities. There are strong parallels here with Rousseau's promotion of equality to strengthen social ties that enhance freedom for all. However, as we have seen in Chapters 1 and 2, in particular, the social contract in England appears to be generally antagonistic towards interventions that pursue alternatives to competitive individualism as a route to freedom.

This chapter seeks to unpack these themes in four sections. In the next section, an introduction to health and health inequalities is provided. In particular, it is argued that social policy focused on both health and health inequalities must move towards conceptualising these as complex. The subsequent section presents a more detailed exploration of the relationship between the political economy and health inequalities, drawing in particular on literature about the social determinants of health. Growing spatial and socioeconomic inequalities, the declining capacity of the state to respond to these, and the growing individualism fostered through the political economy will all be considered here. The following section explores health and health-related policy. It emphasises that a much stronger focus on health as being socially structured and not merely the absence of remediable disease or the treatment of ill-health needs to be adopted in health and social policy, more broadly. Longstanding debates about the need to rebalance policy around the health of populations, rather than the treatment of individual patients, will be considered in relation to priorities for the social contract. The concluding section will consider what health policy and outcomes tell us about the social contract. It will question whether inequalities in such a profoundly important individual and social outcome (concerned with the duration and quality of life) can be used to challenge the nature of a social contract that both produces inequitable health outcomes *and* has free universal access to public healthcare.

Health and health inequalities

'Health' can be conceptualised in a variety of ways. It is not the aim of this book to unpack the associated debate in great detail (for much fuller accounts see, for example, Illich, 1976; Blaxter, 1990; Nettleton, 1995). For our purposes, Sartorius' (2006: 662) summary of three types of definition of health is both convenient and illustrative in relation to the wider discussion around social policy and the social contract:

- Health is the absence of any disease or impairment.
- Health is a state that allows the individual to adequately cope with all demands of daily life (implying also the absence of disease and impairment).
- Health is a state of balance, an equilibrium that an individual has established within him/herself and between him/herself and their social and physical environment.

These are respectively *negative*, *positive* and *functional* definitions of health (Blaxter, 1990). As should be clear, they are not mutually exclusive and ought to be regarded as cumulative. However, when considering these definitions we should also think about how they are used in society. Is there an explicit, or implicit, prioritisation among them for how health is viewed and understood? And does this have implications for how we prioritise and respond to health (including health inequalities) in terms of social policies? It is unlikely to surprise the reader that the functional or health as an equilibrium definition of health most closely aligns with the type of social contract being advocated here, given it acknowledges the significance of social ties and the interdependence between individuals and their environment. The absence of disease and impairment and the ability to cope with daily demands are both important conditions for an individual to maximise their enjoyment of, and potential in, society. The functional definition goes much further than this. For Illich (1976) this means linking the health of populations to political actions that create the environment and circumstances that favour self-reliance, dignity and autonomy for all.

The coronavirus has illustrated how strongly health is understood and framed in terms of the absence of disease and illness. The widespread concern about mortality and morbidity resulting from the virus and the shock that this has provided to the collective psyche have reinforced what is essentially a narrow and negative definition of health (the *absence* of a condition being key here). Ever since the lead-in to the first lockdown in England in March 2020 we have witnessed a policy discourse dominated by health interpreted as the absence of disease and illness. While understandable (to some extent) it is also concerning because a narrow framing of health has been reinforced, which by its nature does not extend to concerns about wider demands on daily life and equilibrium with the wider environment. These wider concerns are central to health outcomes and how they are distributed both unequally and systematically across society. The following quote from the foreword to *Health equity in England: The Marmot Review 10 years on*, illustrates the significance of a social understanding of health to explain patterns of individual outcomes (Marmot et al, 2020a: 5):

> Evidence from around the world shows that health is a good measure of social and economic progress. When a society is flourishing health tends

to flourish. When a society has large social and economic inequalities there are large inequalities in health. The health of the population is not just a matter of how well the health service is funded and functions, important as that is: health is closely linked to the conditions in which people are born, grow, live, work and age and inequities in power, money and resources – the social determinants of health.

When asked on BBC Radio 4's *Today* programme on 27 January 2021 why the UK's death toll from COVID-19 was so high (which at that time had passed 100,000 deaths and the country had the sixth highest death rate behind countries with much smaller populations – Czechoslovakia, Belgium, Gibraltar, San Marino and Slovenia), Michael Marmot replied: 'We came into the crisis in a very bad state.' This is evident through a steep increase in the gap in life expectancy between the top and bottom deciles over the past ten years, to 9.5 years for men and 7.7 years for women (these were 7.5 and 5.4, respectively, in 2010) and with the most deprived expected to spend about twice the proportion of their shorter lives in ill-health (Marmot et al, 2020a). More broadly, health has deteriorated for the population as a whole, with poorer communities, women and those living in the north of England experiencing little or no improvement in life expectancy since 2010, which has contributed to a slowdown to an extent not witnessed in England for 120 years, nor across the rest of Europe or in most other OECD countries during this period (Marmot et al, 2020a). Early indications of outcomes related to COVID-19 are neither promising, nor unexpected, in this context. During the first wave of the virus in England the death rate in the most deprived neighbourhoods was more than double the rate in the least deprived (128.3 compared with 58.8 per 100,000 population) (ONS, 2020). In *Build back fairer: The COVID-19 Marmot Review*, Marmot et al (2020b: 6) highlight that 'widening inequalities in power, money, and resources between individuals, communities and regions have generated inequalities in the conditions of life, which in turn, generate inequalities in health generally, and COVID-19 specifically'. Similarly, Bambra et al (2020) concluded that COVID-19 has 'magnified and exacerbated health inequalities', which they attributed to co-morbidities, occupational exposure, overcrowding, the need to keep on working and a lack of access to health and social care.

As we are beginning to see, health, health inequalities and the COVID-19 crisis provide useful and significant insights into the dynamics and complexity of contemporary society. Kelly (2010) argues that both individual and social levels of explanation are required to capture the significant interactions and linkages between different phenomena. Inequalities in health outcome derive from the linkages between 'persistent and complex causes and relationships that are multi-faceted, between, for instance, early years, education, employment, living environment, income and health' (Marmot, 2010: 84). Lynch (2017) argues that framing the complexity of the causal chain of the social determinants of health around fairness and social structural factors should be done to prompt public support for policies aimed at reducing health inequalities. Life expectancy and healthy life expectancy are two significant indicators of health inequalities that capture fundamental aspects of the contract between individuals and the society they live in. Life is brief and, for those without religious faith, a one-time deal (with society and not god). For these reasons it is extremely important to understand health fully and calibrate policy, social and political economic systems correctly in relation to it. In this respect, Schrecker and Bambra (2015) argue that we must not be drawn into a narrow and individualistic framing of risk and responsibility, given the significance and complexity of the issue. As Salway and Green (2017) argue, there is a danger that system boundaries get mis-specified and key elements are left out. In the next section we will turn to the political economy as a key component of the systems influencing health and health inequalities. For now, and as, for example, Doyal with Pennell (1979), Scambler and Scambler (2015), Wistow et al (2015), Lynch (2017), Salway and Green (2017) and Shrecker (2021) all effectively argue, the ontological and epistemological predisposition informing health-related policy tends towards understanding health as an absence of disease and illness (that is, dealing more with the symptoms rather than causes of poor health), which excludes significant elements of the systems producing inequalities in health outcomes.

Relationship with the political economy

To understand patterns of health and illness we need to understand the context in which these occur, including the mode of production (Doyal with Pennell, 1979). In this respect, Doyal with Pennell (1979) considered that the primary focus on profit under capitalism was the most important determinant of economic and social decision making, which was reflected in patterns of health and illness (see also Harvey, 2021). Scambler and Scambler (2015) highlight how socio-epidemiology makes it clear that a widening health inequalities gap has opened up since the mid-1970s and Navarro (2009) identifies the significance of changes initiated in the Thatcher governments of the late 1970s and early 1980s in the social, political and economic contexts in which mortality inequalities are produced and reproduced. Streeck (2016) describes the current trajectory as one of economic imperialism in which economic social relations (relations of production and exchange) are interacting with, expanding into and becoming dominant over non-economic social relations and the social context. Health inequalities, therefore, provide an example of a social outcome that is a consequence of the significance of economic social relations within the mode of production, with those at the bottom of the distribution being casualties of this. As we have seen, the persistence of social and economic inequalities occurred during a period in which radical changes to the political economy were in no small part responding to agency in the system, given the success of Margaret Thatcher in three general elections and the influence of Thatcherism over all subsequent governments. As Fevre (2016) points out, there was a shift in attitudes away from a collectivist political culture to one in which high taxes, welfare benefits and strong trade unions supporting income equality were increasingly being viewed as holding the country and people back. These changes contributed to the 'phase shift' in inequalities (described in Chapter 1) and are a characteristic of the macro trajectory of complex systems and the social contract over the past 40 years.

In focusing on health and health inequalities, in particular, we can also see how the political economy interacts with, shapes and limits the scope for state intervention in wider social processes (including social and economic inequalities). The changes in culture, politics and economics described in Chapter 2 (in particular) have contributed to and/or reflect the growing influence of the development of neoliberal public policy, which has transformed the health policy environment through (among other things):

- reducing public responsibility for the health of populations;
- increasing the role of choice and markets;
- increasing personal responsibility for health improvement; and
- understanding health promotion as behavioural change (Navarro, 2009).

In this context, Schrecker (2016) highlights the example of the emergence of the 'neoliberal diet' to illustrate the intense marketing by transnational corporations of inexpensive but ultra-processed commercial food products laden with ingredients that are damaging to health. He emphasises the increasing unaffordability of healthy diets for those on declining and insecure incomes and the role of health promotion in assigning responsibility for healthy lifestyles primarily to individuals (Schrecker, 2016). More broadly, these developments have occurred within a context in which markets have expanded into more spheres of social life, disrupting them and leaving them in disarray (Streeck, 2016) and have led to higher levels of inequalities (Sayer, 2016). In short, health occurs within a social contract that has increasingly leaned towards possessive and competitive individualism in the economy and society. The consequences of this within a highly unequal society have been discussed at great length in literature that connects inequalities in status to the extent that people have control over their lives or destiny and how this corresponds to inequalities in health outcomes (see, for example, Marmot,

2004; Whitehead et al, 2016). In this respect, Marmot (2015) argues that a relative lack of control over what is happening in one's life influences our choices about unhealthy and risky behaviours in terms of smoking, drinking, diet and exercise, for example. Targeting localities and people that are losing out in terms of their position on the social gradient is, therefore, a key area for policy development, but crucially this requires intervening in and employing the mechanisms of the political economy to level the gradient. However, the logic and ideology of the neoliberal influence over the political economy are opposed to these kinds of interventions and it is debatable how much popular support there is for moving away from this model. Instead, as we have already seen, the social contract seems to lean more towards Nozick's (1974) and Hayek's (2014 [1959]) concern with individual rights and the view that individual means should be protected as much as possible from state encroachments such as those implied by providing a substructure for equality. However, if we want to see reductions in inequalities in social outcomes, the extent to which the state is seen to have a role in modifying the inequalities that are (re)produced across society should be of much greater concern.

The notion of a social contract, in which greater equality provides the basis for shared common interests and strengthened social ties, can be used to link the social determinants of health to the political economy. The social determinants of health approach is well established in both policy and academic discourse and as Scambler and Scambler (2015: 343) note, there have been 'endlessly repeated statistical associations linking socioeconomic classification to health'. Much less common, but still important within the academic literature, are calls to question the structural and class forces that are key causal factors in producing health inequalities (see, for example, Coburn, 2009; Scambler and Scambler, 2015; Wistow et al, 2015; Lynch, 2017; Schrecker, 2017; Harvey, 2021). Bambra et al (2019) argue that the social determinants of health are themselves shaped by macro-level structural determinants: politics, the economy, the (welfare) state, the organisation of work and the structure of the labour market. As Marmot and colleagues point out (Marmot et al, 2020a, 2020b; 2021), these include longstanding structural racism and inequalities in the social determinants of health for Black, Bangladeshi, Pakistani and Indian British people. Through omitting any consideration of the political causes of socioeconomic status and its relationship to health, Coburn (2009) argues that many theorists of the social determinants of health do not go 'far enough up the causal chain to confront the class forces and class struggles that are ultimately determinant'. In this respect, Navarro (2009) has argued that forgetting or ignoring the scientific contributions of Marxist and Weberian traditions (which consider class a major category of power) carries a huge cost, including the inability to understand our world and how neoliberal policies benefit the dominant classes to the detriment of the dominated classes, thereby increasing inequalities, including health inequalities. Scambler and Scambler (2015) equate this to a changed class/command dynamic of financial capitalism through which health inequalities are the unintended consequence of strategic behaviours of the capitalist elite. The political economy, therefore, forms a key component of a complex systems approach to understand the scale and nature of the challenges facing policy to target health inequalities (and for that matter social policies, more generally). However, health inequalities are often somewhat isolated from the political economy in political and policy debates that do not consider, or respond to, the issues raised here sufficiently.

Marmot is sometimes criticised for not focusing on the mechanisms giving rise to and sustaining differential access to wealth and power (Scambler and Scambler, 2015). However, in his book, *The Health Gap* (2015: 270), he goes as far as stating that:

> It is clear societies have political choices. If they want to increase inequalities of wealth and income they should do the following: transfer publicly owned assets into private hands; be complicit in low general rates of income growth, but engineer the economy so there are runaway salaries at the top; make taxes on income and spending less progressive; reduce taxes on capital, including corporation tax, capital gains and inheritance tax. Sounds rather familiar. It is what we have been doing in the US and the UK. It is hardly surprising that we are having trouble reducing health inequalities.

In the previous section we saw how health inequalities have intensified and increases in life expectancy have stalled under austerity governments. But as this quote from Marmot suggests, there is a wide range of elements in our political economy conducive to producing health inequalities that long pre-date austerity. Indeed, during the New Labour years, when there was sustained investment in public services (especially in the NHS) and a fairly comprehensive programme across government to tackle health inequalities, the life expectancy gap between men in the richest and poorest deciles of the income distribution increased from 7.4 years for men and 5.0 years for women in 2001, to 7.7 and 5.4 years respectively in 2010 (Marmot et al, 2020a). This raises questions about the effectiveness of policy development that does not take a properly calibrated systems focus (that is, integrating the political economy) for issues such as health inequalities. Without following the causal chain to the causes of highly unequal socioeconomic status, a key determinant of health inequalities will be left out of a complex systems approach. As in other areas of social policy, the consequences of socioeconomic status for health (and health inequalities, in particular) are fairly profound, with austerity intensifying the negative impact of economic social relations on the social context.

As things stand, health inequalities appear to be locked into contemporary social and economic relationships by the social contract. Capitalism is inherently competitive and produces winners and losers, which, as we have seen, manifest themselves systematically in terms of health outcomes. As we have moved to an increasingly competitive form of capitalism (in which the decommodifying role of the welfare state has come under sustained attack), the distance between winners and losers becomes greater. Reductions in state interventions in social and economic activities, alongside the deregulation of labour and financial markets (Navarro, 2009), have created obstacles to reducing health inequalities through both reinforcing inequalities and preventing effective government actions to reduce them (Lynch, 2017). In this respect, we can see what Titmuss (1968) would describe as a shift towards allowing the social costs of the system to lie where they fall and a reduced role for welfare to compensate for the disservices and social insecurities that are the result and costs some people pay for the progress others enjoy. The role of the state, which has direct (albeit imperfect) lines of accountability to the public, has been skewed towards serving capital over protecting more vulnerable sections of society. Health inequalities provide a bleak (given they are literally about the difference between life and death) example of the social consequences of this. Chapters 2 and 3 suggested that (until recently at least) part of the strength of the neoliberal ideology has been to create the sense that 'there is no alternative' to the way the economy, and by association society, is organised. Is it the case that there really is no alternative? If so, it suggests that we do not care about/are not sufficiently interested at a societal level in health inequalities and that the communities (including the increased likelihood of some ethnicities living in adverse social conditions; Marmot, 2021) where the worst outcomes occur are not sufficiently on the radar. Health inequalities concern the whole of society and those higher up the social and economic distribution are not only protected from, but also able to enjoy the benefits of, competitive individualism. The political economy, then, is both a protective and a pathogenic mechanism. Whether we want it to remain as such should be a matter of much more concern and mainstream debate. That it is not, is a poor reflection on the society we inhabit.

Health and health-related policy

> If circumstances are good 'healthy' behaviour appears to have a strong influence upon health. If they are bad, then behaviours make rather little difference. (Blaxter, 1990: 216)

Blaxter's conclusion has important policy implications, which Marmot (2015: 1), drawing on his early experiences as a medical practitioner, neatly summarises as: '[W]hy treat people and send them back to the conditions that made them sick?' However, Hunter (2015: 7) argues that attempts to shift the focus of the NHS away from treating people once they are ill has met with little success, at least in part, 'due to powerful interests within the medical profession holding sway over which treatments get prioritised and funded'. More fundamentally, Doyal with Pennell (1979) consider that the medical emphasis on individual causation has acted as a means of defusing the political significance of the 'destruction of health'. Illich's (1976: 274) claim that 'a world of optimal and widespread health is obviously a world of minimal and only occasional medical intervention' may, for some, give insufficient recognition to the positive effects of screening, early intervention and the treatment of patterns of disease and illness. However, Illich's central point that we are all better off if we are not in a position that requires medical attention is not in itself controversial. He goes on to argue that 'healthy people are those who live in healthy homes on a healthy diet in an environment equally fit for birth, growth, work, healing, and dying; they are sustained by a culture that enhances the conscious acceptance of limits to population, of aging, of incomplete recovery and ever imminent death' (Illich, 1976: 274). In the first part of the quote there is a good deal of overlap with the conceptualisation of health inequalities in England discussed in the earlier section in this chapter entitled 'Health and health inequalities' and parallels with Doyal with Pennell's (1979: 35) argument that the 'emphasis on the individual origin of disease is of considerable social significance, since it effectively obscures the social and economic causes of ill health'. The second part of the quote from Illich is no less important as it contextualises a social understanding of health alongside a finite existence. We are all going to die at some point – that is a big part of life; the argument here is about to what extent this is an individual or societal responsibility and how best to respond to this at an individual and societal level. Illich (1976) is on more contentious ground in his argument that the medical establishment had become a major threat to health through impinging on our autonomous, individual coping ability. For those in policy systems dominated by medical hegemony in both health and public health fields, challenging the 'doctor knows best' presumption (see Schrecker, 2021) is much less comfortable ground to tread as it implies that the balance of priorities in health systems is not only wrong but also that the role of the medical profession needs to be substantially reduced in framing and determining health policy.

Concentrating on health inequalities provides a lens on outcomes produced by the social contract. It is revealing, then, as Bambra et al (2011: 403) highlight, that the findings of the 2010 Marmot Review were consistent with the two previous major reviews in this field – the Black Report (1980) and the Acheson Review (1998) – and that 'the impact of earlier research into health inequalities ... has actually had very little real impact on the types of policy implemented'. The coalition government accepted five of the six priority objectives (with the exception of 'Ensure a healthy standard of living for all') of the 2010 Marmot Review, which formed the basis for the public health White Paper in 2010: *Healthy lives, healthy people* (Marmot et al, 2020a). A new set of public health outcome indicators covering the social determinants of health was subsequently developed. However, Marmot et al (2020a: 143) conclude that the absence of a new health inequalities strategy has contributed to much less focus on the social determinants of health than in other countries and that, 'over the last 10 years, prevention services have been cut more than treatment services in public health as well as in the wider arenas related to social determinants'. Given the findings of the health inequalities reviews mentioned here, it is perhaps surprising that there is not a more sustained and meaningful challenge to the role and influence of a medical view of health over health policy and resourcing in England. These reviews point to the material and structural causes of health inequalities and what should be interpreted as the complex causal relationships that intersect with social standing (class) and place, in particular. However, Wistow et al (2015) have argued that an implicit assumption underlying the NHS is that in removing financial barriers to comprehensive medical services there will be better health outcomes for all through identifying and responding to symptoms rather than causes. As we have seen, better health outcomes have not been distributed evenly across the population. The provision of universal health services is only a partial response to the complex structural causes of health inequalities rooted in social and economic factors. However, changing the approach is much easier said than done, which relates, at least in part, to the path dependency of the system.

History matters and Wistow et al (2015) argue that, in the century between the first Public Health Act in 1848 and the creation of the NHS in 1948, a 'public health paradigm' was superseded by one organised around the centrality of personal medical services. The 1848 Act sought to address the causes of infectious diseases such as typhoid and cholera by having clean and continuous water supplies and sanitary systems through the development of an infrastructure of shared central and national responsibilities. Essentially the local democratic arm of government was strengthened through the creation of the modern public health infrastructure and system, which provided a purpose and ability to respond to population health needs. Jumping dramatically forward and by the time the NHS was created, the central state was now deciding the volume of resources and doctors were determining how this would be spent (Klein, 1995). As Klein (1995) notes, in order to secure their participation in the NHS, general practitioners (GPs) were allowed to retain their status as independent (self-employed) contractors partly to assure them that the state (either national or, especially, local) would not interfere in their relationships with patients. Minister for Health, Aneurin Bevan, argued for national rather than local accountability, which is illustrated by his declaration that the sound of a dropped bedpan in an NHS ward should resound in Whitehall and Westminster (Blackman et al, 2008). This position, however, was not a claim for national or political control over service delivery. As part of his strategy to secure the doctors' participation in the NHS he promised to provide them with 'all the facilities, resources, apparatus and help I can, and then leave you alone as professional men and women to use your skills and judgement without hindrance' (quoted in Webster, 1998: 30). As Klein (1995) argued, the political and administrative state was to stop well outside the consulting-room door.

Historically, the NHS and local government structures were built around the skills of providers rather than the needs of users and they sought to privilege internal over external integration through, for example, the transfer of public health and community health services from local authorities to the NHS (Wistow, 2012). In this respect, therefore, the services were structured to reflect their separate identities and purposes rather than the needs of individuals and populations for functional integration (Wistow, 2012). The Health and Social Care Act 2012 returned public health to local government but this occurred within the context of austerity. Meanwhile the continued existence of three separate but interrelated outcome frameworks for social care, public health and the NHS, rather than a single unified framework, is highlighted by Wistow (2012) as a signal of integration remaining on the margins of NHS and local government because their mainstream business is defined in terms of delivering individual services or functions. Despite the *NHS Five Year Forward View* in 2014 stating that integration was a key aim (NHS England, 2014), this has not been fully implemented and fragmentation and divisions remain key features of the health and social care system (Vizard et al, 2021). In particular, Vizard et al (2021) express concerns about the devolution of public health functions to local government, questioning the extent to which the 'levers of control' are within the scope of local authorities.

More generally, government spending as a percentage of GDP declined by seven percentage points between 2009/10 and 2018/19, from 42% to 35% (Marmot et al, 2020a). The resulting austerity has not been felt equally, either by service sector or by place. For example, Vizard et al (2021) assert that, between 2015 and 2020, the NHS budget in England was relatively protected and increased more in real terms than had been planned for that five-year period, but was combined with substantial cuts to local government public health allocations. Comparing expenditure on health during the first and second decades of the 21st century, Vizard et al (2021) demonstrate average increases of 6.6% a year between 1999–00 and 2009–10, compared with 1.7% a year between 2009–10 and 2019–20. Meanwhile, Thomas (2019) cited in Marmot et al (2020a) demonstrates that not only did net expenditure on public health in England decline by £850 million between 2014 and 2019, but also absolute cuts were six times greater in the poorest places compared with the least deprived. Per-person cuts to local authority service spending averaged 24% between 2009–10 and 2017–18 and were highly regressive relative to deprivation, with a reduction of about 35% funding per person in the most deprived quintile and only 15% in the least deprived quintile (Phillips and Simpson, 2018). Consequently, the funding for services most closely aligned with the social determinants of health has been reduced in inverse relationship to the social gradient in health. In an international context, Marmot et al (2020a) conclude that, despite the growing consensus on the importance of the social determinants of health, England has given them much less focus than some other countries.

Despite prevention services and those related to the wider social determinants[1] being cut more than treatment services over the past ten years (Marmot et al, 2020a), the-then Secretary of State for Health and Social Care, Matt Hancock (2018), stated in an address to the International Association of National Public Health Institutes in 2018 that "preventing ill health can transform lives, and transform society for the better too. That might sound radical. It is intended to." This is far from radical stuff! It is, nonetheless, revealing in that Hancock both thought it was and had gone as far as to emphasise this point. In the speech, Hancock went on to consider the significance of people's behaviours for their health and argued that: "I want to see people take greater responsibility for managing their own health … how can we empower people to take more care of their own health? By giving people the knowledge, skills and confidence." He did not, however, consider the nature of the political economy, nor the social determinants arising from this in his analysis and instead essentially isolated behaviours within debates about individual agency and responsibility without due consideration of the social and structural contexts these are situated in. This is both predictable and disappointing. Not because behaviours are unimportant – they are extremely significant for health outcomes – but because they are complex and nested in a wider social structure within a neoliberal political economy. In other words, developing knowledge, skills and confidence around health behaviours (and prevention strategies) must be considered alongside wider systemic drivers such as competitive and possessive individualism in a highly unequal society. In short, the first-order issue is to level the playing field in order to improve the chances of interventions narrowing, as opposed to exacerbating, inequalities. This is significant because, as Curtis (2008) argues, the groups that tend to experience inequalities in health most sharply are those that are hardest to engage in discussions about health. For example, is someone who works as a professional and lives in an affluent and healthy area more or less likely to be receptive to being empowered through knowledge than someone who lives in an unhealthy neighbourhood and whose experiences of and interactions with the state are largely negative through the excessive monitoring and surveillance that comes with living on (or potentially previously living on, given changes to allocation criteria relative to need) incapacity benefits? These are some of the complexities associated with the social gradient of health and without addressing the 'causes of the causes' of ill-health, health professionals in the field of prevention have an uphill battle in encouraging individuals to change their health behaviours. Having not engaged with the significance of the political economy in shaping the causes of the causes, Hancock's approach as Health Secretary, and wider government strategy, sit somewhere between dealing with symptoms and narrowly defined causes of ill-health. That they do so at a time when children's centres have closed, educational funding has declined, precarious working has increased, there is a housing affordability crisis, there has been a rise in homelessness and people have insufficient money to lead a healthy life (Marmot et al, 2020a) means that the government's aims to 'level up' health are not credible.

Marmot et al (2020a) argue that, since 2010, despite the evidence about the overwhelming impacts of the social determinants of health, the government has not acted on this sufficiently, through working to improve the conditions in which people live, in order to improve their health. While I generally agree, this analysis lets the NHS off the hook (albeit recognising that the medical understandings of health and a treatment/sickness service model are well established within the NHS and create a strong path dependency for the policy system). The NHS is, after all, a major player in social policy design and delivery and we should, at the very minimum, question whether it could have done more to turn its attention to the social determinants of health in this period. This would require a more functional (as outlined earlier in this chapter) understanding of health and an inclination to re-examine its priorities. *The NHS long term plan* (NHS, 2019) has outlined a plan for the NHS to have a bigger role in prevention and with higher funding allocated to areas with high inequalities (Marmot et al, 2020a). This is a positive step but takes place after a decade of austerity in which public health has been hit particularly hard.[2] Vizard et al (2021) conclude that, ultimately, the stated drive on prevention and public health in the coalition government's health reforms have not been delivered, while they (Vizard et al, 2021) and Marmot et al (2020a, 2020b) argue that ratcheting up funding for public and preventative health proportionate to need and deprivation is required or health will decline and the burden on health services will increase. Marmot (2015) and Marmot et al's (2020a, 2020b) overarching policy solution to health inequalities (and a healthy society) is *proportionate universalism*. The idea here is relatively straightforward and has strong parallels and complementarity with the response to economic disparities in place, discussed in the previous chapter. Essentially, people and places with the greatest need require resourcing and support proportional to their social and economic circumstances in order to level the consequences, and certain aspects, of the social gradient. There are similarities with the type of social contract being advocated here, although the argument I am making is more explicitly redistributive and concerned with levelling the social gradient. These approaches would require a radical reversal of spending in favour of the most deprived and socially disadvantaged places and a programme of redistributive taxation on income and wealth.

Health, health inequalities and the social contract

The prevailing concept of health and the extent of health inequalities are good indicators of the nature of a society and of the social contract between citizens and the state. The slowdown of improvements in life expectancy in England might have been expected to serve as a focus for greater public concern, given that an equivalent event has not occurred in living memory. While this trend is a new phenomenon, the existence of health inequalities is not. These are more important social outcomes than overall life expectancy from the point of view of a social contract seeking to promote and deliver equality. There are four features of how the social contract currently operates that are strikingly persistent and that need responding to in order to make the challenge of reducing health inequalities more tractable:

- the persistence of the evidence base pointing to the influence of the social determinants of health and material explanations of health inequalities;
- the persistence of a political economy dominated by neoliberalism;
- the persistence of health inequalities in both favourable and unfavourable policy contexts; and
- the persistence of the mode of a personal medical services paradigm at the heart of policy systems.

In this concluding section of the chapter, I will address each of these in turn.

First, if we (as a society) really want to reduce health inequalities, we must do things differently. Since the 1980 Black Report (Black, 1980), the evidence base has been very clear and explicit about the direction policy should take to address health inequalities. There are also strong parallels with the 19th-century origins of public health and the work of Engels and Virchow in this period (Harvey, 2021). Put very simply, social inequalities lead to health inequalities. In order to end the conditions causing health inequalities (see, for example, Marmot, 2010; Scambler and Scambler, 2015; Lynch, 2017; Marmot et al, 2020a), society as a whole needs to challenge and address the inequalities existing within it. To do so, Scambler and Scambler (2015), among others, argue that there is a need to critique and challenge the mechanisms in society that give rise to, and sustain, inequalities in power and wealth, in order to address the inequalities in health and healthcare. Redistribution must, therefore, be part of the 'policy menu'. In complex systems language (Byrne, 2019), this would contribute to changing the longstanding trajectory of the 'possibility space' and moving towards a new 'attractor'. Strategies to tackle health inequalities may, therefore, be more successful when integrating wider aims such as the redistribution of wealth via increased taxation or labour market regulation to address health inequalities related to poverty (Lynch, 2017). However, Salway and Green (2017: 523) suggest that 'we remain deeply wedded to linear models and individualistic interventions'. The individualism developed through the political economy is neatly aligned with policy emphasising individual treatment. Wistow et al (2015) argue that there is a tendency to focus on measuring components as discrete elements, rather than elements of a dynamic and integrated system. In order to address the complexity of health inequalities, the NHS needs radical realignment that fully embeds a complex understanding of the social gradient and social determinants of health in its operating logic (Wistow et al, 2015).

Second, a core argument being developed throughout this book is that the social contract in England is, by and large, unfavourable to equality of condition or outcome, in large part due to the development of a broadly neoliberal trajectory in the political economy over the past 40 years or so. At the start of this period, Doyal with Pennell (1979: 44) argued that:

> Most attempts to control the social production of ill health would involve an unacceptable degree of interference with the process of capital accumulation, and, as a result, the emphasis in advanced capitalist societies has been on the after-the-event curative medical intervention, rather than broadly-based preventive to conserve health.

Their argument was that for preventive medicine to be effective it would need to interfere with the production process itself – hence curative medicine can be seen to deny or minimise the need for this (Doyal with Pennell, 1979). In the years that followed, interference in the production process in favour of social rights weakened, which we have discussed at length in Chapter 2. The key issue in relation to the production of health and health inequalities is how, as Lynch (2017) argues, neoliberalism and the medical model have a common belief in individualism. For this reason, Lynch goes on to argue that reframing social inequality around health medicalises the problem, making it less amenable to systemic or structural solutions (Lynch, 2017). In other words, the political economy and, as Navarro (2009) and

Scambler and Scambler (2015) assert, the material and class-based causes of social inequality, are the first-order issue and we should, therefore, develop our solutions to focus on this. Redistribution through taxation, including a wealth tax, therefore needs to feature more prominently in debates about social and health policy (see, for example, Sayer, 2016; Byrne and Ruane, 2017; Lynch, 2017; Byrne, 2019). However, we should not forget the appeal of individualism as a powerful counterbalance to calls for redistribution. Marmot et al (2020a) cite the work of the Frameworks Institute (2020), which highlights three common public beliefs:

- individualism and that success or failure in life is determined solely by choice, hard work and determination;
- 'them and us' thinking about problems and deficiencies in 'other' people and communities and that if 'they' gain, 'we' lose out; and
- fatalism about addressing deeply entrenched challenges.

These are all mutually reinforcing of the status quo in the political economy and, therefore, changing public understandings and their production is likely to be very challenging. However, using the social contract as a lens on individual and social outcomes provides both a challenge to the legitimacy of a state and society producing persistent health inequalities and also the basis for a more optimistic vision of greater equity in health outcomes, should we choose to pursue greater equality in social and economic terms.

Third, as we have seen, health inequalities in life expectancy grew (albeit at different rates) in the first and second decades of the 21st century. Under New Labour (despite large increases in public expenditure and a detailed and intensive policy agenda), health inequalities targets around life expectancy were not met and there was a slight increase in health inequalities gaps between the top and bottom income deciles. The 2010s, as Marmot et al (2020a: 125) rightly point out, were characterised by a 'lack of national leadership and whole-of-government approaches, the large funding reductions in critical social determinants of health and the difficult economic and social contexts at a local level'. Improvements in life expectancy stalled and inequalities in this increased at a greater rate than in the previous decade. A consistent feature of the favourable and unfavourable policy contexts has been the universalisation of access to 'free' health services (albeit across significantly different policy contexts), which has proved to be a partial response, only, to the structural causes of health inequalities. Wistow et al (2015) argue that this is largely due to the inability of systems focused overwhelmingly on the treatment of ill-health to deal with all the socioeconomic factors that cause and sustain inequalities in health and life expectancy. There is an ontological and epistemological coherence that cuts across dominant strands of methodological, political, economic and policy systems. These are skewed towards a linear and narrowly bounded understanding of the causal chain, in which individual responsibility for socioeconomic status is emphasised and services focus on treating the individual at the point of need. In relation to health inequalities, these factors are negatively reinforcing and go a long way towards explaining the persistence of health inequalities in England.

Fourth, the system is geared towards personal medical services but if health inequalities are considered *the* policy priority in health systems, then the dominant influence of this and the tendency to focus on symptoms over causes of ill-health are a 'category error' (Wistow et al, 2015). Clearly, health inequalities are not the priority driving the complex systems in which they are (re)produced and in which interventions are designed to tackle and reduce them. The NHS plays a significant role in the framing of health around individual patients rather than population health and is a persistent feature of service delivery and organisation that interacts with the political economy. Indeed, Holt-White (2019) identifies the strength of public views about individual responsibility for health as a factor in government's decisions to prioritise spending on the NHS over other areas of provision. This leads Marmot et al (2020a) to identify engaging the public in the social determinants of health as one of their key recommendations for action. However, there is a long way to go in this respect and the NHS provides a powerful synecdoche for the way that collectivism functions in the English social contract. For example, Matt Hancock (2018) summed this up well: "Ultimately, at the heart of our public provision for healthcare there's a social contract. A social contract at the heart of our NHS. We, the citizens, have a right to the healthcare we need, when we need it, free at the point of use." Similarly, in her maiden Conservative Party Conference speech as Prime Minister and leader of the Party, Theresa May (2017) was right to state:

> That it is this party that has invested in the National Health Service and upheld its founding principles through more years in government than any other. ... It is the very essence of solidarity in our United Kingdom. An institution we value. A symbol of our commitment to each other, between young and old, those who have and those who do not, the healthy and the sick.

This is both factually true and on deeper analysis is revealing about the role of the NHS in the social contract. That both Hancock and May valued the NHS in this way is very significant and suggests that it is an institution that sits comfortably within a neoliberal society and political economy. Governments from both the centre-right and the centre-left value the NHS as a form of collectivism that does not unduly challenge the notion of individual rights and responsibilities in society. Ultimately, the NHS deals with symptoms rather than the much more complex and deeply ingrained social inequalities causing them.

In conclusion, health inequalities are very challenging to narrow. They are a moving target and occur in an unequal society. The better-off are in a better position to make choices and experience life in ways that improve their health more than those in the middle of the socioeconomic distribution and much more than those towards the bottom. This is the social gradient in health and society, and it corresponds to other factors such as: where one lives; access to services; inequalities in income, wealth and power; and inequalities in condition, opportunity and outcomes. In the next chapter we will discuss these kinds of issues more fully in terms of social mobility. For now, it is worth introducing a question that is uncomfortable for many in debates about social mobility: To improve the chances of social circulation, should policy measures move beyond seeking to improve the individual agency of those at the bottom of the distribution to consider how to hold back the progress of those with much better life chances through the 'brute luck' (Dworkin, 2000) of birth? In other words, limiting the progress of those at the top contributes to levelling the social gradient and, therefore, improves the chances of those lower down the distribution to match the pace of, and potentially start to catch up with, those towards the top. However, this means thinking about taking redistributive actions (for example in terms of income, wealth, inheritance and land taxes) that could potentially impact on life expectancy at the top of the distribution. This is quite controversial territory as it is literally about life and death. However, those in less privileged positions continue to disproportionately face the sharp end of the wedge when it comes to matters of life and death (and poor health throughout life). If we all have a relatively equal stake in society, we might want to question why the scythe falls so systematically relative to socioeconomic status. In so doing we might also consider the legitimacy of a social contract in which these persistent social outcomes exist.

6

Social mobility

Introduction

Social mobility is a big deal in debates about social policy in England. As Calder (2016) has argued, it has had a privileged position as a policy priority across the policy spectrum. However, despite a 'shared shorthand' among political leaders and the media for the need for more mobility, there is disagreement about why it is important, ranging from fairness to economic efficiency, individual freedom and anxiety about an underclass (Payne, 2017). If we (as a society) are prioritising social mobility as a goal, we should consider how it is being framed and, perhaps more importantly, what we are not focusing on as a result of our preoccupation with it. These issues form the basis of the first section of this chapter in which debates about social mobility are analysed using the framing of the social contract adopted here. The second section moves the discussion on to consider the relationship between social mobility and social policy. In the third section we will return to debates about the significance of the political economy and develop this relative to the ongoing discussion about social mobility, the social contract and to policy responses connected to these. The chapter then concludes.

Social mobility and the social contract

As we have already seen, social mobility occupies an unusually significant place in policy debates in England. At first sight it also has a close alignment with the type of social contract being advocated for here. In essence, social mobility is about the circulation of people from different backgrounds in society and, therefore, involves movement up and down the social hierarchy both within generations and across them, which many consider to be a measure of fairness in society. However, social mobility is one of the most misunderstood processes of our time, despite it moving up the political agenda to the extent that media coverage of it increased tenfold over the past decade (Payne, 2017). Payne (2017) contends that there are actually high rates of mobility in Britain (given most of us have been socially mobile in terms of labour market movement) but that does not mean that everyone has an equal chance of getting on. In other words, a population can be highly socially mobile but the position people find themselves in, in a free society, and the contract this is based on, can be far from equal or mutually beneficial. Calder (2016: 4) argues that 'the value of social mobility is taken as a given', in part because it is less charged and contentious than equality. Consequently, the concept can be viewed as a core pillar of the social contract that has been adopted without sufficient critical engagement. As a policy agenda it is much more closely aligned with the ideological gloss of the neoliberal political economy than with pursuing equality.

Payne's (2017) review of the evidence base shows that about three quarters of the population are socially mobile in absolute terms (that is, they occupy both better and worse positions than their parents during their lifetime). This is not that surprising because people lead dynamic lives and have ups and downs during them (although in general the tendency is upwards over the lifecourse). Payne's (2017: 2) summary of the evidence base suggests that, in absolute terms, 'mobility rates are high; rates of upward mobility show little sign of falling; downward mobility is increasing; there are nevertheless considerable inequalities in who gets to be mobile; [and] there are "pockets" of low mobility'. Changes in the occupation structure, with professional and managerial work more than doubling between the 1920s and 1990s from 15% to 37%, created considerably more 'room at the top' for upward mobility and career progression (Payne, 2017). However, as Boliver and Byrne (2013), Brown (2013), Calder (2016), Payne (2017) and Friedman and Laurison (2019) all argue, *relative* mobility (which is a more stretching goal as it compares the movement of people across occupational class relative to their class of origin) has shown much less sign of becoming equal over time. Boliver and Byrne (2013) suggest that the reason for this is fairly straightforward: when there is more room at the top, it enables more people to avoid falling down. However, not all countries are equal in this respect and in 2015 there was a wider gap between the *relative* life chances of rich and poor people in the UK than in any other country in the OECD, leading Calder (2016: ix and 2) to state that:

> [W]e are a brand leader in social immobility. And everyone seems to find this scandalous ... it is not OK not to be affronted by it ... [especially when] ... a commitment to equality of opportunity is, ostensibly at least, part of the non-negotiable fabric of the kind of society we like to see ourselves as being.

For a more egalitarian form of social mobility, we need to have the conditions for a greater degree of equality of opportunity for relative mobility. However, the route to achieving this turns our attention to some fairly entrenched protective mechanisms associated with (in)equality of condition that stop people from falling down.

In, *How inequality runs in families*, Calder (2016) argues that the family is often presented as a social unifier, with individual families equal stakeholders in society. However, he continues that not only is 'the family a major engine of class fate. Class fate is rife and especially in countries like the UK that are characterised by widening income inequality' (Calder, 2016: 99). Family has a privileged status as part of the private sphere, given the significance of individual property rights and the importance placed on what is generally considered a family's own business in terms of parental rights to interact with and raise their children and what is within reach of the state. For example, Friedman and Laurison (2019: 90–1) highlight inherited or gifted funds as an example of the inequality in resources that are largely hidden from public view, downplayed and not much talked about but that often act as a 'pivotal early-career lubricant buying them a freedom of choice and allowing them to manoeuvre on to more promising career tracks, focus on developing valuable networks, resist exploitative employment or take risky opportunities'. In this light, family autonomy should not be considered sacred as families are not islands nor insulated from wider social dynamics (Calder, 2016), but are strongly associated with inequalities in life chances. In considering whether inequalities damage society, Crouch (2011) concludes that not only do some individuals and families have greater capacity to make the world according to their preferences but also the concentration of privileges can diminish the lives of others. This is by no means a zero-sum game but Bourdieu (1986), and the wealth of educational sociologists following in his footsteps, identify the impact of accumulated history and capital over time (and between generations of families) on opportunities and outcomes. Through considering this within the complexity frame of reference we might view these as a trajectory within the social contract that has significant implications in limiting the potential for policy systems to affect a more equitable form of social mobility. As Bourdieu (1986: 241) states, accumulated capital and history 'makes the games of society – not least, the economic game – something other than simple games of chance'.

More than 40 years ago, Therborn (1980) identified a bourgeois sociological interest in social mobility, which, he argued, did not seek to affect the class structure while affirming competitive individualism. This understanding is consistent with the subsequent tendency in England towards developing a 'deficit model' (that is, seeking to improve individual education, skills and so on where they are lacking) of working-class (im)mobility, which Brown (2013) considers will inevitably fail because it cannot compensate for wider social and economic inequalities. Reay (2017) also highlights the declining economic and political power of the working classes as key to how educational inequalities relate to wider social, economic and political inequalities. Reay (2017: 116) argues that:

The nature of social mobility in English society is a consequence of the way society is historically organised 'as a whole'. Social mobility, particularly in deeply unequal societies, is always about failure as much as it is about success. You become more equal in relation to privileged others, but at the cost of those you love and care for becoming less equal in relation to you.

In a strongly classed society such as England, a sense of belonging to the working class carries connotations of being less, and as Reay's quote suggests, there is also shame in escaping, therefore raising class should be the collective desire (Reay, 2017). Instead, social mobility has fulfilled an inculcation into the ruling-class 'ego-ideology' for those born into or permitted to enter this (Therborn, 1980). The shift in the use of 'meritocracy' as a pejorative term to a positive ideal (Allen, 2011) is highly salient here. Michael Young's (1958) *The rise of the meritocracy* was, in part, a satire about the ego of those at the top relative to their merit and the need for reassurance that people occupied their position in society due to merit as opposed to privilege. In this respect, at least, there is certainly much for those at the top of society to be insecure about. For example, in *The class ceiling*, Friedman and Laurison (2019) analysed the Labour Force Survey and conducted interviews with employers and employees to explore access to elite occupations in Britain. They summarised their key findings as follows:

> that people from working-class backgrounds earn less in top jobs than their privileged colleagues; that this can only be partially attributed to conventional measures of 'merit'; and that more powerful drivers are rooted in the misrecognition of classed self-representation as 'talent', work cultures historically shaped by the privileged, the affordance of the 'Bank of Mum and Dad', and sponsored mobility premised on the class–cultural homophily. (Friedman and Laurison, 2019: 185)

This relates to the advantages provided through the significant inequalities that are entrenched in society and how they are reproduced in both accessing (which Friedman and Laurison describe as 'getting in') and progressing in (which they call 'getting on') elite positions. Under these circumstances, Fevre (2016: 263) asserts that 'inequality is validated and perpetuated', with characteristics associated with failure and success being used to provide equal opportunities for self-determination and self-development. In short, success is characterised under the conditions of class–cultural homophily, which 'loads the deck' in favour of those coming from more privileged backgrounds and provides a strong trajectory and path dependency in the system.

Calder's (2016) notion of the need for a 'rear-view mirror' to understand the implications of class inequality for class fate becomes very significant in light of the analysis just described. Interactions between conditions, opportunities and outcomes are critical to understanding social mobility. In so doing, we should question whether people have a realistic opportunity of becoming the best candidate for a job, rather than appointing the best candidate on the day (Calder, 2016). However, this involves serious critical engagement with the notion of equality of condition and how it impacts on the potential for equity of opportunities and outcomes from different backgrounds such as class, race, gender and disability. Boliver and Byrne (2013) question whether those at the top will be as keen on upward social mobility given that changes in the occupational structure (which will be discussed more fully in Chapter 7) increasingly necessitate downward mobility and, therefore, threaten the intergenerational transmission of social standing. It is, after all, a key part of human nature for parents to want the best for their children. Consequently, Calder (2016) concludes that, given we are so saturated in the influence of inequalities on family circumstances, through intergenerational transfers of wealth and other forms of capital, it would be 'science fiction' to consider an alternative version of society with a 'perfectly horizontal playing field'. Pure equality of opportunity is, therefore, far-fetched (Calder, 2016) and in this light the concern to increase social mobility is something of a diversion from the far more important, and in fact prerequisite, goal of reducing social inequality (Boliver and Byrne, 2013). Politically this is significant because the social mobility agenda can be interpreted as post-hoc sour grapes among, or on behalf of, those losing out in a social contract skewed towards competitive and possessive individualism. In this respect, Therborn (1980: 62) emphasises the power of ideology in workers' conscious or unconscious acceptance of capitalism as a 'going concern' in which 'inferior individual performance results in a lack of success for attaining power and wealth'. He argues that the legal existence of equality of opportunity leads to people blaming themselves and others for not working hard enough or being clever enough (Therborn, 1980). More fundamentally, the 'bourgeois alter-ideology' cuts across framing individual responsibility for social mobility and extends to interpreting attacks on capitalism as being economically irrational and negatively impacting on the material wellbeing of all (Therborn, 1980). 'Alter-ideologies' is a term Therborn uses to refer to 'attempts to mould the dominated according to the rulers' image of them, and into resistance to the opposition of the ruled'. Essentially, this can be viewed as the pre-emptive process of delegitimising alternative conceptions of the social contract. In this example, the wide inequalities in economic, cultural, social, educational and political position are marginalised. The implications for the social contract are to reinforce the trend towards competitive and possessive individualism, without sufficiently questioning the make-up of the playing field these occur within – the consequences of which, as Brown (2013) argues, are that without a positional and relational theory of relative social mobility, we reduce policy debate to a 'deficit model' of what working-class students and family lack rather than disturbing the privileges of the middle classes.

Social mobility and social policy

In this section we will focus on two key issues relating to social mobility and social policy in England. First, it will be argued that the nature of social mobility and social circulation in the country has consequences for the design and nature of a wide range of social policies, including how these interact with the social contract and the political economy. Second, we will explore some policy responses to the issue of social mobility, albeit relatively briefly. The rationale for the brevity stems from the argument put forward in the previous section, namely that social inequality should be the more pressing concern.

The relative lack of social mobility or circulation at the top of society was the focus of the Social Mobility and Child Poverty Commission's (2014) report, *Elitist Britain*, which described a 'closed shop' leading to declining levels of public trust and engagement. The report highlighted a dramatic over-representation of those attending independent schools and Oxbridge across the top of British public life, including politics, business, the media, the public sector and sports. Reay (2017) highlights continuity between the situation now and when Jackson and Marsden (1968) were writing *Education and the working class*, about the 1950s and 1960s, arguing that elitism remains at the core of our education system, extending from private schools into our elite universities and to the top of professions. Similarly, Friedman and Laurison (2019) identify parallels with Turner's (1960) notion of 'sponsored' mobility at the top of society. They state that many believe that this kind of elite closure has waned given the expansion of higher education, a decline in the aristocracy, rising rates of absolute social mobility and achievements of feminism, but their research suggests that in elite occupations sponsorship continues to exist and does so not in the shadows but as a normalised practice. There is an oversupply of appointable candidates for elite occupations, which points to the significance of 'signalling' one's familiarity with the culture of those in elite positions (Friedman and Laurison, 2019). Brown (2013) argues that in a system of mass higher education, candidates are excluded for lacking the personal qualities that constitute employability rather than the appropriate credentials. This is starkly illustrated by Friedman and Laurison's (2019) finding that someone from a working-class background with a first-class degree attending a Russell Group university is less likely to end in an elite occupation than someone with either an upper or a lower second-class degree from a family with a professional or managerial background.

Clearly, then, there is a strong tendency towards social closure at the top of English society, limiting circulation into and out of this group across generations. Private schools play a role here and, as Reay (2017) argues, are not just about elitism and exclusivity – they create a form of 'monopoly privilege', ring-fencing high-status positions. These processes can be viewed as part of the post-democratic social contract in England and as an environment in which there is a good deal of mobility contained within this section of society, often to the detriment of effective, let alone equitable, political, economic and social outcomes. For example, Wilks (2015) describes the corporate takeover, or colonisation, of government via a 'revolving door' through which people with corporate backgrounds enter into government and civil servants and ministers with knowledge of government contracts and processes are recruited out. Wilks (2015) argues that these are unified through an ideology based on preferences for a small state and putting business and free-market interests at the heart of policy making. Davis (2018: 124) describes mobility here as something that connects modern elites as they exploit insider knowledge across organisations and 'leap from one sinking institution or sector to another'. Pretty much any issue of *Private Eye* will provide examples of this English tendency to fail sideways among the elite. *Elitist Britain* (Social Mobility and Child Poverty Commission, 2014) also highlighted wider issues arising from the perception that public life is conducted by the few who are very familiar with each other but far less familiar with the day-to-day challenges facing 'ordinary' people. Institutions derive their authority from how inclusive they are and we have a 'closed shop' leading to declining levels of public trust and engagement (Social Mobility and Child Poverty Commission, 2014). As a consequence, Davis (2018) concludes that (elite) mobility is a powerful commodity that leads to a lack of transparency and accountability for those in powerful positions.

The appointment of Baroness Harding (Oxford graduate, daughter of a hereditary peer, Conservative life peer, wife of a Conservative MP and board member of the Jockey Club[1]) as a head of NHS Test and Trace and then chair of the National Institute for Health Protection, apparently without interview, is an example of how the closed shop at the top of, and incompetence within, public life has flourished during the COVID-19 crisis. Harding has a background in business (and famously as chief executive of TalkTalk said she did not know whether customers' data was encrypted during a 2015 cyber-attack when up to four million people's personal and banking details were accessed (Komami, 2015) and became chair of NHS Improvement in 2017, while retaining her Conservative Party peerage. NHS Test and Trace was awarded about £22 billion of public money in 2020/21 (NAO, 2020c) and operates a fairly complex governance model across the public sector, with considerable contracting out to the private sector. The service has been widely criticised for failing to meet targets and provide the type of knowledge and support required in order to keep track, and on top, of the virus during 2020 (Blakely, 2020, Creasy, 2020, NAO, 2020a, 2020c). The lack of anticipation of a sharp rise in testing demand in September 2020 when schools and universities reopened and people returned to work after the summer led to inadequate steps to prepare for this (NAO, 2020c), and is just one example of its shortcomings. Given the established track-and-trace experience of local authorities and the statutory duty to control local disease outbreaks (NAO, 2020c), it is questionable why the UK did not follow international trends to involve local government more in these services from the outset. England was unique (among 15 other countries reviewed by government) in outsourcing tracing capacity, which comparators generally built from existing tracing and public health expertise, further substantiating concerns from local government stakeholders about their lack of involvement in the design and implementation of test-and-trace services (NAO, 2020c). Instead, the private sector was used and developed a call-centre model that has, at times, been barely used (NAO, 2020c). An opportunity to restore much-needed capacity to local government has been missed by those in a position to signal their way to the top and who instead remained wed to a narrow ideological preference for a small state, even during widespread spending of public money.

Two further issues emerged during the response to the COVID-19 crisis that are fairly typical of the tightly controlled public agenda and close-knit relationship between politicians and business interests in English policy making. First, the governance arrangements have become complex and fragmented, with poor coordination between central and local agencies (with many local authorities starting their own tracing systems independently of NHS Test and Trace). The UK2070 Commission (2020) has highlighted the confusion created in a highly centralised system of governance but one that relies on local action. Second, accountability and competence in these emerging systems of governance are both lacking. As we have seen, commissioning and contracting out services has become a key feature of the English state, which self-reinforces the tendency towards post-democracy. The Labour MP Stella Creasy (2020) has illustrated through parliamentary questions the 'many cogs' (themselves a result of contracting out) in this system that are out of alignment with each other, as Deloitte provided COVID-19 testing but did not manage access to this, Serco provided a proportion of test locations but did not schedule access to tests, Randox performed laboratory tests but was not involved in the public securing a test. As Creasy (2020) demonstrates, the contracts with these companies bizarrely excluded service penalties, which also goes some way towards explaining the apparent failings of the test-and-trace system in England. To be clear, this is a systems failure and one that is axiomatic of the complex governance arrangements existing in the UK and the selective use of competition in the allocation of public funds for services. For example, of the £18 billion in procurement contracts issued largely for PPE and test-and-trace services, £10.5 billion was awarded to companies in the 'so-called VIP lane' for contracts, to people known personally to ministers, peers and MPs, often to firms with little or no record for such work (Jenkins, 2021). The then Secretary of State for Health and Social Care, Matt Hancock, was found to have acted unlawfully by a high court judge in February 2021 for not publishing details of multi-billions of pounds of COVID-19-related contracts and refused to apologise for this (Merrick, 2021). Even considering the emergency situation, the apparent lack of accountability and arrogance at the top of government and business[2] is revealing of the make-up of the kind of social contract that these contracts occur in. Not only is social closure a persistent feature of the social contract but it also (re)produces the 'possibility space' for policy development and implementation within the nexus.

A further example is provided by Friedman and Laurison's (2019) analysis of the Labour Force Survey, in which they cite Weeden and Grusky's (2005) notion of 'micro-class reproduction' to explain the contribution of children following in their parents' occupational footsteps to the exclusivity of certain fields. People with parents as doctors are a 'staggering' 24 times more likely to become doctors than those with parents doing any other kind of work and, despite the standardised pay and training in the NHS, are also more likely to experience job progression (Friedman and Laurison, 2019). This is not to question the 'merit', such as the effort, qualifications and skills of people in these positions. But as Friedman and Laurison (2019) state, people do not have an equal capacity to realise their talent, nor chance for that merit 'to land' and, therefore, argue that the privileged enjoy a critical head start. More fundamentally it is striking that medicine is by some distance the profession with the strongest micro-class reproduction (law is the next highest, with children of lawyers 17 times more likely to enter this profession) given the argument in the previous chapter about the privileged position held by the NHS relative to other public services in the social contract. The persistence of medical framings of health has largely dominated how we understand and respond to health in policy terms, despite well-established calls for a more complex social and material understanding of health. This suggests that widening the gene pool might produce a better understanding and appreciation of the conditions making people sick and assist the medical profession (and by association health systems) to be less captivated with patient-focused responses to population health problems.

Turning now to education policy and the education system has a key function to prepare children for the division of labour and make the population fit for the requirements of capitalism (Fevre, 2016). That it does so for children and families from very unequal footings is a longstanding feature of debates about education policy. For example, in *The wealth of nations*, Smith (1776) highlighted that parents were buying their sons education and training not because jobs needed these investments but to effectively transmit privilege to them and create a barrier to keep poorer competitors out (Fevre, 2016). Similarly, Reay (2017: 26) points out that education cannot compensate for society because the education system was not set up to do that; it operates instead as an 'academic sieve, sorting out the educational winners from the losers in a crude and often brutal process that prioritises and rewards upper- and middle- class qualities and resources'. Hierarchical class advantage, then, has been designed into the expansion of access to education in England and the subsequent reforms of this (see Fevre, 2016: 129–43), and despite 150 years of state schooling, working-class trajectories remain markedly different from those of the upper and middle classes (Reay, 2017). In this respect there is a close alignment between the social contract and paternalistic conceptions of need (see, Dean, 2010), in which education provides skills and opportunities for 'someone like you'. Even the Education Act 1944, which responded to a greater impetus for social equality but did so by creating three types of secondary schools (grammar, secondary modern and technical schools – although very few of the last of these opened) (Fevre, 2016), can be viewed in this light. Blackman (2017: 15) argues that these developments were 'partly a reactionary response to demands for more inclusive social policies further to the growth of mass democracy,' and sit within Thane's (1978) view of British social policy's long history of separating people into deserving and undeserving 'us' and 'other' categories.

The Conservative governments' education policy post-2015 sought to raise social mobility through education and a commitment to equality of opportunity through raising educational standards across the board (Lupton and Obolenskaya, 2020). However, Lupton and Obolenskaya (2020) found a 'system under strain', in which the ratio of pupils to teachers rose and very little impact was made on reducing inequalities in terms of spending, access, experiences or outcomes. The latest Social Mobility Commission's (2019) *State of the nation* report makes a series of recommendations in the following areas:

- early years (for example, extend eligibility for the offer of 30-hour childcare);
- schools (for example, identify and share good practice in schools in areas of poverty and deprivation);
- further education and apprenticeships (for example, increase spending on disadvantaged 16- to 19-year-olds through a student premium);
- higher education (for example, limit unconditional offers and make more use of contextualised offers for widening participation); and
- working lives (for example, invest in skills, jobs and infrastructure for areas with low social mobility).

These are worthy areas for social policy but fail to target inequalities in condition sufficiently to level the playing field or intervene in the political economy to change the rules of the game. Gamsu (2021) provides some more radical policy recommendations focusing on private schools, which include removing charitable status from private schools and creating a 'People's Education Endowment' through nationalising and redistributing endowment wealth. These changes would lead to private schools becoming reliant on fee income alone, making many of them economically unviable, leading to closure or integration into the state system (Gamsu, 2021). As Gamsu (2021) concedes, this would require legislation and redistributive taxation and measures across society, which, in turn, would need popular support that may be building as the COVID-19 pandemic has exacerbated inequalities and emphasised the need for children from widely different positions to 'catch up' on lost education.

For now, I will conclude this section with a radical challenge to higher education policy, which has been provided by Blackman (2017) in his report entitled *The comprehensive university*. Since the post-1992 expansion of higher education in the UK, many more children from working-class backgrounds have gone to university but Reay (2017) argues that exclusion from the system has shifted to exclusion within it. In this respect, Blackman (2017) argues that given higher education institutions claim to be engines of social mobility, selectivity in these should come under the same scrutiny as for schools, because they entrench class privilege to a greater extent than they extend opportunities. Decisions to send children to independent schools are in essence concerned with separating these children from children in general to increase their chances of doing well later in life and the hierarchical nature of higher education fulfils a similar function and is a continuation of this trajectory (Blackman, 2017). Blackman (2017: 29) states that in higher education, highly selective institutions are viewed as 'high status' or elite institutions, and this contributes to social stratification and segregation, which leads to less selective universities and the students attending these (who are more likely to be working class and Black) essentially being viewed as lower status. Despite the democratic intentions of widening access, there has been an intensification of class and racial inequalities between different levels of higher education, leading to an increasingly polarised system in which working and lower-middle classes are relegated to universities the more privileged do not want to attend (Reay, 2017). Blackman's (2017) proposal is to have open or basic matriculation entry (that is, to introduce a comprehensive system) and universities with a disproportionately high number of entrants from more affluent backgrounds would have targets to rebalance them towards the sector average. Citing Astin (2016), Blackman (2017) highlights the need for universities to attach much more priority to 'excellence' in 'developing smartness' and the academic growth of average or underprepared students, arguing that this would enhance productivity in the economy, as well as fairness.

Social mobility and the political economy

In this section we will return to the discussion about a political economy that is inherently competitive, seeks to commodify people within a market economy *and* has produced high levels of inequality. These high levels of inequality would have been considered unusual (at best) during the 1970s but are now a long-established feature of the complex systems cutting across the political economy and social policy. In Chapter 1 this was described as a 'phase shift' in the trajectory of society, which we explore here in relation to, and interaction with, the social mobility policy agenda. As we have seen, there is a tendency towards social closure at the top of society in a system rigged towards those in more privileged positions, which makes the notion of fair competition highly questionable. However, we have also seen that the individualism in the political economy has, at least in part, responded to the desires and beliefs of a population about, for example, freedom, responsibility, merit and competition in society. A key consequence of this, according to Srnicek and Williams (2016), is that we are constructed as competitive subjects driven to constant self-improvement through perpetual education and the requirement to be employable.

Herbert Spencer's[3] view of the 'demoralising effects of government' preventing self-reliance and interfering with human rights was influential over the Thatcher governments' shift to neoliberalism (Fevre, 2016). In short, an unfettered form of capitalism was increasingly seen as the best guarantor of individualism and freedom by the electorate (Fevre, 2016). Under New Labour, renewed attempts to mitigate the harshness of the political economy were often framed around notions of 'social investment'. Investing in individuals' capacity (or human capital) was viewed as a legitimate form of social spending, in for example education, because it would deliver both individual and societal returns downstream. However, this approach did little to challenge the individualism and competition at the heart of the political economy. Subsequently, the Conservative-led coalition government's debt to Hayek's (1960) model of market individualism is apparent through it making no attempt to create a level playing field and instead using policy measures aimed at those who have failed to make the most of market opportunities (Brown, 2013). Reay (2017), therefore, stresses that all recent governments of different political persuasions have prioritised creating aspirational students and have done so in a deeply unequal society, which makes working-class students responsible for their success through the 'cruel optimism' of social mobility.

Jessop (2020: 202–3) summarises key features of the neoliberal political economy as:

- liberalisation and deregulation, making markets more competitive;
- privatisation of state-funded or -owned activities and the use of market proxies in the residual public sector;
- internationalisation to promote competition; and
- reductions in direct taxes for greater consumer freedom and sovereignty.

Srnicek and Williams (2016) argue that neoliberalism has not simply been externally imposed but has been built on very real desires of the population, tapping into beliefs about meritocracy, hard work, freedom and the distrust of politicians, unions and bureaucracies. In this respect, Owens and St Croix (2020) cite Littler's (2017) claim that neoliberal political and cultural formations have closely aligned meritocratic social mobility with social justice and highlight the central position of the 'responsible individual' within meritocratic policy discourse. Consequently, the political economy functions around individual rights and concepts of freedom associated with these. The logic of the political economy is, therefore, generally antagonistic towards social rights and the egalitarian conditions Rousseau viewed as a necessary foundation for freedom.

Wealth and access to educational opportunities provide a good example of the priorities embedded in the system. Housing wealth and overall wealth are much more unequal than income inequalities (see, for example, Sayer, 2016; Byrne and Ruane, 2017) and Owen et al (2021) argue that the 2007/08 financial crisis marked a structural change in housing wealth inequalities, with new levels of spatial inequality emerging in house-price appreciation. Wealth provides access to selective education, which acts as a protective mechanism around sustaining higher socioeconomic status across generations. Wealth (and the potential to purchase more expensive housing) also provides more choice relative to accessing the state sector, which Byrne (2005) described as a 'fitness landscape' of highly differentiated school examination performance, which originated in the catchment area of comprehensive secondary schools. The potential to move to better-performing local educational systems and catchment areas means that middle-class parents are in a much better position to use the readily and freely accessible information online that will help people 'find the right home near the right school'. These types of factors led Hamnett and Butler (2013: 1) to highlight the very different housing market characteristics of different areas that contributed to 'distinct social geographies of class, income and ethnicity which operate at a variety of different spatial scales'. In this context, it is no surprise that socioeconomic inequalities in educational attainment remain clear and persistent (Marmot et al, 2020a). There is a need to enhance social rights to decommodify us as economic actors and provide more equal starting points for everyone to fulfil their potential, but we are strongly wed to a system geared to the transfer of individual property rights.

Social mobility provides a good example of the ecological dominance of the market and capital in interaction with social policy and public service provision. As we have already seen, the lack of mobility at the very top of society is a key feature of the social contract. For example, the close links between Whitehall and international finance are demonstrated through the past five Permanent Secretaries to the Treasury working before or after in international finance (in the IMF, the World Bank or investment banks) (Davis, 2018). In this respect, there is a common understanding of economic theory between a highly influential arm of the state and global finance. Streeck (2016) characterises this kind of understanding as representing markets as a technical arrangement for economic convenience that has far-reaching implications and repercussions for society and the distribution of power, status, opportunities, ways of life and identities. The nature of social mobility in England (that is, some movement in absolute terms, but inequalities in relative mobility and a tendency towards social closure at the top of society) is both reproduced by, and reproduces, the political economy that is so central to the social contract. Hutton (2015), for example, argues that the Treasury has an inbuilt scepticism about public spending and prioritises reductions in debt first, tax cuts second and creating public benefit and goods and infrastructure as the residual. Therefore, its capability to create public value and advance the public interest is limited (Hutton, 2015). The austerity programme that developed after 2010 provides an extreme example of this and one in which the role of the state to decommodify us has been further reduced. Blakeley (2020: 71) argues that austerity was 'about maintaining the political and economic power of the British ruling class at a time of deep fragility', rather than the best approach to reducing government debt. In so doing, they have reinforced a tendency in the political economy towards what Mason (2019: 64) describes as defining human nature as essentially economic and the worker as 'human capital'.

There are, however, serious and growing questions about the extent to which neoliberalism can fulfil its part of the deal in the social contract in creating sufficient opportunities for 'responsible' and 'hard-working' individuals with merit. In this respect, Brown et al (2011) claim that social mobility highlights a crisis in the neoliberal 'opportunity bargain', which Brown (2013) argues is no longer able to bear the weight of social and political expectations. He describes this as a prolonged positional struggle akin to a traffic jam, in which aspirational working- and middle-class people and families just want to do the best for themselves but become disappointed with institutions, posing a 'legitimation crisis' to market competition. At the same time, the development of a strong tendency towards wealth extraction and rentierism in the economy (see, for example, Sayer, 2016; Christophers, 2018) has contributed to a reward structure in which personal success is not aligned with institutional success or the best interests of society (Davis, 2018). As Friedman and Laurison (2019: 227) conclude, we should be asking questions about the 'legitimacy of an economic system that too often allocates profoundly unequal rewards based on the accident of social origin'. In this light, Boliver and Byrne (2013) assert that at the very least we should think again about whether we are prepared to accept wide disparities in income and wealth, and the considerable educational and other advantages they can buy, at a time when opportunities for social mobility are about to close down. Brown (2013) argues that mobility studies need to move beyond focusing on origins and destinations via education to include inequalities in condition and by so doing focus on how societies reward those in different destinations and organise the competition for a livelihood. Marmot et al (2020a: 71) demonstrate a concerning trend in which 'in-work poverty has increased, mainly due to low wages, inflation, rising housing costs and the low level of benefits; benefits are meant to compensate for low wages but are currently too low to lift working people out of poverty'. We should, for example, question why some social care workers, who look after some of the most vulnerable people in society, are paid the minimum wage. This reflects very badly on the legitimacy of the political economy and the social contract in terms of the stake these workers have in society and how they are valued for fulfilling such a vital role. However, this is part of the trajectory of the UK as one of the most unequal of European post-industrial societies, in which a flexible labour market has been pursued, alongside crippling the capacity of trade unions to act effectively and to organise in new domains of employment (Byrne, 2019). Social mobility, through encouraging aspirations to move up in a society in a rigged competition, encourages us to take our eye off the ball in terms of labour market conditions in general and at the bottom, in particular, leading Berardi (2019: 161) to identify that 'the current social pathology is largely seen as an effect resulting from exploitation, economic competition, and the precariousness of salaries'.

Complexity science helps us to understand systems, their complexity and how they intersect with one another (Castellani, 2018). Capital through neoliberalism and the prioritisation of economic over social relations exerts ecological dominance over the nexus. The political economy plays an important role in the deal people get out of society and is a key system that shapes other systems and the 'possibility spaces' of these to a greater extent than they influence it. As we have seen, this tends towards the logic of competitive individualism while doubling down on creating an unequal playing field for this to take place on. Not only does this impact on the life chances of people, with place, social class, ethnicity and gender being important characteristics, but it also deals social policy a very bad hand in providing more equitable outcomes for individuals and groups from less advantaged backgrounds. So, when Boris Johnson (2013) stated at the Margaret Thatcher lecture that economic inequality is an inevitable by-product of humans being 'very far from equal in raw ability, if not spiritual worth', he reveals prejudicial views about valuing worth stemming from misinterpreting social hierarchy as natural. Boliver and Byrne (2013: 1) argue that in this situation inequalities in pay and outcomes are viewed as fine as long as equality of opportunity exists to allow fair competition for unequal outcomes, 'but the logic immediately breaks down as soon as we realise that one generation's unequal outcomes are the next generation's unequal starting points'. We are, in short, very far from the conditions needed to make an accurate judgement of the kind that Johnson does. Education, employment and labour market individualism exist largely for narrow elites (Fevre, 2016). As Friedman and Laurison (2019: 226) argue, the notion of a 'prevailing wind' associated with an advantaged class background 'acts as an energy-saving device, allowing some to get further with less effort'. In a system that is geared towards competitive individualism, the secure footing that this provides can be incredibly beneficial across social, economic, cultural, psychological and political spheres. Levelling the playing field, therefore, is a prerequisite for making moral judgements about the worth and merit of people (should we be of the inclination to do so). Furthermore, the notion of competition that cuts across the economic system is also problematic in terms of producing limited economic growth (see Chapter 2) and for the legitimacy of the system to deliver opportunities across society. As Krugman has stated, cited by Shaxson (2018), 'a government wedded to the ideology of competition … is as unlikely to make good economic policy as a government committed to creationism is to make good science policy'.

Conclusion

> Social mobility … ensnares and works on both the individual psyche and collective consciousness. (Reay, 2017: 102)

This quote from Reay highlights both the significance and effects of social mobility in the social contract. It is an example of a policy priority that, despite a focus on fairness, aligns with the individualistic ideology of the political economy that stresses personal responsibility without meaningfully seeking to address the unequal footing upon which this takes place. Social mobility, therefore, provides a very good synecdoche for social policy in 21st-century England. The tendency towards the survival of the fittest in the political economy and social contract set a direction of travel and momentum that social policy is expected to address in order to produce more egalitarian outcomes. However, this is an example of social policy being 'tagged on' (see Byrne, 2005) to the market and, as such, social mobility plays a role in creating a degree of legitimacy for the social contract, without disturbing its trajectory.

The way the term 'social mobility' is employed tends to only (or at best largely) refer to upward mobility rather than social circulation. This misconception about the nature of social mobility sits much more comfortably with the social contract in England than the notion of relative equality of opportunity. The latter requires a more redistributive social contract that pays close attention to the significance of equality of condition in order to achieve a more equitable form of social circulation. Social mobility effectively allows politicians to dodge this issue and, therefore, crowds out a focus that seeks to level the playing field through challenging largely inherited protective mechanisms. For example, Calder (2016) describes post-1997 politicians as typically focusing on the unfairness of life chances in the UK and social mobility, rather than reducing income inequality, as the route to a fair society; leading to a focus on education rather than income inequalities or the privilege being preserved in families. Furthermore, as Brown (2013) argues (citing Hutton, 2010 and Stiglitz, 2012), social mobility is problematic because the neoliberal opportunity bargain cannot resolve the central challenge of educational and social inequalities. The accumulation of wealth, power and different forms of social and cultural capital across time, place and (especially) families is too significant for the notion of equality of opportunity to be anything other than a chimera. Thus, a key difference with health inequalities (as discussed in the previous chapter) is that social mobility is the wrong high-level policy issue to focus on from the perspective of developing a more egalitarian social contract. In examining social mobility, we must ask whether the type of contract that exists between citizens and the state and the individual and social outcomes produced through this are sufficiently equitable to secure our common interests. If not, we should also question whether the state needs to develop a more active role in tackling the excess of the market and the protective mechanisms that exist within families. Given that Calder (2016: ix) demonstrates that family remains a 'highly reliable predictor of how we do in life, where we end up, and how long we live', it should be a prime target for intervention.

7

The intergenerational contract

Introduction

In this chapter we will explore intergenerational aspects of the social contract by considering the situation now and looking ahead to future prospects. Fraser's (2016) account of a crisis of social reproduction (which includes social capacities such as giving birth to and raising children, care for family and friends, maintaining households and communities and sustaining social connections) in financialised capitalism provides a useful context for this discussion. Fraser (2016: 113) argues that finance capital disciplines 'states and publics in the immediate interests of private investors not least by demanding public disinvestment from social reproduction'. This disinvestment not only is highly significant for care across generations but also has wider implications for the social systems this is situated in. The argument in Chapters 1 and 2 about the tendency in the political economy to seek out and remove redundant or spare capacity from social systems based on a narrow (market-oriented) view of economic efficiency has salience here. Following Fraser's (2016) argument, the mode of economic production is putting strains on people in and out of work and to the extent that we have developed a 'liberal-individualistic' and 'gender-egalitarian' imaginary where everyone deserves equal opportunities to realise their talents in the sphere of production and where social reproduction is an obstacle to advancement. In other words, and consistent with the argument made in Chapters 1 to 3, the social sphere has been squeezed through developments in the political economy and the social contract is increasingly struggling to deliver the equality of opportunity to progress in the meritocratic way the rhetoric suggests is central to the social contract. The move away from relegating women to the private sphere is undoubtedly progress but as Fraser (2016) argues we also need to reinvent the production–reproduction distinction in capitalism. Without doing so, the inequalities in experience relative to socioeconomic status across production and reproduction will likely extend. In the next section of this chapter, we will consider the intergenerational nature of the social contract from the perspective of the opportunities for the future for younger generations. We will also consider the implications of the notions of 'wellbecoming' and 'wellbeing', given the tendency towards individualism in the system they are occurring within, and we will explore how these may be affecting and shaping younger people. The following section considers ageing in society and connotations of this for the social contract and the role of social policy.

The subsequent section will explore some routes and conditions for change in the social contract. In particular, we will consider the turn to applied postmodernism and a focus on identity-based politics, with implications for a hegemonic (class-based) route for social change. We will also briefly explore some possible implications of technological developments associated with automation for the development of the social contract in the near future. The chapter then concludes.

The intergenerational contract: young and relatively young

In the previous chapter, concerns about the extent of social circulation *and* of declining opportunities for future generations relative to those of their parents were raised. In this section we will explore the latter more fully, first by considering the position as it is now and then exploring potential future developments. In both respects it important to set this in a historical context. Byrne (2019) argues that one of the most important aspects of post-industrial society is that parents of young adults and young adults themselves are looking at a future in which they are going to be materially worse off than their predecessors for the first time since the late 19th century. The section will conclude by exploring debates about child wellbeing and how this concept relates to broader trends in society.

In advanced capitalist democracies, concerns about how inequalities impact on opportunities across generations have been growing in recent years. For example, prior to the COVID-19 pandemic the OECD (2019) was reporting multiple pressures facing the middle classes in many OECD countries, including technological change, the automation of jobs and the cost of living rising faster than earnings. In the wake of the pandemic, the IMF (2021) has highlighted that COVID-19 has worsened pre-existing inequalities and may cause income gaps to persist from generation to generation. Both of these reports call into question trust in governments if action is not taken to improve intergenerational standards of living. Essentially, the social contract (that is, the deal between the state and society) needs to adapt to these trends. If not, the current form of capitalism, and its influence over the nexus, is facing a crisis of legitimacy. Whether capitalism is able to adapt sufficiently (given its intrinsic prioritisation of profit, competition and economic efficiency) is questionable. It is also highly questionable whether capitalist-led adaptation is desirable when there is an inbuilt tendency to prioritise economic over social relations (as discussed in Chapter 2). We will return to this discussion in the concluding chapter.

In many respects, England and the UK are at the forefront of debates about inequalities in generational living standards. Obolenskaya and Hills (2019) demonstrate that inequality over the past 20 years has plateaued, especially when compared with the sharp increases in inequality in the 20 years before then. They also argue that this is somewhat of a mirage as the nature and depth of inequalities have changed markedly for some groups, for example the income share of the top 1% was much higher in 2015 than 20 years earlier. While housing costs increased as a proportion of income for all income deciles between 1996/97 and 2016/17, the largest increase was for the most deprived decile and nearly 40% of families in this group were spending at least a third of their income on housing costs, compared with about 2% for the least deprived (Judge and Bell, 2018). Bourquin et al (2020) highlight wide discrepancies in the growth of incomes across generations, with the over 60s increasing theirs on average by 28% between 2002–03 and 2018–19, and the under 60s increasing theirs by just 7%. In the working-age population, millennials are 20–25% less likely to move jobs (and, therefore, miss out on pay rises) than members of 'Generation X' and are only half as likely to own their own home by age 30 as baby boomers (Resolution Foundation, 2018). Johnson et al (2021) cite Cribb and Simpson (2018) to acknowledge the collapse in home ownership for people in their late 20s and early 30s (falling from 55% to 35% between the mid-1990s and 2017) as real house prices rose by 170%, while declining growth in younger people's pay, income and wealth was a major social change after 2005 affecting the better off and worse off within younger age groups (Obolenskaya and Hills, 2019). Furthermore, Johnson et al (2021) argue that the response to the 2007/08 financial crisis opened up the generational divide through ultra-low interest rates and quantitative easing pushing up asset prices. They also argue that fiscal policy after the pandemic would do well not to repeat this. In short, significant inequalities are being experienced between, and within, generations, with a general trajectory towards younger generations not doing as well as their parents.

The Social Mobility Commission (2016: iii) concluded that 'the 20th century expectation that each generation would be better off than the preceding one is no longer being met'. The Resolution Foundation (2018) identifies pessimism about young adults' chances of improving on their parents' lives with housing, work and pensions being the aspects of life in which this pessimism is most marked. These developments have become part of the social contract and Byrne (2019) usefully employs complexity language to describe the 'phase shift' in the 'possibility space' so that younger generations are hit by the downward trend in real wages, welfare cuts (massively accelerated by austerity) and the transformation of the housing system (with increased purchasing and renting costs). As Jessop (2018: 1737) states, neoliberal strategies have 'produced a seriously weakened "real economy" and hypertrophied rent-seeking financial sector'. He argues that 'successive governments have failed to provide adequate technical and vocational support to address workers shortages, to protect worker and union rights to prevent the race to the bottom and spur productivity-boosting capital investment ... to overcome the housing crisis ... and to moderate uneven regional development'. Fraser (2009) highlights that the ideal of the male-breadwinner family wage within the androcentrism of welfare provision in state-organised capitalism has been replaced once and for all by the neoliberal norm of the two-earner family. However, in 'disorganised' neoliberal capitalism, depressed wages, decreased job security, declining living standards and an increase in the number of hours worked have accompanied the increased participation of women in labour markets (Fraser, 2009). Therefore, while social reproduction continues to have a gendered nature, the critical distinction is that for those who can afford to pay for it, it is commodified (through low/minimum wages to those providing it), and for those who cannot it is privatised (that is, carried out in person) (Fraser, 2016). These trends are all features of the trajectory of the political economy over the past 40 years (which were described in Chapters 1 to 3) and have, therefore, been a long time in the making and a quite visible product of the social contract that is seemingly immune from meaningful or sustained challenge. They have occurred alongside the reduction in corporation and top-rate taxes in this period (Jessop, 2018). Hood and Waters (2017) demonstrate that, between 2010 and 2015, tax and benefit reforms resulted in a negative impact for the poorest half of the UK, with the poorest quintile experiencing the most negative impacts. A key issue highlighted by Sayer (2016) and Streeck (2016) is that there is money in the economy and society but that it is increasingly concentrated in fewer private hands and not used to encourage growth and increase standards of living. As Sayer (2016), in particular, argues, those towards the bottom of the income and wealth distribution spend a much higher proportion of their income than those hoarding wealth at the top of society and, therefore, increasing their spending power has a greater benefit for the economy and society. Keynesian critiques of the negative impact of neoliberal taxation policy and austerity reforms on aggregate demand should, therefore, be included alongside discussions about declining standards of living.

Alongside these issues, the notion of child wellbeing has grown in significance in recent years (see Bradshaw, 2002; The Children's Society, 2020; Gromada et al, 2020). In part this has been in response to the tension between 'wellbeing' and 'wellbecoming' as concepts that inform societal development and policy. The latter plays an important role in the justification for public spending as a form of social investment within the political economy and is logically consistent with the individualism in the social contract and with the notion of social mobility (as discussed in the previous chapter) more specifically. In competitive and possessive individualistic societies, rights and responsibilities are geared towards neoliberal concerns with wellbecoming and the development of economic actors to succeed and consume in the global economy. Han's (2017) focus on neoliberalism's attention towards the psyche is instructive here. His argument is that the psyche is being exploited and, through the digital revolution and big data, 'the surveillance state and the market are merging' (Han, 2017: 65). Through self-optimisation and compulsive achievement, we exploit ourselves, with burnout and depression defining our times, but in so doing help to optimise neoliberalism as a system (Han, 2017). 'Wellbeing' is an alternative concept, which is concerned with quality of life, being in equilibrium with and flourishing in one's environment, and is associated with dimensions such as life satisfaction, positive relationships, self-acceptance, having a purpose in life and autonomy (Dodge et al, 2012). For young people, the UK fairs less well than its European counterparts in terms of wellbeing and The Children's Society (2020) highlights the potential significance of associations with child poverty levels and fear of failure. Austerity has played a role here as funding for local authority children and young people's services fell by 29% between 2010/11 and 2017/18 and in the most deprived local authorities (in England) these services fell almost five times faster than in the least deprived local authorities (Marmot et al, 2020a). Over a similar period (2009–10 and 2017–18), children's happiness with life as a whole became significantly lower and declined in terms of happiness with appearance, school, schoolwork and friends (The Children's Society, 2020). The only area not declining significantly was happiness with family (Children's Society, 2020). Family largely relates to the private sphere and could be interpreted as providing some protection and shielding from public, social and economic spheres of influence. How these negative outcomes impact on later life remains to be seen. However, there are concerns about how poor wellbeing impacts on transitions to adulthood, not least through the effects of COVID-19 lockdowns and disruptions to education, which are exacerbating and intensifying inequalities in childhood development (see, for example, Araujo et al, 2020; Marmot et al, 2020b).

While recognising the significance and seriousness of a lack of wellbeing and poor mental health, it is also important to consider some of the potential consequences of these on generational outlooks. Millennials have been a key focus of the (largely) right-wing media in recent years. They are often characterised as the so-called 'woke'[1] or 'snowflake'[2] generation, depending on which side of the culture war one is on. Of course, many (including myself) are not taking sides here and the culture war is in many ways a phoney war being stoked up by both sides. However, as we shall see in the section later in this chapter on routes and conditions for change, it is capturing and diverting attention from more pressing issues. For now, there are three concerns about how the dynamics of wellbecoming and wellbeing (albeit to a lesser extent) are interacting with the expectations that millennials have about the social contract. Each of these stems, at least in part, from a perspective informed through working and teaching in an elite higher education institution for about 15 years. First, inequalities in experience, assets and resources can become lost through a focus on individual wellbeing and/or wellbecoming. These inequalities are highly significant and for those towards the bottom of the distribution they intensify the negative consequences of the two remaining concerns.

Second, there is a tension between creating aspirations and expectations[3] around individual wellbeing and wellbecoming (including about opportunities, quality of life and public sector service provision) when intergenerational standards of living appear to be declining, inequalities are rising and we have disinvested in public services in a broader context of lean systems geared towards economic efficiency and removing redundant spare capacity (see Chapter 2). We may well question whether the bar is being set at a level higher than many can achieve at an individual level and to demands for more bespoke and responsive service delivery than we currently fund. In other words, raising aspirations (through a *me* as opposed to *we* intentionality [see Chapter 1] in the competitive individualistic context of the political economy and the social contract) creates dynamics and a diversity of demands on the system that it lacks the capacity to deal with.

Third, as Lukianoff and Haidt (2019) argue, there is a danger that, focusing on experiential and subjective knowledge over objective knowledge, while expounding the belief that people are fragile and are weakened by unpleasant and upsetting experiences, is decreasing young people's resilience and ability to cope with difficult ideas and hurt feelings (cited in Pluckrose and Lindsay, 2020). They describe this as a form of reverse cognitive behavioural therapy. Without seeking to demean the significance of mental health, the issue here is that the world has never been a *fair* place and does not bend to the vast majority of our individual wills. In fact, we seem to be placing more demands on it to do so at the same time as the capacity of the system to respond to these demands (in terms of opportunities and supports) is increasingly limited. None of this is good preparation for the flexible labour market that struggles to provide opportunities to meet societal expectations, unless of course one is able to rely on the brute luck of birth as a protective mechanism (in terms of networks and capital either for employment and/ or for economic and social security within the family unit).

The intergenerational contract: ageing

In this section we will consider ageing, how it relates to the social contract and implications for social policy. As Walker (2018) argues, ageing is inevitable but it is also malleable. This means that there is a role for policy to affect the malleability in positive ways. However, as Walker (2018) also argues, socioeconomic factors, in particular, leave 'biological imprints' on later-life physical development. In other words, inequalities, and especially deprivation, take their toll over the lifecourse. We have covered a lot of ground in discussing the role of the political economy in heightening and then maintaining high levels of inequality in England and also seen how this negatively impacts on life expectancy and healthy life expectancy relative to a social gradient in health inequalities. These are directly related, through their cumulative yet differential impacts, to ageing across the lifecourse.

Moreira (2017) highlights pessimistic and optimistic views of the ageing society in policy and academic debates. The former is largely based on the notion of declining economic participation later in life and increasing 'dependency ratios' through which the economically active will have to increase their productivity in order to generate more income to sustain the pension schemes and welfare programmes needed to sustain older, 'dependent' non-workers (Moreira, 2017). The more optimistic view emphasises the opportunities emerging from ageing populations and moving to increasingly age-integrated social relations linked to flexible retirement policies, policies for the active involvement of older people in economic and social life, and support for health-maintenance activities and social relations (Moreira, 2017). We will explore the nature, and some of the challenges, of demographic ageing in society later in this chapter. Before we do so we should consider the notion of health-maintenance activities and social relations more fully. Walker (2018) argues that social policy can play an important role in modifying the ageing process at earlier stages of the lifecourse so that old age is less restricting physically and mentally. This approach is based on targeting the impact of risk factors to reduce the severity and prevalence of chronic conditions later in life (Walker, 2018). Walker (2018) identifies the following as the types of policies that would contribute to an agenda of active ageing across the lifecourse: taxation policies on smoking, alcohol and sugar; a national physical exercise programme; long-term calorie restriction and weight loss programmes; and programmes for cognitive stimulation. He also argues that this requires moving beyond age-segmented policy to a lifecourse approach and a seismic shift from acute sickness services to prevention, in order to mitigate against the cumulative effects that physical and mental illness and/or injuries have on a person's functional capacity. This approach is consistent with global developments, such as the WHO's healthy ageing agenda, which sets out a comprehensive set of public policy responses to population ageing (Vizard et al, 2021). There is also a good deal of overlap between the health inequalities research discussed in Chapter 5 and the healthy ageing agenda. In short, creating the conditions to lead a healthy life results in longer lives with a lower proportion of time spent in poor health, which is mutually beneficial to an active ageing agenda.

By 2066, the total number of people aged 65 years and older is projected to increase by 8.6 million people to 20.4 million people (26% of the population), which is broadly equivalent to the size of the population of London today (ONS, 2018). The 85 years and over age group are projected to increase fastest, from 1.6 million people in 2016 (2% of the total population), doubling to 3.2 million in 2041 and then reaching 5.1 million people by 2066 (ONS, 2018). In contrast, the population aged 16 to 64 years is projected to increase by only 2% over the next 25 years and by 5% by 2066 (ONS, 2018). Hills (2017) cites the Office for Budget Responsibility's long-term spending projections to highlight a potential 1% increase of GDP on public spending per decade between 2022–23 and 2062–63 due to the pressures of an ageing population. He emphasises that there are vast and increasing uncertainties that may both overstate (for example, the impact of increases in life expectancy on the state pension age resulting in slower increases in state pension spending than predicted) and understate (for example, increases in health conditions such as dementia, diabetes, coronary heart disease, stroke and arthritis among the over 65s) the projected costs. The ONS (2018) highlights that health requirements increase steeply from about 65 years of age and social care requirements increase with age, especially as people reach older, old age. However, Moreira (2017) warns against the uncertainty of expertise and expert calculations of ageing, citing the failure of past actuarial assumptions leading to population ageing being a 'knowledge-related problem'. The successful implementation of a coordinated approach to active ageing would be a prime example of how actuarial assumptions about ageing may be wrong, given the likely savings on health and social care from a healthier and more active population.

If actuarial calculations are broadly correct, Hills (2017: 247–8) concludes that:

> an ageing population and the structure of our welfare state mean we will have to spend more just to stand still in terms of services in relation to needs and living standards. That leaves us with two choices in the long run – cutting services in relation to needs or raising more revenue.

The current trajectory is towards the former, with the ONS (2018) reporting a steady decline in local authority spending on adult social care in recent years with, for example, a 24% decrease in the number of people receiving domiciliary care services between 2009 and 2015 in England. In these circumstances the need for care has not decreased and Age UK (2020) has estimated that 1.4 million people who need care no longer access it. The difference between social care and healthcare is stark here, with people with assets over £23,250 having to pay for care themselves, rely on family or friends to provide it or go without (SCIE, 2020). The provision of informal care has clear implications for families. In England, most care is provided informally by carers who are unpaid family members, friends or neighbours, with an estimated value of between £58.6 billion and nearly £100 billion a year (NAO, 2018b). Using the last available Census data, the National Audit Office highlights that the number of unpaid carers in England increased by 11% between 2001 and 2011, to 5.4 million people (NAO, 2018b). Given the changes to allocation criteria under successive austerity governments, this number is likely to have increased significantly. Of these 5.4 million people more than one million people provided 50 or more hours of unpaid care a week (NAO, 2018b). The impact on active ageing across the lifecourse for those providing this level of support while working in paid employment is extremely detrimental.

Age and ageing in England are not uniform across place and this creates different dynamics alongside those of inequalities in the capacity of public services and private means to respond to these. McCurdy (2019) highlights that gaps have grown considerably over the past 20 years, with the poorest and richest areas ageing slowest and middle-income areas the fastest – the average age for a UK region being 40.1 years old, with London (35.3 years old) the youngest region and the South West of England (43.9 years old) the oldest. At the local authority level of aggregation, these age gaps increase significantly, with the gap between the oldest local authority (North Norfolk, with an average age of 53.8 years) and youngest (Oxford, with an average age of 29 years) being nearly 25 years. An active ageing agenda must take into account the spatial variations in ageing in order to calibrate a lifecourse approach to demographics.

A key aim of the welfare state has always been to smooth out variations in the incomes and living standards people get from the market during their lifecourse (Hills, 2017). This 'life-cycle smoothing' is provided largely through universal services such as health and education and benefits such as pensions, with contributions into the system generally outpacing the risks it insulates us from until later in life (Hills, 2017). In this respect, Hills (2017) argues that much of what social policy does relates to lifecycle variations in resources and needs and the dominant effect is to redistribute income between people's own lifecycles rather than between people. However, we might question whether the balance is entirely right here, as the move to a more preventative and active ageing approach earlier in life may well reduce costs later in life. As Walker (2018: 269) concludes: 'It is not that successive governments have openly opposed a life-course approach to ageing but, rather, if they have even contemplated it, the ideological and/ or practical challenges of doing so have proved too daunting.' He argues that the influence of major corporations, which benefit from the status quo, need to be factored into this equation too. The decline in public spending as a proportion of GDP between 2008/09 and 2018/19, from 42% to 35%, is also a major barrier to the kind of approach advocated by Walker. He highlights the neoliberal political economy and anti-welfare state paradigm of individual entrepreneurial freedom, private property rights and free markets as providing a major barrier to the collective approach required to mobilise active ageing policy. Once again, we can see how (after Fraser, 2016) social reproduction has been limited by the nature of production in financial capitalism. Removing capacity from the former in the search for profit through economic efficiencies has ramifications across the complex systems that our lifecourses develop within. As in other areas of the social contract, the consequences are not equitable and are patterned relative to inequalities. The unequal distribution of age-associated chronic conditions are biological imprints of socioeconomic factors across the lifecourse (Walker, 2018).

Routes and conditions for change

Taylor-Gooby (1994) declared that postmodernism represented 'a great leap backwards' in relation to the social policy discipline. His central argument was that, in viewing the universal themes of modern society as obsolete (particularly themes such as inequality) and focusing instead on diversity, postmodernism acts as an 'ideological smokescreen' for some of the most important trends in capitalism and social policy. It is important to recognise that social policy analysis has not whole-heartedly embraced postmodernism and instead incorporates an emphasis on discourse, diversity and a disillusionment with the validity of universalistic policy solutions and institutional models of welfare (Villadsen, 2011). However, here we are concerned with how social policy interacts with the political economy and the social contract and in these areas the impact of the turn towards postmodernism has some profound implications. In their highly critical account of postmodernism, Pluckrose and Lindsay (2020) argue that it has evolved into a more actionable and applied form, alongside social justice activism[4] and intersectionality, as a moral community that seeks to delegitimise bad discourses and replace them with better ones. A particular problem, identified by Pluckrose and Lindsay (2020), is the postmodern tendency to focus on oppressive language and discourse, which fits within Crouch's (2000) classification of a negative activism of blame and contempt. The emergence of a specialised language that delegitimises 'bad' discourse causing social injustice has become a key battleground for social justice activism (Pluckrose and Lindsay, 2020). In this respect, Pluckrose and Lindsay (2020) contrast the identity-first intersectional approaches to politics that dictate what people must believe and the language they should use, with the civil rights movement of universalistic equal rights. Telling people what not to think and say[5] is not a great strategy for academics and politicians who are far more immersed in these debates than most people. Castellani (2018) argues that therapeutic ways of managing threats and aggressions and positive messages are more effective in changing people's behaviours than punishing tones. None of this is meant to discount that identity-based prejudice exists in societies, although we should also recognise that historically we are living in one of the most tolerant times in terms of identities of gender, sexuality and ethnicity (see, for example, Castellani, 2018; Mason, 2019; Pluckrose and Lindsay, 2020). We would do well to remember, as Crouch (2020) asserts, that people on the liberal left have been on the winning side (often with the tacit support of neoliberals) on cultural issues around, gender, sexuality, race, multiculturalism and the role of religion in social life but often without realising it.

Why does the argument set out here matter to debates about social policy? Put simply, a primary focus on discourse is the wrong battle for our times, both strategically and materially, given that it fragments and distracts attention from the political economy. Fraser (2009: 113) sums this up well by arguing that capitalism would much rather 'confront claims for recognition over claims for redistribution'. Srnicek and Williams (2016) and Mitchell and Fazi (2017) argue that the postmodern and post-structuralist focus on identity politics has diverted attention from capitalism while failing to turn into a hegemonic movement to challenge neoliberalism. This does not have to be an either/or and the reality is not straightforward. A critical distinction to be made here is that historical and structural power imbalances globally (see, for example, Fraser, 2009, 2016; Castellani, 2018; Virdee, 2019), in gender (Fraser, 2009, 2016) and ethnicity (Bonilla-Silva, 1997; Virdee, 2019), provide path dependencies in (and resulting from) the social contract that interact with social policy and political economic systems at different scales and across sectors. However, it is hard to disagree with Fraser (2009) when she describes an over-extension of a critique of culture and a downplaying of a critique of the political economy. These are important issues to confront and Mitchell and Fazi (2017: 10) state that insufficient attention has been focused on capitalism, meaning that 'marginality is no longer described in class terms but in terms of identity ... class struggle has ceased to be seen as the path to liberation'. Fraser (2016) has characterised these trends as leading to the emergence of a 'progressive neoliberalism'; Mason (2019) is much more strident in referring to postmodernism as a 'slave ideology for the neoliberal system', through critiquing sexism, racism, colonialism and patriarchal certainty in science but not doing so in the name of overthrowing the system that produced them. If Fraser (2009) is right that dominant claims for justice have shifted from redistribution to the recognition of identity and difference, then we need to redress the balance. Mitchell and Fazi (2017) argue that discarding identity politics in favour of class-based anti-capitalist understandings of emancipation is not in contradiction with the struggle against racism, patriarchy, homophobia, transphobia and other forms of prejudice and discrimination. The application of Rousseau's conception of a social contract with a high degree of equality is highly salient here as equality is considered to be an enabling condition for the freedom and moral development of humans. As we saw in Chapter 1, Thompson (2017: 272) described this as a new form of cognition proposed by Rousseau, valuing 'interdependent, non-dominant and non-exploitative and egalitarian social relations'. The theory is, if we are more materially equal this will enhance social ties and free us up to lead the kind of lives we choose to, regardless of our background and/or identity.

On a personal note, and as someone who wants to see greater equality in terms of class, disability, gender, ethnicity and sexuality, I should, in theory, be reasonably receptive to the identity-based social justice activism just described. That I am not should be of concern to its proponents because I am, more or less, a fellow-traveller in terms of not wanting to see discrimination and prejudicial treatment and outcomes for people based on their identity. However, an excessive focus on discourse becomes tiresome and offputting to my socially liberal[6] mind, and for those with a less egalitarian vision for society there is a strong tendency to interpret social justice activism as a form of control by a liberal elite of 'thought-police'. There is no doubt that the political right has been stoking, tapping into and exploiting these issues. Crouch (2020) argues that changes in contemporary societies are bringing conservatism back to the fore through representing pessimistic nostalgia, which claims to defend apparently threatened national cultures and gender relations from liberal internationalism. Castellani (2018) describes this as contributing to a rise in 'global strongarms' (for example, Donald Trump, Recep Tayyip Erdoğan and Viktor Orbán – and to this we should add Boris Johnson) who come to power in democratic countries and are the chosen form of government within which people seek to pursue their happiness. Crouch (2020) argues that there has long been a large minority of people in society who are socially conservative, but the basic guarantee of economic and social security provided by liberal societies acted as a dam holding these attitudes back. Globalisation and deindustrialisation have taken their toll on the working classes and it is clear that the appeal of the alt-right has increased as cultural issues have grown in significance for this group (Couch, 2020). Byrne (2019: 18–19) concludes that in a post-industrial age:

> there has been a reduction in the direct appreciation of the relationship between employment and exploitation … exploitation is rampant but the workplace and political organisations which confronted it are much weaker … class is weaker as an emergent and expressed form of post-industrial capitalism BUT the generative mechanisms of capitalist social relations which produces class is up and running at full steam ahead.

So, as Crouch (2020) argues, we are not seeing a triumph of culture over the economic but a new configuration of the two. The concern here, as Fraser (2016) highlights, is that under the current mode of financial capitalism, emancipation has joined marketisation to undermine social protection. Byrne (2019) summarises a core strand of argument among academics such as Colin Crouch, Peter Mair and Robert Unger that in post-industrial and democratic capitalism, while social reform remains on the agenda the necessity of profound social change has been abandoned.

In this final part of the chapter, we will briefly explore a key development facing the social contract and social policy that does offer the possibility of profound social change. This is the development of artificial and machine intelligence and the automation of jobs and services. Research into automation suggests that enhanced productive capacity could lead to between 47% and 80% of current jobs being automatable in the next two decades (Srnicek and Williams, 2016). New jobs will emerge to replace these but whether they will do so on a scale to fill these gaps is highly questionable. This would lead to levels of unemployment that are potentially both economically and socially unmanageable and make the 'survival of the fittest' a much more brutal competition than it is now. Under these circumstances, the social contract will have to adapt significantly and the potential for a new trajectory and 'possibility space' emerging are enhanced. Whether, for example, this is an equality-preserving contract or one in which a strong sovereign authority is required to preserve the social order will be key to the role of the state relative to the interactions with the political economy.

The current trajectory is not promising. Neoliberalism and the market (see Mason, 2019) have been central to the values we want machine intelligence to work within and express. Furthermore, Bridle (2019) argues that not only is computation increasingly layered across and hidden within objects, it also constitutes power for the small number of people controlling these technologies. Mason (2019) argues that we need to decide what values we want machine intelligence to express and that there is a chance to develop a form of 'utopian socialism' if we use technological advancement cooperatively and to reduce the number of hours that are required for work. Debates about automation include the possibility of enhanced equality through post-work (Srnicek and Williams, 2016) or job-guarantee (Mitchell and Fazi, 2017) futures that rely on the profits of the 'second-machine' age being put into public as opposed to private hands. The idea of a post-work future is based on the idea that as a consequence of automation the global economy will not be able to produce enough jobs and, therefore, we should move towards a post-work consensus, in which we no longer rely on jobs for income (Srnicek and Williams, 2016). Srnicek and Williams (2016) argue that through a universal basic income (UBI), people will have the money to enjoy their free time and build communities and engage in politics. Mitchell and Fazi (2017) agree about the threat from automation and similarly argue that it is the role of the state to create a framework that will advance the interests of its citizens relative to this. They differ in the response, however, arguing for a job guarantee instead of a UBI, whereby anyone who is willing to work will receive an unconditional job offer for a socially acceptable wage. The labour force will provide a supplement to a wide range of social and infrastructural expenditure using the proceeds of automation to fund this (Mitchell and Fazi, 2017).

While these visions of the future are fairly utopian, they are also proactive in facing the consequences of automation head on and seeking to manage this for the benefit of society and social relations. They are, therefore, consistent with the approach to the political economy proposed here as the significance of the social sphere over the economy is stressed, and that the latter should be put to work for the former. Fraser's (2016) focus on the current struggles over reproduction are relevant here. She argues that this extends beyond the family and strengthening social reproduction encompasses a wide range of services (for example, health and social care), unconditional basic income, rights (including trade union rights) for migrants and domestic workers (who often take on paid reproductive labour), a shorter working week and greater parental leave (Fraser, 2016). As Fraser (2016: 116) concludes, 'taken together, these claims are tantamount to the demand for a massive reorganisation of the relations between production and reproduction: for social arrangements that could enable people of every class, gender, sexuality and colour to combine social-reproductive activities with safe, interesting and well-remunerated work'. Automation may well be the best bet for achieving these ends given that it will demand a collective response.

Conclusion

In this chapter we have explored some of the intergenerational dynamics that exist within the nexus and that co-evolve with the trajectory of the political economy and the social contract. Capitalism, as influenced by neoliberalism, is failing to produce equitable intergenerational transfers of income, wealth, living standards and opportunities. There is a 'me' intentionality within the system, associated with wider dynamics towards wealth extraction (that is, into private hands), competition and individualism. At the same time, debates about identity have become a preoccupation that distract attention from the mismanagement of the economy as a means for social equality (that is, putting the economy to work for society as a whole as opposed to working in the interests of capital). This provides a far from promising context for social policy development and raises questions about the legitimacy of social policy delivery in the face of heightened expectations and an intractable political economy. The kind of approach needed to successfully embed active ageing, for example, seems beyond the means of social policy given that intergenerational and intragenerational inequalities remain stubbornly high and the capacity of the state and the space afforded to social reproduction to respond to these have both been reduced. Looking ahead, the COVID-19 pandemic and automation both provide opportunities to challenge the nature and organisation of the system, with the latter, in particular, having the potential to 'shake things up' to the extent that the nexus may move to a new attractor state. How this is managed, and in whose interests, will be as critical for the future of social policy as for the future of employment, given the relationship between society and the economy.

8

Conclusion

In a book with social policy in the title, there may not have been as much focus on policy as some readers might have expected. This is not because it is being argued that social policies do not matter. They do, and frequently make real differences to people's lives (including some of the most vulnerable people in society) and for both good and for ill. On balance, and despite the surveillance and conditionality associated with much contemporary policy making (as illustrated, for example, by the UN Special Rapporteur, 2019), I believe that social policy has a positive impact on society, although it has not been the purpose of this book to tally up and keep a score of the impact of social policies. This is incredibly challenging methodologically and relates to the complexity and interactions between the political economy, social policies, individuals, their life histories, places, communities, professions, labour markets, housing, public and private amenities and services, and so on. These are part of a wider complex whole and the agency, structures and cultures that cut across and constitute complex systems. Instead, the approach here has been to situate social policy as a field of study within broader debates about the political economy and the social contract. In so doing, there has been a tendency to focus on the macro-trajectory of England as a nation within the UK and the broader global context. The intention has been to contextualise the role and efficacy of social policy and encourage us to consider changing the conditions[1] in which social policies are delivered to make these somewhat more tractable to policy levers. Micro and individual agency in systems undoubtedly matters but the significance of the macro, given the influence of the political economy outlined here, means that the role of social policy is best framed as trying to hold back the tide (and seeking to prevent the most vulnerable in society from getting swept away). In order to make social policy more effective we need to pay more attention to the conditions it operates within and that it is trying to affect but, in so doing, also plays a role in legitimating and maintaining. In this respect the Marxist interpretation of the function of the welfare state and social policy, more generally, as preserving capitalism through smoothing off its sharper edges is instructive.

I do not want to conclude by simply repeating the refrain that the social contract is broken as it both lets society off the hook and underestimates the strength and adaptability of the status quo. Put simply, if the social contract was broken, the nature and direction of society would not have persisted with the relative ease that it has, albeit within a political system that is far from perfect and increasingly post-democratic. England and the UK have had more than 40 years of governments subscribing to some form of neoliberalism and competitive and possessive individualism. Income inequalities increased markedly throughout the 1980s and have remained at roughly this level ever since. In this period the shift from government to governance began in earnest through the privatisation and contracting out of public services, resulting in more fragmentation and complexity and less accountability for their delivery. Following the application of Rousseau's conceptualisation of the social contract (outlined in Chapter 1) as a lens to test the position people find themselves in, in a free society, we can conclude that England is a long way short of an equality-preserving contract that enhances freedom through non-exploitative human relations.

The social contract as it stands, therefore, both creates significant social problems associated with inequalities and ties the hands of social policy as an effective means for meeting the size of the challenges accumulated in society. This is a 'double whammy' and is crucial for contextualising the impact and effectiveness of social policy. These are features of (and continuities within) the social contract that are contributory factors to the situation we find ourselves in now. The COVID-19 pandemic has made these issues more visible but whether that will be sufficient to escape the inherent entropy in our social, economic and policy systems is an entirely different question. Changing direction is difficult and made all the more so when we lack a hegemonic movement coordinating and driving this. Where does this leave and/or take us looking ahead? It is not possible to rip things up and start again. Any change that occurs, no matter how radical this is, will be built upon the trajectory and previous path dependency of the system. A change in kind (as opposed to in degree) of the nature of the nexus and complex systems constituting this (a 'phase shift') requires sustained support across a wide range of interests and stakeholders and will have to be achieved through a democratically elected government seeking to influence the range of interests cutting across the nexus.

In the next section we will explore some attitudes about social justice, inequality and fairness in England and relate these to pressing issues in the social contract, relative to the COVID-19 pandemic and the impact this has had, and is likely to have, on the social contract. The concluding section will propose some high-level recommendations consistent with the application of social contract theory outlined in Chapter 1 (that is, mediating on what Rousseau got right, in a contemporary setting).

Social attitudes and crisis

In this section we will explore recent attitudes about inequality, fairness and social justice outlined in the British Social Attitudes (BSA) survey (Curtice et al, 2020). These provide a useful illustration of the type of social contract that could be considered to be desirable in England. Given the strong links between capital and politics both globally and nationally (as discussed in Chapters 1 to 3), public attitudes are a necessary but far from sufficient condition for change. Nevertheless, desiring change and having a strong popular alternative vision of the social contract are minimum conditions for shifting the nature of the social contract towards a more egalitarian and equality-preserving character. The section concludes with consideration of the impact of the COVID-19 pandemic on the trajectory of society and the nature of the social contract.

One of the headline findings from the BSA survey (Curtice et al, 2020) is that only 24% of English respondents think that income distribution in Britain is fair (22%) or very fair (2%), compared with 65% thinking it is unfair (52%) or very unfair (13%). However, there is a relatively even split between whether people think it is right or wrong for those with a higher income to buy better healthcare and education, which suggests less concern with how income inequalities are used as protective mechanisms for social outcomes. Curtice et al (2020: 2) cite Wlezien (1995) and Curtice (2010) to suggest that 'voters react like a thermostat to changes in public spending and soon lose whatever enthusiasm they may have had for higher taxes and spending once the public expenditure taps have been turned on'. Over the course of the past 40 years, attitudes to public spending and taxation have fluctuated. Just over a third of people wanted higher public spending and taxation at the start of the Thatcher governments (which were seeking to reduce public spending) but this had nearly doubled by the end of her time in office and more or less remained at this level through the course of the Major government and the early years of New Labour, when they were committed to previous levels of public spending (Curtice et al, 2020). As Labour began spending more on public services and then following the 2007/08 financial crash (with the large public expenditure incurred through this) and into the early austerity years, the proportion of people wanting higher public spending and taxation had declined again to about a third of the population (Curtice et al, 2020). By the end of a decade of austerity, attitudes had once again reversed, with growing demand for higher spending and taxation. Trends in attitudes about the generosity of benefits relative to dependency on these, social security and deservingness, and the level of unemployment benefits follow relatively similar patterns over the past 40 years or so, which correspond with those around public expenditure (Curtice et al, 2020). Despite the changing attitudes about tax, spending and benefits these should be interpreted as both pragmatic and conservative given that they resonate within and contribute towards the ongoing trajectory of the political economy and the social contract when viewed with a broad lens. For example, public attitudes appear to play a role akin to the Marxist interpretation of the function of the welfare state. We might view these attitudes as equivalent to a sailing boat changing tack to plot a steady course within the trajectory of the system and thereby helping to sustain it. To mix metaphors, Curtice et al (2020: 4) argue that unless the COVID-19 pandemic has persuaded voters to 'reset the level of their tax and spend thermostat', then the increased spending to meet the costs of the public health crisis is likely to meet a negative public reaction in time. In other words, public attitudes allow for a certain amount of deviation within the 'possibility space' of the social contract but not for a significant change in trajectory.

In Chapter 2 we explored Fevre's (2016) argument that neoliberalism emerged in large part through the growing acceptance that the forces of collectivism were seen to be threatening to put human progress into reverse. This standpoint still has real purchase and runs entirely counter to Rousseau's philosophy that equality and collectivism are the basis from which true freedom (that is, *freedom to*) can emerge. The attitudes expressed in the BSA survey need to be interpreted within this context and represent a degree of homeostasis within a political economy that is heavily influenced by neoliberal ideals (and the appeal of *freedom from*). Despite its flaws (and the 'first past the post' electoral system is a significant one), democracy is the route to changing the nature of the social contract and the social outcomes produced through this. There appears to be something about the ballot box that brings out the innate conservativism in England and the comfortable marriage between neoliberalism (that is, competitive individualism) and conservatism (that is, pragmatic possessive individualism) has prospered through this. The only Labour governments in my lifetime were the Callaghan government (for one year) and the New Labour government between 1997 and 2010, both of which accepted the turn to neoliberalism. More recently, the election of four successive austerity governments since 2010 demonstrates a reaffirmation not only of the neoliberal trajectory but also of a doubling, tripling and quadrupling down on what the UN Special Rapporteur on Poverty (2019: 1) described as deliberately removing the 'glue' holding British society together and replacing it with 'a harsh and uncaring ethos'. Nevertheless, the attitudes described here suggest that some fissures are emerging in the social contract and furthermore Curtice et al (2020) highlight that there is an overall dissatisfaction with the status quo in England as more than three quarters of respondents to the BSA survey feel that the distribution of social inequality across society is not what it ought to be. While these provide some promising green shoots for a more egalitarian social contract, we must treat them with caution given they coincide with the election of a Conservative government in 2019 that had been instrumental in the austerity programme of the previous ten years (albeit with a new leader, promising to 'get Brexit done' and to 'level up').

We will conclude this section by considering some of the implications of the COVID-19 pandemic and crisis for the social contract. Fraser (2016) demonstrates how different crises in capitalism led to the shift from 19th-century liberal capitalism to state-managed capitalism in the 20th century and to the current financialised capitalism. The 2007/08 financial crisis did not initially lead to a reinvention of capitalism,[2] but more recently the OECD (2019) and the IMF (2020) appear to be aligning with calls for increased state management of capitalism in the aftershock of the effects of austerity, with the COVID-19 pandemic potentially adding further momentum to this. As Blakeley (2020) argues, the fiscal response from the global north to the pandemic demonstrates that governments can issue bonds and create money and, therefore, do not face limits to spending in the way that neoliberals often assert. Balogun et al (2021) cite Tussell (2021) in identifying that £31.2 billion of public money had been spent on COVID-19 contracts to fund the private sector by June 2021, once again demonstrating the selective intervention of the state in market economies. Furthermore, while the rich world can do this, poorer and less powerful countries cannot (Blakeley, 2020).

Madgavkar et al (2020: 2) highlight that countries such as 'the US and UK that were typically lower spenders on the social contract before the pandemic have raised their expenditure by significantly more than countries like Denmark, which previously had ranked among the high spenders'. This finding appears to corroborate the argument in Chapters 2 and 3 about the implications of the neoliberal logic of economic efficiency removing 'redundant' spare capacity from systems, reducing the resilience of these to shocks to the system. More fundamentally, Marmot et al (2020b) describe the conditions in England prior to the pandemic as consisting of an unhealthy population, a defunded public service and poor political leadership and governance. They argue that:

> The levels of social, environmental and economic inequality in society are damaging health and well-being. As the UK emerges from the pandemic it would be a tragic mistake to attempt to re-establish the status quo that existed before ... social and regional health inequalities, and health deteriorating for the most deprived people, are markers of a society that is not functioning to meet the needs of its members. (Marmot et al, 2020b: 4–5)

One hope emerging from the crisis is that it has focused attention on the social contract in the way that Rousseau proposed – as a lens on whether mutually beneficial social outcomes are being achieved. It is clear that those who are doing less well out of society have done less well out of the pandemic. Marmot et al (2020b: 8), for example, highlight that the 'deep-rooted inequalities in society which manifest in overcrowded households and unsafe working conditions will have made it harder to manage the pandemic, as has the fact that the UK government's response to maintaining people's incomes, while welcome, was less generous than in many European countries'. On the other hand, Leslie and Shah (2021) demonstrate that the richest 10% of families increased their wealth by £40,000 over the median family during the pandemic and the wealth gap now stands at 55 times the typical household income. They also argue that wealth gaps seem set to persist, with wealthier households looking likely to maintain higher saving rates following the pandemic. Key findings from Marmot et al (2020b) suggest that the likely impact of the pandemic will include:

- an adverse impact on young people's social and emotional development and an educational gap;
- widening inequalities long term through social/economic impacts on family income and training/employment prospects;
- higher COVID-19 death rates mirroring local authority deprivation and underlying socioeconomic inequalities;
- systemic disadvantages, including living conditions, among minority ethnic communities through structural racism;
- divisions between key workers and elementary workers in terms of working conditions; and
- a new health crisis of pandemic-associated behaviour change and declines in mental health.

If we are to talk, as the government frequently does, about 'building back better' from the pandemic, the analysis of the preceding argument is that we must do so in ways that 'build back fairer' (Marmot et al, 2020b). Because the pandemic has so exposed the inequities in the social contract, there is arguably no better time to do so.

Whether the differential experiences and outcomes (both current and future) will lead to a significant change in the social contract is debatable. Madgavkar et al (2020) argue that there has been a 'sudden and massive' movement in the social contract through increased government expenditure on: public sector wages, total social spending, unemployment, active labour market programmes, family and other social policies, healthcare, housing, pensions, education and gross fixed capital formation. They calculate that the UK increased its expenditure in these areas by 38% in 2020, compared with 2019. Madgavkar et al (2020: 4) argue, therefore, that the 'social contract may be momentarily stronger and more effective in buffering risks and guaranteeing basic needs for individuals than it has previously been this century'. However, they question whether the 23% increase in public debt to GDP ratio in 2020 is financially sustainable. Indeed, Curtice et al's

(2020) findings about public attitudes to public spending also question the extent to which this level of spending can be sustained with popular support. Nonetheless, for the social contract to undergo a 'phase shift', as opposed to adapt to a crisis, the renewed role for state action and public spending needs to be sustained.

A more equitable social contract?

In this final section we will explore some proposals that seek to alter the trajectory of the social contract and the political economy and would, therefore, change the conditions in which social policies intervene. As indicated in the introduction to the chapter, these require popular support, and the current social contract is much more closely aligned with a notion of 'survival of the fittest' rather than with pursuing greater equality as a normative goal in society. The extent to which society, as a whole, is a willing accomplice or along for the ride or in opposition to the nature of the contract is debatable and complex to untangle. For those seeking a radical departure from the current trajectory there are rays of hope, ranging from: longstanding crises in capitalism (see, for example, Streeck, 2016), climate change (see, for example, Sayer, 2016) and the more recent financial crisis (see, for example, Fraser, 2009); growing concerns about inequalities for the legitimacy of governments (OECD, 2019); through to some of the attitudes expressed in the BSA survey (Curtice et al, 2020) discussed in the previous section; and, of course, to the COVID-19 pandemic (see, for example, Madgavkar et al, 2020). In the BSA survey (Curtice et al, 2020), respondents are asked about the type of society Britain ought to be in terms of patterns of social inequality and out of the five options provided there is a strong preference towards the most egalitarian distribution presented, that is, a 'society with most people in the middle'. Whether it is possible to harness these rays of hope in a society so geared towards competitive and possessive individualism is highly debatable. The logical corollary to this is that we need to adjust the gearing and mechanisms in society in order to change direction. Currently, good policy design[3] is generally calibrated to the nature of complex systems. A core argument put forward here is that this does not go far enough and that we also need to recalibrate complex systems in order to make them more tractable to well-meaning policy objectives. The kinds of policy goals and initiatives that would go a long way towards recalibrating the social contract, the political economy and the complex systems cutting across these, towards a more mutually beneficial and egalitarian contract, could include the following:

- Reverse the 'phase shift' in inequalities that played a major role in moving England to a new 'attractor state' and 'possibility space' during the 1980s.

- Specifically, reduce inequalities to 0.24 on the Gini coefficient for household income within ten years. This will be stretching to the say the least, but the timespan is equivalent to that during which the increase in inequalities occurred.
- Reduce the gap in typical household wealth between the top 10% of households and the median household from 55 times greater than household income (Leslie and Shah, 2021) to 20 times greater.
  - The introduction of a range of redistributive taxation measures targeting assets held through land, housing and family should be used to target excessive wealth and unearned income.
  - Increase corporation tax towards the levels at the higher end of the distribution of OECD countries. This would mean increasing this tax from 19% to about 30%.
  - Introduce an additional top level of income tax at 60% for people on an annual income over £250,000.
  - These measures are intended to level the social gradient of socioeconomic inequalities and to limit the impact of protective mechanisms held within wealthier families.
- Return government spending as a percentage of GDP to pre-austerity levels, to 42% within ten years and to 50% by 2030.
- Return public service delivery 'in-house' as the default position and make social value the dominant logic for the contracting out of services that cannot be, or are better delivered externally.
  - Not only will this simplify the fragmented governance and accountability of complex systems, it will also move public services away from a profit-logic that is largely incompatible with social systems.
  - This would also provide a meaningful role for local democracy through enhancing and devolving control of public services and resources to the local arm of government.
- Create a regional economic development strategy based on proportionality and redistribution, in order to address regional and local spatial imbalances and the allocation of 'disbenefits' associated with the progress of some parts of the country at the expense of others.
  - Allocate funds on a needs-based formula related to disparities in social outcomes (for example, educational and health inequalities) and disparities in economic, social and cultural infrastructure and *not* on the basis of competitive bidding for pools of central government funds.
- Give local government control of healthcare commissioning, including the return of outsourced care to the public sector. This should be based on proportionate universal allocation of funding, to be provided to areas according to deprivation and need.
  - This proposal is intended to move the operating logic of health systems away from a sickness/treatment model and towards focusing on the

social determinants of health through locally accountable institutions. The medical understanding of health is vital but should work within a much broader social understanding of health and place.

• Abandon social mobility as a high-level policy goal and concentrate instead on the relationship between equality of opportunity, condition and outcomes.

Of course, these initiatives are widely out of step with the current trajectory of society and the social contract. However, that is precisely the point. In order to move to a more equitable society we need a step change in the ways things are done. I am absolutely convinced that the social contract can be improved 'for the many and not the few'.[4] The analytical use of the social contract has demonstrated that society produces highly patterned and inequitable outcomes relating to social inequalities. However, this does not seem to matter sufficiently to tackle these inequities and inequalities in a comprehensive and sustained manner. The appeal of competitive individualism, no doubt, plays a significant role here. This does not necessarily have to run counter to claims for greater equality. After all, competition is most thrilling and rewarding when it is closely fought and from a fair and level playing field. We also need to raise the bar in terms of what we expect out of the deal we all make in order to surrender our sovereignty to be members of a political community. We are, in theory, all equal participants in a political community. Yet, health and wellbeing in terms of quality and duration of life, opportunities to participate in labour market activities we choose to pursue, living in comfortable surroundings, having spare capacity (in terms of time and resources) to pursue leisure activities and so on, could all much more closely reflect our formally equal status. The key problem facing those of us on the left ideologically and politically is that not enough people have sufficiently high expectations about the role of society and the state in producing more equal outcomes. After more than 40 years of individualism and the notion that collectivism holds more people back than it helps holding sway over the social contract, it might be time to reconsider and reset the equilibrium.

Notes

Introduction

1   Although the latest life expectancy figures show that life expectancy is stalling (Marmot et al, 2020a).

2   How this is managed and what it means in terms of work and unemployment is open to debate, but Srnicek and Williams (2016) and Mitchell and Fazi (2017) offer positive ways forward to manage this that have the potential to enhance social ties, which we will explore in Chapter 7.

3   Essentially my individual bias, tastes and preferences. These are things we all have, are somewhat innate and, therefore, are fairly ingrained and hard to change. This is really significant to discussions about the social contract and also to debates about social policy, although it will be argued here that while they are generally central to the former, they are much underrepresented in the latter and to the detriment of the discipline.

4   Castellani et al (2015) have argued that, in complex systems approaches, both social reality and data are best seen as 'self-organising, emergent, non-linear, evolving, dynamic, network-based, interdependent, qualitative and non-reductive'.

5   Disposable income takes into account the impact of taxation and cash benefits. The Gini coefficient is a measurement of inequality in society, in which 0 would equate to all households receiving equal income and 1 would mean that a single household possessed all income.

6   A 'phase shift' is a complexity term and relates to a change in *kind* rather than *degree* in a social system.

7   As will become clear, I am not arguing that a diversity of experience is negative, far from it, but that if people do not have a relatively equal basis from which to pursue their life choices then at a minimum we need to consider the implications of this for the make-up and nature of society.

8   Hobbes' solution was for a strong individual sovereign who would offer a credible threat of sanctions for non-compliance (Hartz and Nielsen, 2015).

9   We might interpret 'general' as public and social and 'particular' as private and individual interests.

10 Whether that is in terms of enhancing the income/wealth of the poorest in society, which it is argued stifles motivation and causes dependency, or taking income/wealth from the richest, which is often constructed as unmeritocratic or a form of theft of private property.

11 Note the use of *reduce* here – the state continues to have an important (albeit reduced) function to redistribute resources to mitigate against extremes of inequality at the bottom of the income distribution.

Chapter 2

1   And to a lesser extent, gender and ethnicity, given the persistence of strands of patriarchy and racism across society, and to a much lesser extent disability.

2   In this respect, freedom is generally constructed as *freedom from* external constraints in neoliberalism.

3   See Crouch (2020) for a discussion of 'posts' as 'parabolas'. Post-democracy means that we have moved past peak democracy, in the same way post-industrial means a move beyond peak industrial society. In these cases, democracy and industry still exist and function in society but are in decline.

4   We return to rentiers later in the discussion. For now, rentier capitalism is concerned with the profits (economic rent) stemming from the ownership of different types of property rather than the productive use of labour or capital.

Chapter 3

[1] However, it is important to recognise, as Fox Gotham (2009) emphasises, that alongside deregulation a range of state institutions and agencies created policy and legal-regulatory frameworks to facilitate subprime lending.

[2] In the 2005 general election, Labour received 35.5% of the vote in England and the Conservatives 35.7%, but under the 'first past the post' electoral system, Labour received 355 seats compared with the Conservatives' 198. In all other elections in this period, the party with the highest percentage of votes won the most seats, but not proportionately so (Cracknell and Pilling, 2021).

Chapter 4

[1] However, it is important to recognise that by far the greatest spatial disparities occur at the neighbourhood and Lower Layer Super Output Area (LSOA) level.

[2] The cost may well rise again in the future (see Atkins, undated).

[3] Lund (2016) reports that over the course of the 20th century the price of land as a proportion of housing cost grew from 5% in 1930 to about 40% by the late 1990s, and Policy Exchange (2013) estimates that the cost was as much as 55% by 2013.

Chapter 5

[1] For example, HM Treasury's (2015) *Spending review and autumn statement 2015*, estimated that local authorities would face 'a real terms reduction of 71 percent for early intervention services between 2010/11 and 2019/20'.

[2] It is also worth noting that *The NHS long term plan* made it clear that the social determinants of health were the responsibility of local government and not the NHS (NHS, 2019).

Chapter 6

[1] As MP for Newmarket (flat horse-racing's headquarters and seat of the Jockey Club) and Secretary of State for Health and Social Care (between 2018 and 2021) Matt Hancock has received tens of thousands of pounds in donations from wealthy racehorse owners, trainers and other members of the sport's establishment (Conn, 2020).

[2] Alex Bourne, a former neighbour of Matt Hancock, with no previous experience in producing medical devices, won a contract to supply test tubes to the NHS, many of which had to be recalled due to being faulty, and joked in a private text exchange to Hancock, 'Matt Hancock – never heard of him' (Lawrence, 2021).

[3] Herbert Spencer is thought to have coined the term 'survival of the fittest'.

Chapter 7

[1] Woke means being alert to injustice and discrimination in society, although it has been increasingly used as pejorative term by opponents.

[2] The term 'snowflake' is used to mean an overly sensitive or easily offended person.

[3] Noting that homeostasis (that is, adapting our satisfaction, happiness and aspiration to our environment) has an impact on (see, for example, Cummins, 2010; Dodge et al, 2012) the level of expectation about wellbeing relative to socioeconomic position.

[4] They provide a detailed critique of the implications of the 'scholar activism' that has emerged and draws on postmodernism and intersectionality. Their core argument is that by reducing inquiry to an assumed outcome of prejudice (across intersections), complexity and nuance are flattened in order to promote identity politics based on 'truths' that are situated within cultural constructs and different descriptions of reality that cannot be measured against one another (Pluckrose and Lindsay, 2020).

[5]   Of course, this does not include hate speech, which expresses hate or encourages violence towards people based on identity.

[6]   My political philosophy is broadly socialist libertarian, that is, highly economically redistributive, which provides the material conditions for people to lead the lives they want to, unencumbered by economic constraints or moral judgement.

Conclusion

[1]   Of course, social policies can and do play a role in changing these conditions.

[2]   Recognising the huge investment of public money was (paradoxically) used to preserve neoliberalism.

[3]   And there are many examples of not-good policy design that, for example, fail to take into account the nature of and interactions between the political economy, social inequality and policy outcomes.

[4]   Although recent election results suggest that 'the many' are nowhere near as convinced!

Bibliography

Abrahamson, V. and Raine, R. (2009) 'Health and social care responses to the Department of Health Heatwave Plan', *Journal of Public Health*, 31(4): 478–489.

ACEVO (Association of Chief Executives of Voluntary Organisations) (2011) *Powerful people, responsible society: The report of the Commission on Big Society*, London: ACEVO.

Acheson, D. (1998) *Independent inquiry into inequalities in health*, London: The Stationery Office.

Age UK (2020) '1.4 million requests for care from older people turned down since the PM promised to "fix care, once and for all"', https://www.ageuk.org.uk/latest-press/articles/2021/1.4-million-requests-for-care-from-older-people-turned-down-since-the-pm-promised-to-fix-care-once-and-for-all/ (last accessed 29 September 2021).

Alcock, P. with May, M. (2014) *Social policy Britain*, London: Palgrave Macmillan.

Allen, A. (2011) 'Michael Young's The Rise of the Meritocracy: A philosophical critique', *British Journal of Educational Studies*, 59(4): 367–382.

Amnesty International (2020) *As if expendable: The UK government's failure to protect older people in care homes during the COVID-19 pandemic*, London: Amnesty International.

Araújo, L., Veloso, C., Souza, M., Azevedo, J. and Tarro, G. (2020) 'The potential impact of the COVID-19 pandemic on child growth and development: A systematic review', *Jornal de Pediatria*, doi: 10.1016/j.jped.2020.08.008.

Agrawal, S. and Phillips, D. (2020) *Catching up or falling behind? Geographical inequalities in the UK and how they have changed in recent years*, London Institute for Fiscal Studies.

Artaraz, K. and Hill, M. (2016) *Global social policy: Themes, issues and actors*, London: Palgrave.

Astin, A.W. (2016) *Are you smart enough? How colleges' obsession with smartness shortchanges students*, Sterling, VA: Stylus.

Atkins, G. (undated) 'High Speed 2 costs', https://www.instituteforgovernment.org.uk/explainers/high-speed-2-costs.

Atkinson, T. (2013) *Wealth and inheritance in Britain from 1896 to the present*, CASE working paper 178, London: London School of Economics and Political Science.

Baker, A., Epstein, G. and Montecino, J. (2019) *The UK's finance curse costs and processes*, Sheffield: Sheffield Political Economy Research Institute.

Balogun, B., Jozepa, I., Booth, M., Ward, L. and Powell, T. (2021) *COVID-19 contracts and the public inquiry into the handling of the outbreak*, London: House of Commons Library.

Bambra, C., Smith, K., Garthwaite, K., Joyce, K. and Hunter, D. (2011) 'A labour of Sisyphus? Public policy and health inequalities research from the Black and Acheson Reports to the Marmot Review, *Journal of Epidemiology and Community Health*, 65(5): 399–406.

Bambra, C., Smith, K. and Pearce, J. (2019) 'Scaling up: The politics of health and place', *Social Science and Medicine*, 232: 36–42.

Bambra, C., Hayre, J., Pollock, A. and Brown, H. (2020) *COVID-19 and health inequalities: Independent SAGE report 21*, London: Independent SAGE.

Barnett, N., Giovannini, A. and Griggs, S. (2021) *Local government in England: 40 years of decline*, London: Unlock Democracy.

BBC (2019) 'Thatcher: A very British revolution', BBC 2, 10 June.

BBC (2021) *Today*, Radio 4, 27 January.

Beatty, C. and Fothergill, S. (2016a) *The uneven impact of welfare reform: The financial losses to people and places*, Sheffield: Centre for Regional Economic and Social Research.

Beatty, C. and Fothergill, S. (2016b) *Jobs, welfare and austerity: How the destruction of industrial Britain casts a shadow over present-day public finances*, Sheffield: Centre for Regional Economic and Social Research.

Beatty, C. and Fothergill, S. (2017) 'The impact on welfare and public finances of job loss in industrial Britain', *Regional Studies, Regional Science*, 4(1): 161–180.

Beatty, C. and Fothergill, S. (2018) *The contemporary labour market in Britain's older industrial towns*, Sheffield: Centre for Regional Economic and Social Research.

Belfield, C., Cribb, J., Hood, A. and Joyce, R. (2016) *Living standards, poverty and inequality in the UK: 2016*, London: Institute for Fiscal Studies.

Berardi, F. (2019) *Futurability: The age of impotence and the horizon of possibility*, London: Verso.

Bevan, G. and Hood, C. (2006) 'What's measured is what matters: Targets and gaming in the English public health system', *Public Administration*, 84(3): 517–538.

Bevir, M., Rhodes, R. and Weller, P. (2003) 'Traditions of governance: Interpreting the changing role of the public sector', *Public Administration*, 81(1): 1–17.

Bhaskar, R. (2008) *A realist theory of science*, London: Verso.

Black, D. (1980) *Inequalities in health*, London: Department of Health and Social Security.

Blackman, T. (2006) *Placing health: Neighbourhood renewal, health improvement and complexity*, Bristol: Policy Press.

Blackman, T. (2017) *The comprehensive university: An alternative to social stratification by academic selection*, Oxford: HEPI.

Blackman, T., Wistow, G. and Wistow, J. (2008) *Accountability for health: A scoping paper for the LGA Health Commission*, London: Local Government Association.

Blakeley, G. (2020) *The corona crash: How the pandemic will change capitalism*, London: Verso.

Blakemore, K. and Warwick-Booth, L. (2013) *Social policy: An introduction*, Maidenhead: Open University Press.

Blaxter, M. (1990) *Health and lifestyles*, London: Tavistock/Routledge.

BMA (British Medical Association) (2020) *The role of private outsourcing in the COVID-19 response*, London: BMA.

Boliver, V. and Byrne, D. (2013) 'Social mobility: The politics, the reality, the alternative', *Soundings: a journal of politics and culture*, 55: 50–59.

Bonilla-Silva, E. (1997) 'Rethinking racism: Toward a structural interpretation', *American Sociological Review*, 62: 465–480.

Bourdieu, P. (1986) 'The forms of capital', in Richardson, J. (ed) *Handbook of theory and research for the sociology of education*, Westport, CT: Greenwood, pp 241–258.

Bourquin, P., Joyce, R. and Norris Keiller, A. (2020) *Living standards, poverty and inequality in the UK: 2020*, Report R170, London: Institute for Fiscal Studies.

Boyson, C., Taylor, S. and Page, L. (2014) 'The National Heatwave Plan – a brief evaluation of issues for frontline health staff', *PLOS Currents Disaster*, edition 1, doi: 10.1371/currents.dis.aa63b5ff4cdaf47f1dc6bf44921afe93.

Bradshaw, J. (2002) *The well-being of children in the UK*, London: Save the Children.

Bridle, J. (2019) *New dark age: Technology and the end of the future*, London: Verso.

Briggs, A. (1961) 'The welfare state in historical perspective', *European Journal of Sociology*, 2: 221–258.

Broughton, J. (2019) *Municipal dreams: The rise and fall of council housing*, London: Verso.

Brown, P. (2013) 'Education, opportunity and the prospects for social mobility', *British Journal of Sociological Education*, 34(5–6): 678–700.

Brown, P., Lauder, H. and Ashton, H. (2011) *The global auction: The broken promises of education, jobs and incomes*, New York: Oxford University Press.

Burawoy, M. (2005) 'For public sociology', *American Sociological Review*, 70(1): 4–28.

Burchardt, T., Obolenskaya, P. and Hughes J. (2020) *The Conservatives' record on adult social care: Spending, policies and outcomes in England, May 2015 to pre-COVID 2020*, London: Centre for Analysis of Social Exclusion.

Burns, D., Earle, J., Folkman, P., Froud, J., Hyde, P., Johal, S., Rees Jones, I., Killett, A. and Williams, K. (2016) *Why we need social innovation in home care for older people*, CRESC Public Interest Report, Cardiff: WISERD.

Byrne, C. (2017) 'Neoliberalism as an object of political analysis: An ideology, a mode of regulation or a governmentality?', *Policy and Politics*, 45(3): 343–360.

Byrne, D. (2005) *Social exclusion*, Maidenhead: Open University Press.

Byrne, D. (2019) *Class after industry: A complex realist approach*, Basingstoke: Palgrave Macmillan.

Byrne, D. and Ruane, S. (2017) *Paying for the welfare state in the 21ˢᵗ century: Tax and spending in post-industrial societies*, Bristol: Policy Press.

Cabinet Office (2010) *The coalition: Our programme for government*, London: Cabinet Office.

Cabinet Office (2013) *State of the estate in 2012*, London: Cabinet Office.

Cabinet Office (2017) *Race disparity audit*, London: Cabinet Office.

Calder, G. (2016) *How inequality runs in families: Unfair advantage and the limits of social mobility*, Bristol: Policy Press.

Callaghan, G. (2008) 'Evaluation and negotiated order: Developing the application of complexity theory', *Evaluation*, 14(4): 393–405.

Campbell, D. (1979) 'Assessing the impact of planned social change', *Evaluation and Program Planning*, 2(1): 67–90.

Castellani, B. (2018) *The defiance of global commitment: A complex social psychology*, Abingdon: Routledge.

Castellani, B., Rajaram, R., Buckwalter, J., Ball, M. and Hafferty, F. (2015) *Place and health as complex systems: A case study and empirical test*, New York: Springer.

Chakrabortty, A. (2019) 'If you can't abide Jeremy Corbyn, learn from the moral of Ed Miliband', https://www.theguardian.com/commentisfree/2019/aug/20/jeremy-corbyn-moral-ed-miliband (last accessed 22 August 2019).

Christophers, B. (2018) *The new enclosure: The appropriation of public land in neoliberal Britain*, London: Verso.

Christophers, B. (2020) 'The PPE debacle shows what Britain is built on: Rentier capitalism', https://www.theguardian.com/commentisfree/2020/aug/12/ppe-britain-rentier-capitalism-assets-uk-economy (last accessed 15 September 2021).

Citizens Advice Bureau (2015) *A nation of renters: How England moved from secure family homes towards rundown rentals*, London: Citizens Advice.

Clarke, J. (2008) 'Living with/in and without neo-liberalism', *Focaal*, 51: 137–145.

Coburn, D. (2009) 'Income inequality and health', in Panitch, L. and Leys, C. (eds) *Morbid symptoms: Health under capitalism*, Pontypool: The Merlin Press.

Conn, D. (2020) 'Horse racing, Tory donations and a swift return from lockdown', https://www.theguardian.com/sport/2020/jun/16/horse-racing-tory-donations-and-a-swift-return-from-lockdown-matt-hancock (last accessed 26 January 2021).

Cope, Z. (2019) *The wealth of (some) nations: Imperialism and the mechanics of value transfer*, London: Pluto Press.

Corbett, S. and Walker, A. (2013) 'The Big Society: Rediscovery of the social or rhetorical fig leaf for neo-liberalism', *Critical Social Policy*, 33(3): 451–472.

Cracknell, R. and Pilling, S. (2021) *UK election statistics: 1918–2021: A century of elections*, London: House of Commons Library.

Creasy, S. (2020) 'Private companies face no accountability for the failure of test and trace – however poorly the service is run', https://www.polit icshome.com/thehouse/article/private-companies-face-no-accountabil ity-for-the-failure-of-test-and-trace-however-poorly-the-service-is-run (last accessed 26 January 2021).

Cribb, J., Disney, R. and Sibieta, L. (2015) *The public sector workforce: Past, present and future*, London: Institute for Fiscal Studies.

Cribb, J. and Simpson, P. (2018), 'Barriers to homeownership for young adults', in Emmerson, C., Farquharson, C. and Johnson, P. (eds) *The IFS green budget*, https://www.ifs.org.uk/publications/13475.

Crisp, R., Ferrari, E., Fothergill, S., Gore, T. and Wells, P. (2019) *Strong economies, better places: Local and regional development for a Labour government*, London: Labour Party.

Crouch, C. (2000) *Coping with post democracy*, London: The Fabian Society.

Crouch, C. (2011) *The strange non-death of neoliberalism*, Cambridge: Polity Press.

Crouch, C. (2016) *The knowledge corrupters: Hidden consequences of the financial takeover of public life*, Cambridge: Polity Press.

Crouch, C. (2020) *Post-democracy: After the crisis*, Cambridge: Polity Press.

Cummins, R. (2010) Subjective wellbeing, homeostatically protected mood and depression: A synthesis, *Journal of Happiness Studies*, 11: 1–17.

Curtice, J. (2010) 'Thermostat or weathervane? Public reactions to spending and redistribution under New Labour', in Park, A., Curtice, J. Thomson, K. Phillips, M., Clery, E. and Butt, S. (eds) *British social attitudes: The 26th report*, London: Sage.

Curtice, J., Hudson, N. and Montagu, I (eds) (2020) *British Social Attitudes: The 37th report*, London: National Centre for Social Research.

Curtis, S. (2008) 'How can we address health inequality through healthy public policy in Europe?', *European Regional and Urban Studies*, 15(4): 293–305.

Curtis, S., Oven, K., Wistow, J., Dunn, C. and Dominelli, L. (2018) 'Adaptation to extreme weather events in complex health and social care systems: The example of older people's services in England', *Environment and Planning C: Politics and Space*, 36 (1): 67–91.

Davis, A. (2018) *Reckless opportunists: Elites at the end of the establishment*, Manchester: Manchester University Press.

Dean, H. (2010) *Understanding human need*, Bristol: Policy Press.

Department of Environment (1977) *Housing (Homeless Persons) Act 1977*, London: HM Government.

Department for Environment, Food and Rural Affairs (2012) *UK climate change risk assessment: Government report*, London: Defra.

Department for Environment, Food and Rural Affairs (2014) *The national flood emergency framework for England*, London: Defra.

Department of Health and Social Care (2016) *Childhood obesity: A plan for action*, London: HM Government.

Department of Health and Social Care and Department for Education (2017) *Transforming children and young people's mental health provision: a green paper*, London: HM Government.

Disability Rights UK (2017) 'Disability Rights UK response to the Work and Pensions Committee inquiry on Personal Independence Payment (PIP)', https://www.disabilityrightsuk.org/disability-rights-uk-response-work-and-pensions-committee-inquiry-personal-independence-paym ent-pip (last accessed 8 September 2019).

Dodge, R., Daly, A., Huyton, J. and Sanders, L. (2012) 'The challenge of defining wellbeing', *International Journal of Wellbeing*, 2(3): 222–235.

Dorling, D. (2011) *Injustice: Why social inequality persists*, Bristol: Policy Press.

Dorling, D. (2013) *Unequal health: The scandal of our times*, Bristol: Policy Press.

Dorling D. (2017) *The equality effect: Improving life for everyone*, Oxford: New Internationalist Publications.

Doward, J. (2019) 'Grayling under fire as serious crimes committed on parole soar by 50%', https://www.theguardian.com/society/2019/jan/ 12/chris-grayling-probation-reforms-serious-crimes-committed-on-par ole-soar (last accessed 8 April 2021).

Doyal, L. with Pennell, I. (1979) *The political economy of health*, London: Pluto Press.

Dworkin, R. (2000) *Sovereign virtue: The theory and practice of equality*, Cambridge, MA: Harvard University Press.

Edminston, D. (2018) *Welfare, inequality and social citizenship: Deprivation and affluence in austerity Britain*, Bristol: Policy Press.

Fevre, R. (2016) *Individualism and inequality: The future of work and politics*, Cheltenham: Edward Elgar.

Foresight Land Use Futures Project (2010) *Final project report*, London: Government Office for Science.

Fox Gotham, K. (2009) 'Creating liquidity out of spatial fixity: The secondary circuit of capital and the subprime mortgage crisis', *International Journal of Urban and Regional Research*, 33(2): 355–371.

Frameworks Institute (2020) *Social determinants of health (UK)*, Washington, DC: Frameworks Institute.

Fraser, N. (2009) 'Feminism, capitalism and the cunning of history', *New Left Review*, 56: 97–117.

Fraser, N. (2016) 'Contradictions of capital and care', *New Left Review*, 100: 99–117.

Friedman, S. and Laurison, D. (2019) *The class ceiling: Why it pays to be privileged*, Bristol: Policy Press.

Gamble, A. (2003) *Between Europe and America: The future of British politics*, Basingstoke: Palgrave Macmillan.

Gamsu, S. (2021) *Why are some children worth more than others? The private-state school funding gap in England*, London: Commonwealth.

Gough, J. (1957) *The social contract: A critical study of its development*, Oxford: Clarendon Press.

Gray, M. and Barford, A. (2018) 'The depth of the cuts: The uneven geography of local government austerity', *Cambridge Journal of Regions, Economy and Society*, 11(3): 541–563.

Grimshaw, D. and Rubery, J. (2012) 'The end of the UK's liberal collectivist social model? The implications of the coalition government's policy during the austerity crisis, *Cambridge Journal of Economics*, 36(1): 105–126.

Gromada, A., Richardson, D. and Rees, G. (2020) *Childcare in a global crisis: The impact of COVID-19 on work and family life*, New York: United Nations.

Hall, S. and Wojcik, D. (2021) '"Ground zero" of Brexit: London as an international financial centre', *Geoforum*, 125: 195–196.

Hamnett, C. and Butler, T. (2013) 'Distance, education and inequality', *Comparative Education*, 3: 317–330.

Han, B.-C. (2017) *Psycho-politics: Neoliberalism and new technologies of power*, London: Verso.

Hancock, M. (2018) 'Prevention is better than cure: Matt Hancock's speech to IANPHI', https://www.gov.uk/government/speeches/prevention-is-better-than-cure-matt-hancocks-speech-to-ianphi (last accessed 21 September 2021).

Harris, T., Hodge, L. and Phillips, D. (2019) *English local government funding: Trends and challenges in 2019 and beyond*, London: Institute for Fiscal Studies.

Hartz, E. and Nielsen, C.F. (2015) 'From conditions of equality to demands of justice: Equal freedom, motivation and justification in Hobbes, Rousseau and Rawls', *Critical Review of International Social and Political Philosophy*, 18(1): 7–25.

Harvey, D. (2005) *A brief history of neoliberalism*, Oxford: Oxford University Press.

Harvey, M. (2021) 'The political economy of health: Revisiting its Marxian origins to address 21st-century health inequalities', *American Journal of Public Health*, 111(2): 293–300.

Hay, C. (2020) 'Brexistential angst and the paradoxes of populism: On the contingency, predictability and intelligibility of seismic shifts', *Political Studies*, 68(1): 187–206.

Hayek, F. (1960) *The constitution of liberty*, London: Routledge.

Hayek, F. (2014 [1959]) 'The meaning of the welfare state', in Pierson, C., Castles, F. and Naumann, I. (eds) *The welfare state reader*, Cambridge: Polity Press, pp 72–78.

Hemerijck, A. (2016) 'Foreword', in de la Porte, C. and Heims, E. (eds) *The sovereign debt crisis, the EU and welfare state reform*, London: Palgrave Macmillan, pp v–xv.

Hiley, D. (1990) 'The individual and the general will: Rousseau reconsidered', *History of Philosophy Quarterly*, 7(2): 159–178.

Hill, M. and Hupe, P. (2014) *Implementing public policy*, London: Sage.

Hills, J. (2017) *Good times, bad times: The welfare myth of them and us*, Bristol: Policy Press.

Hirschman, A. (1970) *Exit, voice, and loyalty: Responses to decline in firms, organizations, and states*, Cambridge, MA: Harvard University Press.

HM Government (2011) *Open public services: White paper*, Cm 8145, Norwich: The Stationery Office.

HM Government (2017) *UK climate change risk assessment, 2017*, Norwich: The Stationery Office.

HM Treasury (2015) *Spending review and autumn statement 2015*, London: HM Treasury.

HM Treasury (2016) *Northern powerhouse strategy*, London: HM Treasury.

HM Treasury (2019) *Country and regional analysis*, London: HM Treasury.

Hobbes, T. (1985) *Leviathan*, MacPherson, C. (ed), London: Penguin Books.

Hodge, G. and Greve, C. (2018) 'Contemporary public–private partnership: towards a global research agenda', *Financial Accountability and Management*, 34(1): 3–16.

Holmwood, J. (2000) Three pillars of welfare state theory: T.H. Marshall, Karl Polanyi and Alfa Myrdal in defence of the national welfare state, *European Journal of Social Theory*, 3(1): 23–50.

Holt-White, E. (2019) *Public opinion on the determinants of and responsibility for health*, London: The Health Foundation.

Hood, A. and Waters, T. (2017) *The impact of tax and benefit reforms on household incomes*, London: Institute for Fiscal Studies.

Huang, C., Vaneckova, P., Wang, X., FitzGerald, G., Guo, Y. and Tong, S. (2011) 'Constraints and barriers to public health adaptation to climate change', *American Journal of Preventive Medicine*, 20(2): 183–190.

Hunter, D. (2015) *The health debate*, Bristol: Policy Press.

Hunter, J. (2017) *Rebooting devolution: A common-sense approach to taking back control*, Newcastle: IPPR North.

Hutton, W. (2010) *Them and us: Changing Britain – why we need a fair society*, London: Little Brown.

Hutton, W. (2015) *How good we can be: Ending the mercenary society and building a great country*, London: Abacus.

Hyde, M. (2019) 'Kylie Jenner: Who'd want to be a matte lip billionaire?', https://www.theguardian.com/lifeandstyle/lostinshowbiz/2019/mar/07/kylie-jenner-whod-want-to-be-a-matte-lip-billionaire (last accessed 23 September 2021).

Hyde, M. (2020a) 'Do not adjust your set: Gwyneth Paltrow is spreading Goop all over TV', https://www.theguardian.com/lifeandstyle/lostinshow biz/2020/jan/16/do-not-adjust-your-set-gwyneth-paltrow-is-spreading-goop-all-over-tv (last accessed 23 September 2021).

Hyde, M. (2020b) 'How do you know when the Oscars have gone vegan? Answer: They keep telling you', https://www.theguardian.com/lifeandst yle/lostinshowbiz/2020/jan/30/oscars-gone-vegan-they-keep-telling-you (last accessed 23 September 2021).

Hyde, M. (2021) 'Decor without decorum – this is home economics, Johnson-style', https://www.theguardian.com/commentisfree/2021/apr/ 27/decor-home-economics-johnson-no-10-flat-refurb (last accessed 30 May 2022).

IFS (Institute for Fiscal Studies) (2015) 'Recent cuts to public spending', https://www.ifs.org.uk/tools_and_resources/fiscal_facts/public_ spending_survey/cuts_to_public_spending (last accessed 5 March 2017).

Illich, I. (1976) *Limits to medicine, medical nemesis: The exploration of health*, London: Marion Boyars Publishers.

IMF (International Monetary Fund) (2020) *World economic outlook: The great lockdown*, Washington, DC: IMF.

IMF (2021) *Fiscal monitor: A fair shot*, Washington, DC: IMF.

Independent Panel on Pandemic Preparedness and Response (2021) *COVID-19: Make it the last pandemic*, IPPPR.

Intelligence and Security Committee of Parliament (2020) *Russia*, London: The Stationery Office.

IPCC (Intergovernmental Panel on Climate Change) (2014) *Managing the risks of extreme events and disasters to advance climate change adaptation: Special report of the Intergovernmental Panel on Climate Change, Geneva, Switzerland*, Geneva: IPCC, http://www.ipcc.ch/pdf/special-reports/srex/SREX_Full _Report.pdf (last accessed 1 February 2022).

IPCC (2021) *Climate change 2021: The physical science basis: Contribution of Working Group I to the Sixth Assessment Report of the Intergovernmental Panel on Climate Change*, Cambridge: Cambridge University Press.

Jackson, B. and Marsden, D. (1968) *Education and the working class*, London: Routledge.

Jenkins, S. (2019) 'The City may thrive despite Brexit, but the rest of us won't', https://www.theguardian.com/commentisfree/2019/feb/22/city-free-port-brexit-deal-bankers (last accessed 27 April 2021).

Jenkins, S. (2021) 'The billions spent by the UK government in fighting Covid need proper scrutiny', https://www.theguardian.com/commen tisfree/2021/feb/23/billions-uk-government-spent-covid-scrutiny (last accessed 12 April 2021).

Jessop, B. (1996) 'Post-Fordism and the state', in Greve B. (eds) *Comparative welfare systems*, London: Palgrave Macmillan.

Jessop, B. (2000) 'From the KWNS to the SWPR', in Lewis, G., Gewirtz, S. and Clarke, J. (eds) *Rethinking social policy*, London: Sage.

Jessop, B. (2015) 'Crisis, crisis-management and state restructuring: What future for the state?', *Policy and Politics*, 43(4): 475–492.

Jessop, B. (2016) *The state: Past, present, future*, Cambridge: Polity Press.

Jessop, B. (2017) 'The organic crisis of the British state: Putting Brexit in its place', *Globalizations*, 14(2): 133–141.

Jessop, B. (2018) 'Neoliberalization, uneven development and Brexit: Further reflections on the organic crisis of the British state and society', *European Planning Studies*, 26(9): 1728–1746.

Jessop, B. (2020) *Putting civil society in its place: Governance, metagovernance, and subjectivity*, Bristol: Policy Press.

Johnson, B. (2013) *3rd Margaret Thatcher lecture*, https://www.youtube.com/watch?v=Dzlgrnr1ZB0

Johnson, P., Joyce, R. and Platt, L. (2021) *The IFS Deaton review of inequalities: A new year's message*, London: Institute for Fiscal Studies.

Jones, M. (2019) 'Spaces of welfare localism: Geographies of locality making', in Whitworth, A. (eds) *Towards a spatial social policy: Bridging the gap between geography and social policy*, Bristol: Policy Press.

Judge, L. and Bell, T. (2018) *Housing stress is up – and has shifted:. Our debate on social housing needs to keep up*, London: Resolution Foundation.

Kelly, M. (2010) 'The axes of social differentiation and the evidence-base on health equity', *Journal of the Royal Society for Medicine*, 103(7): 266–272.

Kenny, M. (2015) 'The return of "Englishness" in British political culture – the end of the unions?', *Journal of Common Market Studies*, 53(1): 35–51.

Kirton, G. and Guilaume, C. (2019) 'When welfare professionals encounter restructuring and privatization: The inside story of the Probation Service of England and Wales', *Work, Employment and Society*, 33(6): 929–947.

Klein, R. (1995) *The new politics of the NHS*, Harlow: Longman.

Khomami, N. (2015) 'TalkTalk hacking crisis deepens as more details emerge', https://www.theguardian.com/business/2015/oct/23/talktalk-hacking-crisis-deepens-as-more-details-emerge.

Lancet Commissions (2015)' Health and climate change: Policy responses to protect public health', http://dx.doi.org/10.1016/S0140-6736(15)60854-6 (last accessed 1 February 2022).

Lawrence, F. (2021) 'Covid test kit supplier joked to Hancock on WhatsApp he had "never heard of him"', https://www.theguardian.com/world/2021/mar/11/covid-test-kit-supplier-joked-matt-hancock-whatsapp-never-heard-of-him-alex-bourne (last accessed 12 April 2021).

Leach, S., Stewart, G. and Jones, G. (2018) *Centralisation, devolution and the future of local government in England*, Abingdon: Routledge.

Lees, L. (2014) 'The urban injustices of New Labour's "new urban renewal": The case of the Aylesbury Estate in London', *Antipode*, 46(4): 921–947.

Lefebvre, H. (2003) *The urban revolution*, Minneapolis, MN: University of Minnesota Press.

Leslie, J. and Shah, K. (2021) *(Wealth) gap year: The impact of the coronavirus crisis on UK household wealth*, London: Resolution Foundation.

Lessnoff, M. (1990) 'Introduction: Social contract', in Lessnoff, M. (eds) *Social contract theory*, Oxford: Basil Blackwell, pp 1–26.

Littler, J. (2013) 'Meritocracy as plutocracy: The marketizing of "equality" within neoliberalism', *New Formations: A Journal of Culture/Theory/Politics*, 80–1: 52–72.

Lukianoff, G. and Haidt, J. (2019) *The coddling of the American mind: How good intentions and bad ideas are setting up a generation for failure*, London: Penguin Books.

Lund, B. (2016) *Housing politics in the United Kingdom: Power, planning and protest*, Bristol: Policy Press.

Lupton, R. and Obolenskaya, P. (2020) *The Conservatives' record on compulsory education: Spending, policies and outcomes in England, May 2015 to pre-COVID 2020*, London: Centre for Analysis of Social Exclusion.

Lupton, R. and Power, A. (2004) What we know about neighbourhood change: *A literature review: CASE report 27*, London: Centre for Analysis of Social Exclusion.

Lupton, R., with Hills, J., Stewart, K. and Vizard, P. (2013) *Labour's social policy record: Policy, spending and outcomes*, London: Centre for Analysis of Social Exclusion.

Lynch, J. (2017) 'Reframing inequality? The health inequalities turn as a dangerous frame shift', *Journal of Public Health*, 39(4): 653–660.

Madgavkar, A., Tacke, T., Smit, S. and Manyika, J. (2020) 'COVID-19 has revived the social contract in advanced economies – for now. What will stick once the crisis abates?', https://www.mckinsey.com/industries/pub lic-and-social-sector/our-insights/covid-19-has-revived-the-social-contr act-in-advanced-economies-for-now-what-will-stick-once-the-crisis-aba tes (last accessed 21 September 2021).

Marmot, M. (2004) *The status syndrome: How social standing affects our health and longevity*, New York: Owl Books.

Marmot, M. (2010) *Fair society, healthy lives: Strategic review of health inequalities in England post-2010*, London: Marmot Review.

Marmot, M. (2015) *The health gap: The challenge of an unequal world*, London: Bloomsbury.

Marmot, M. (2021) 'The Sewell report cited my work – just not the parts highlighting structural racism', https://www.theguardian.com/commentisfree/2021/apr/07/sewell-report-structural-racism-research (last accessed 21 September 2021).

Marmot, M., Allen, J., Boyce, T., Goldblatt, P. and Morrison, J. (2020a) *Health equity in England: The Marmot Review 10 years on*, London: Institute of Health Equity.

Marmot, M., Allen, J., Boyce, T., Goldblatt, P. and Morrison, J. (2020b) *Build back fairer: The COVID-19 Marmot Review*, London: Institute of Health Equity.

Marshall, T. (1950) *Citizenship and social class and other essays*, Cambridge: Cambridge University Press.

Martin, R. (2010) 'Uneven regional growth: The geographies of boom and bust under New Labour', in Coe, N. and Jones, A. (eds) *Economic geography of the UK*, London: Sage, pp 29–46.

Martin, R. (2015) 'Rebalancing the spatial economy: The challenge for regional theory', *Territory, Politics, Governance*, 3(3): 235–272.

Marx, K. (1852) 'The eighteenth Brumaire of Louis Bonaparte', https://www.marxists.org/archive/marx/works/1852/18th-brumaire/index.htm (last accessed 2 September 2021).

Mason, P. (2019) *Clear bright future: A radical defence of the human being*, Milton Keynes: Allen Lane.

Massey, D. (1979) 'In what sense a regional problem?', *Regional Studies*, 13: 223–243.

Massey, D. (1980) 'The pattern of landownership and its implications for policy', *Built Environment*, 6: 263–271.

Massey, D. (1991) 'The political space of locality studies', *Environment and Planning A*, 23: 267–291.

May, T. (2017) '2017 Speech at Conservative Party Conference', https://www.ukpol.co.uk/theresa-may-2017-speech-at-conservative-party-conference/.

McCurdy, C. (2019) *Ageing, fast and slow: When place and demography collide*, London: Resolution Foundation.

Merrick, R. (2021) 'Matt Hancock dismisses ruling that he broke the law over lucrative Covid contracts as just "delayed paperwork"', https://www.independent.co.uk/news/uk/politics/matt-hancock-covid-contracts-law-b1805248.html.

Meslin, E. Carroll, A. Schwartz, P. and Kennedy, S. (2014) Is the social contract incompatible with the social safety net? Revisiting a key philosophical position, *Journal of Civic Literacy*, 1(1): 1–15.

MHCLG (Ministry of Housing, Communities and Local Government) (2019) *The English indices of deprivation*, London: MHCLG.

Minton, A. (2019) 'Grenfell and the place of housing in modern life', in Whitworth, A. (ed) *Towards a spatial social policy: Bridging the gap between geography and social policy*, Bristol: Policy Press.

Mitchell, W. and Fazi, T. (2017) *Reclaiming the state: A progressive vision of sovereignty for a post-neoliberal world*, London: Pluto Press.

Moreira, T. (2017) *Science, technology and the ageing society*, Abingdon: Routledge.

Morin, E. (1981) *La méthode. 1. La nature de la nature* [Method. 1. The nature of nature], Paris: Seuil.

Murray, C. (1984) *Losing ground: American social policy, 1950–1980*, New York: Basic Books.

Murray, C. (1990) *The emerging British underclass*, London: Institute of Economic Affairs, Health and Welfare Unit.

Murray, C. (1994) *Underclass: The crisis deepens (choice in welfare)*, London: Institute of Economic Affairs.

NAO (National Audit Office) (2018a) *The financial sustainability of local authorities*, London: NAO.

NAO (2018b) *Adult social care at a glance*, London: NAO.

NAO (2020a) *Investigation into government procurement during the COVID-19 pandemic*, London: NAO.

NAO (2020b) *Exiting the European Union: The cost of EU exit preparations*, London: NAO.

NAO (2020c) *The government's approach to test and trace in England – interim report*, London: NAO.

NAO (2021) *The adult social care market in England*, London: NAO.

Navarro, V. (2009) 'What we mean by social determinants of health', *Global Health Promotion*, 16(1): 5–16.

Nelson, J. (1995) *Post-industrial capitalism*, New York: Sage.

Nettleton, S. (1995) *The sociology of health and illness*, Cambridge: Polity Press.

Newman, I. (2014) *Reclaiming local democracy: A progressive future for local government*, Bristol: Policy Press.

NHS England (2014) *NHS five year forward view*, London: NHS England.

NHS (2019) *The NHS long term plan*, London: NHS England.

Nozick, R. (1974) *Anarchy, state and utopia*, New York: Basic Books.

Oatley, T. (2019) 'Towards a political economy of complex interdependencies', *European Journal of International Relations*, 25(4): 957–978.

Obolenskaya, P. and Hills, J. (2019) *Flat-lining or seething beneath the surface? Two decades of changing economic inequality in the UK*, London: Centre for Analysis of Social Exclusion.

OECD (Organisation for Economic Co-operation and Development) (2017) *OECD: Economic surveys*, Paris: OECD Publishing.

OECD (2019) *Under pressure: The squeezed middle class*, Paris: OECD Publishing.

ONS (Office for National Statistics) (2018) 'Living longer – how our population is changing and why it matters: Overview of population ageing in the UK and some of the implications for the economy, public services, society and the individual', https://www.ons.gov.uk/peopl epopulationandcommunity/birthsdeathsandmarriages/ageing/articles/ livinglongerhowourpopulationischangingandwhyitmatters/2018-08-13 (last accessed 29 September 2021).

ONS (2020) *Deaths involving COVID-19 by local area and socioeconomic deprivation: Deaths occurring between 1 March and 31 May 2020*, London: ONS.

Osborne, D. and Gaebler, T. (1992) *Reinventing government: How the entrepreneurial spirit is transforming the public sector*, Reading, MA: Addison-Wesley.

Osborne, S. (2006) 'The new public governance?', *Public Management Review*, 8(3): 377–87.

Oven, K., Curtis, S., Reaney, S., Riva, M., Stewart, M., Ohlemuller, R., Dunn, C., Nodwell, S., Dominelli, L. and Holden, R. (2012) 'Climate change and health and social care: Defining future hazard, vulnerability and risk for infrastructure systems supporting older people's health care in England', *Applied Geography*, 33: 16–24.

Owen, G., Chen, T., Heaton, T., Price, G. and Zhang, M. (2021) *The rise of housing wealth inequality: How the financial crisis initiated a new era of growing regional inequalities in gross housing wealth in England and Wales*, Housing Studies Association Conference, Week 1: Cities and Devolution, Session 2, 5 November.

Owens, J. and de St Croix, T. (2020) 'Engines of social mobility? Navigating meritocratic education discourse in an unequal society', *British Journal of Educational Studies*, 68(4): 403–424.

Oxfam (2021) 'Passing the buck on debt relief: How the failure of the private sector to cancel debt is fueling a crisis across the developing world', https://oxfamilibrary.openrepository.com/bitstream/handle/10546/621 026/mb-passing-buck-debt-relief-private-sector-160720-en.pdf?seque nce=4&isAllowed=y (last accessed 21 September 2021).

Page, R. (2018) 'A "radical" crisis for the subject of social policy?', http:// www.social-policy.org.uk/50-for-50/radical-crisis/ (last accessed 16 August 2021).

Payne, G. (2017) *The new social mobility: How politicians got it wrong*, Bristol: Policy Press.

Pearce, J. (2013) 'Financial crisis, austerity policies and geographical inequalities in health', *Environment and Planning A*, 45: 2030–2045.

Peck, J. (2003) 'Geography and public policy: Mapping the penal state', *Progress in Human Geography*, 27(2): 222–232.

Peck, J. (2013) 'Explaining (with) neoliberalism', *Territory, Politics, Governance*, 1(2): 132–157.

Peck, J., Theodore, N. and Brenner, N. (2009) 'Postneoliberalism and its malcontents,' *Antipode*, 41(1): 94–116.

Phillips, D. and Simpson, P. (2018) *Changes in councils' adult social care and overall service spending in England, 2009–10 to 2017–18*, London: Institute for Fiscal Studies.

Pierson, P. (1996) 'The new politics of the welfare state', *World Politics*, 48(2): 143–179.

Pluckrose, H. and Lindsay, J. (2020) *Cynical theories: How activist scholarship made everything about race, gender and identity – and why this harms everybody*, Durham, NC: Pitchstone Publishing.

Polanyi, K. (2018) *Economy and society: Selected writings*, Cambridge: Polity Press.

Policy Exchange (2010) *Making housing affordable*, London: Policy Exchange.

Policy Exchange (2013) *Taxing issues? Reducing housing demand or increasing housing supply*, London: Policy Exchange.

Porter, S. (2013) 'Capitalism, the state and health care in the age of austerity: a Marxist analysis', *Nursing Philosophy*, 14(1): 5–16.

Poulantzas, N. (2014) *State, power, socialism*, London: Verso.

Public Health England (2015) 'Flooding health guidance and advice', https://www.gov.uk/government/collections/flooding-health-guidance-and-adv ice (last accessed 5 March 2017).

Public Health England (2016) *Cold weather plan for England 2016*, London: Public Health England.

Public Health England (2017) *Exercise Cygnus*, London: Public Health England.

Public Health England (2018) *Heatwave plan for England 2018*, London: Public Health England.

Raikes, L. (2018) *Future transport investment in the north*, Manchester: IPPR North.

Raikes, L. (2019) *Transport investment in the northern powerhouse*, Manchester: IPPR North.

Raikes, L. (2020) *The devolution parliament: Devolving power to England's regions, towns and cities*, Manchester: IPPR North.

Raikes, L. and Giovannini, A. (2019) 'The devolution parliament', https://www.ippr.org/blog/the-devolution-parliamentIPPR (last accessed 10 September 2021).

Raikes, L., Giovannini, A. and Getzel, B. (2019) *Divided and connected: Regional inequalities in the north, the UK and the developed world*, Manchester: IPPR North.

Rawls, J. (1971) *A theory of justice*, Cambridge, MA: Harvard University Press.

Rawls, J. (1990) *Contractarian justice*, in Lessnoff, M. (ed) *Social contract theory*, Oxford: Basil Blackwell.

Rawls, J. (1999) *A theory of justice: Revised edition*, Cambridge, MA: The Belknap Press of Harvard University Press.

Reay, D. (2017) *Miseducation: Inequality, education and the working classes*, Bristol: Policy Press.

Reed, M. and Harvey, D. (1992) 'The new science and the old: Complexity and realism in the social sciences', *Journal of Theory and Social Behaviour*, 22: 356–379.

Resolution Foundation (2018) *A new generational contract: The final report of the intergenerational contract*, London: Resolution Foundation.

Rhodes, R. (1997) *Understanding governance: Policy networks, governance, reflexivity and accountability*, Buckingham: Open University Press.

Rousseau, J.-J. (1993) *The social contract and the discourses*, London: David Campbell Publishers.

Salway, S. and Green, J. (2017) 'Towards a critical complex systems approach to public health', *Critical Public Health*, 27(5): 523–524.

Sartorius, D. (2006) The meanings of health and its promotion, *Croat Medical Journal*, 47(4): 662–664.

Sayer, A. (2016) *Why we can't afford the rich*, Bristol: Policy Press.

Scambler, G. (2011) 'Tackling health inequalities and its pros, cons and contradictions: A commentary on Blackman, Wistow and Byrne, *Social Sciences and Medicine*, 72(12): 1975–1977.

Scambler, G. (2018) 'Introduction', in Scambler, G. (ed) *Sociology as applied to health and medicine*, London: Palgrave, pp xxv–xxvii.

Scambler, G. and Scambler, S. (2015) Theorizing health inequalities: The untapped potential of dialectical critical realism, *Social Theory and Health*, 13(3–4): 340–354.

Schrecker, T. (2014) 'Changing cartographies of health in a globalizing world', *Medicine Anthropology Theory*, 1(1): 145–180.

Schrecker, T. (2016) '"Neoliberal epidemics" and public health: Sometimes the world is less complicated than it appears', *Critical Public Health*, 26(5): 477–480.

Schrecker, T. (2017) 'Was Mackenbach right? Towards a practical political science of redistribution and health inequalities', *Health and Place*, 46: 293–299.

Schrecker, T. (2021) 'What is critical about critical public health? Focus on health inequalities', *Critical Public Health*, doi: 10.1080/09581596.2021.1905776.

Schrecker, T. and Bambra, C. (2015) *How politics makes us sick: Neoliberal epidemics*, Basingstoke: Palgrave Macmillan.

SCIE (Social Care Institute for Excellence) (2020) *Beyond COVID: New thinking on the future of social care*, London: SCIE.

Scottish Government (2021) *After Brexit: The UK internal market act and devolution*, Edinburgh: Scottish Government.

Shankley, W. and Finney, N. (2020) 'Ethnic minorities and housing in Britain', in Byrne, B., Alexander, C., Khan, O., Nazroo, J. and Shankley, W. (eds) *Ethnicity, race and inequality in the UK: The state of the nation*, Bristol: Policy Press.

Shaxson, N. (2018) 'The finance curse: How the outsized power of the City of London makes Britain poorer', https://www.theguardian.com/news/2018/oct/05/the-finance-curse-how-the-outsized-power-of-the-city-of-london-makes-britain-poorer (last accessed 29 March 2019).

Skills for Care (2020) *The size and structure of the adult social care sector and workforce in England*, Leeds: Skills for Care.

Slater, T. (2018) 'The invention of the "sink estate": Consequential categorization and the UK housing crisis', *The Sociological Review*, 66(4): 877–897.

Sinfield, A. (1978) Analyses in the social division of welfare, *Journal of Social Policy*, 7(2): 129–156.

Smith, A. (1776) *The wealth of nations*, London: W. Strahan and T. Cadell.

Social Mobility and Child Poverty Commission (2014) *Elitist Britain*, London: Social Mobility and Child Poverty Commission.

Social Mobility Commission (2016) *State of the nation 2016: Social mobility in Great Britain*, London: Social Mobility Commission.

Social Mobility Commission (2019) *State of the nation 2018 to 2019*, London: Social Mobility Commission.

Spicker, P. (2014) *Social policy: Theory and practice*, Bristol: Policy Press.

Srnicek, N. and Williams, A. (2016) *Inventing the future: Postcapitalism and a world without work*, London: Verso.

Starke, P. (2006) 'The politics of welfare state retrenchment: A literature review', *Social Policy and Administration*, 40(1): 104–120.

Stewart, K., Cooper, K. and Shutes, I. (2019) *What does Brexit mean for social policy in the UK? An exploration of the potential consequences of the 2016 referendum for public services, inequalities and social rights*, London: Centre for Analysis of Social Exclusion.

Stiglitz, J. (2012) *The price of inequality*, London: Allen Lane.

Stoker, G. (1998) 'Governance as theory: Five propositions', *International Social Science Journal*, 50(155): 17–28.

Stone, J. (2016) 'Tories refused to build social housing because it would "create Labour voters", Nick Clegg says', https://www.independent.co.uk/news/uk/politics/tories-refused-to-build-social-housing-because-it-would-create-labour-voters-nick-clegg-says-a7223796.html.

Streeck, W. (2016) *How will capitalism end?*, London: Verso.

Suteanu, C. (2005) 'Complexity, science and the public – the geography of new interpretation', *Theory, Culture and Society*, 22: 113–140.

Taylor-Gooby, P. (1981) The state, class ideology and social policy, *Journal of Social Policy*, 10(4): 433–452.

Taylor-Gooby, P. (1994) 'Postmodernism and social policy: A great leap backwards?', *Journal of Social Policy*, 23(3): 385–404.

173

Taylor-Gooby, P. (2002) 'The silver age of the welfare state: Perspectives on resilience', *Journal of Social Policy*, 31(4): 597–621.

Taylor-Gooby, P. (2016) 'The divisive welfare state', *Social Policy and Administration*, 50(6): 712–733.

Telford, L. and Wistow, J. (2020) 'Brexit and the working class on Teesside: Moving beyond reductionism', *Capital and Class*, 44(4): 553–572.

Thane, P. (1978) *The Origins of British Social Policy*, London: Groom Helm.

The Children's Society (2020) *The good childhood report 2020*, London: The Children's Society.

Therborn, G. (1980) *The ideology of power and the power of ideology*, London: Verso.

Thomas C. (2019) *Hitting the poorest worst? How public health cuts have been experienced in England's most deprived communities*, London: IPPR.

Thompson, E. (1981) 'The politics of theory', in Samuel, R. (ed) *People's history and socialist theory*, London: Routledge and Kegan Paul, pp 396–408.

Thompson, M. (2017) 'Autonomy and common good: Interpreting Rousseau's general will', *International Journal of Philosophical Studies*, 25(2): 266–285.

Titmuss, R. (1968) *Commitment to welfare*, London: Allen and Unwin.

Tomaney, J. (2016) 'Limits of devolution: Localism, economics and post-democracy', *The Political Quarterly*, 87(4): 546–552.

Tomaney, J. and Marques, P. (2013) 'Evidence, policy and the politics of regional development: The case of high-speed rail in the United Kingdom', *Environment and Planning C*, 31: 414–427.

Travers, T., Sims, S. and Bosetti, N. (2016) *Housing and inequality in London*, London: Centre for London.

Turner, T. (1960) Sponsored and contest mobility and the school system, *American Sociological Review*, 25(6): 855–67.

UK2070 Commission (2020) *Go big: Go local: The UK2070 report on a new deal for levelling up the United Kingdom*, Nottingham: UK2070 Commission.

United Nations (2019) *Visit to the United Kingdom of Great Britain and Northern Ireland: Report of the Special Rapporteur on extreme poverty and human rights*, New York: United Nations, General Assembly and Human Rights Council.

Usmani, A. (2017) 'The left in Europe: From social democracy to the crisis in the euro zone: An interview with Leo Panitch', *New Politics*, 14(54), https://newpol.org/issue_post/left-europe-social-democracy-crisis-euro-zone-interview-leo-panitch/.

Van Gunsteren, H. (1978) 'Notes on a theory of citizenship', in Birnbaum, P., Lively, J. and Parry, G. (eds) *Democracy, consensus and social contract*, London: Sage, pp 9–36.

Varoufakis, Y. (2017) *Adults in the room: My battle with Europe's deep establishment*, London: Vintage.

Verkerk, J., Teisman, G. and Van Buuren, A. (2015) 'Syncronising climate adaptation processes in a multilevel governance setting: Exploring synchronisation of governance levels in the Dutch Delta', *Public Management Review*, 43(4): 579–596.

Villadsen, K. (2011) 'Ambiguous citizenship: "Postmodern" versus "modern" welfare at the margins', *Distinktion Journal of Social Theory*, 12(3): 309–329.

Virdee, S. (2019) 'Racialized capitalism: An account of its contested origins and consolidation', *The Sociological Review*, 67(1): 3–27.

Vizard, P. and Obolenskaya, P., with Hughes, J., Treebhoohun, K. and Wainwright, I. (2021) 'Health from May 2015 to preCOVID 2020: Policies, spending and outcomes', in Vizard, P. and Hills, J. (eds) *The Conservative governments' record on social policy from May 2015 to pre-COVID 2020: Policies, spending and outcomes*, London: Centre for Analysis of Social Exclusion, pp 151–164.

Walker, A. (2018) 'Why the UK needs a social policy on ageing', *Journal of Social Policy*, 47(2): 253–273.

Warren, J., Stephenson, C. and Wistow, J. (2021) 'Editorial: "After industry" the economic and social consequences of deindustrialization', *Frontiers in Sociology*, doi: 10.3389/fsoc.2021.645027.

Warren, J. and Wistow, J. (2017) 'Policy, practice and difference within welfare regimes: Evidence from the UK', in Greve, B. (ed) *Handbook of social policy evaluation*, Cheltenham: Edward Elgar Publishing.

Webster C. (1998) *The National Health Service: A political history*, Oxford: Oxford University Press.

Weeden, K. and Grusky, D. (2005) The case for a new class map, *American Journal of Sociology*, 111: 141–212.

Whitehead, M., Pennington, A., Orton, L., Nayak, S., Pettricrew, M., Sowden, A. and White, M. (2016) 'How could differences in "control over destiny" lead to socio-economic inequalities in health? A synthesis of theories and pathways in the living environment', *Health and Place*, 39: 51–61.

Wilcox, Z., Nohrova, N. and Bidgood, E. (2014) *City views: How do Britain's cities see London*, London: Centre for Cities.

Wilks, S. (2015) *The revolving door and the corporate colonisation of UK politics*, London: The High Pay Centre.

Williams, F. (1989) *Social policy: A critical introduction*, Cambridge: Polity Press.

Wistow, G. (2012) 'Still a fine mess? Local government and the NHS 1962 to 2012', *Journal of Integrated Care*, 20(2): 101–114.

Wistow, J., with Blackman, T., Byrne, D. and Wistow, G. (2015) *Studying health inequalities: An applied approach*, Bristol: Policy Press.

Wistow, J., Curtis, S. and Bone, A. (2017) 'Implementing extreme weather event advice and guidance in English public health systems', *Journal of Public Health*, 39(3): 498–505.

Wlezien, C. (1995) 'The public as thermostat: Dynamics of preferences for spending', *American Journal of Political Science*, 39: 981–1000.

Work and Pensions Committee (2018) *PIP and ESA assessments: Seventh report of the session 2017–19*, London: House of Commons Work and Pensions Committee.

Yamamura, K. (2017) *Too much stuff: Capitalism in crisis*, Bristol: Policy Press.

Young, M. (1958) *The rise of the meritocracy 1870–2033: An essay on education and society*, London: Thames and Hudson.

Index

References in **bold** type refer to tables. References to
endnotes show the page number, the note
number and the chapter number (154n3[ch1]).

A

Acheson Review 104
Age UK 137
ageing 135–139
agency 3–4, 13, 52, 53
agglomeration 73, 83, 92
Agrawal, S. 76, 78
Alcock, P. 14, 16, 65
Allen, A. 116
alt-right 141
alter-ideologies 117
American individualism 35
Amnesty International 60, 61
Artaraz, K. 53, 57, 67
Astin, A.W. 123
Atkinson, T. 5
Atos 46–47
austerity 40–43, 46, 56, 65, 66, 68,
   126, 134
automation 142–143

B

baby boomers 132
Baker, A. 74
Balfour Tower 76
Bambra, C. 40, 78, 97, 98, 100, 103
Barford, A. 65–66, 80
Barlow Commission 73, 92–93
Barnett, N. 64, 65, 86
Beatty, C. 78, 80
behaviours 106
Bell, T. 132
benefit allocation 2
Berardi, F. 34, 36, 37, 54, 127
Bevan, A. 105
Bevan, G. 43
Bevir, M. 43, 44
Black Report 103, 108
Blackman, T. 105, 122, 123
Blair, T. 38–39, 75
Blakeley, G. 32, 33, 55, 56, 120, 126, 149
Blakemore, K. 19
Blaxter, M. 96, 102
Boliver, V. 114, 117, 127, 128
Bonvilla-Silva, E. 91
Bourdieu, P. 2, 12, 115
Bourquin, P. 132
Bretton Woods Agreement 53
Brexit 63, 66–69

Bridle, J. 142
Briggs, A. 24
British Medical Association (BMA) 61
British Social Attitudes (BSA) survey
   146–148, 151
Broughton, J. 37, 38, 76, 87, 88, 89, 91
Brown, P. 115, 117, 118, 124, 126,
   127, 129
Building back fairer (Marmot) 97
Burawoy, M. 17–18
Burchardt, T. 59
Burns, D. 46
Butler, T. 125
buy-to-let mortgages 90
Byrne, D. 3, 4, 5, 24, 25, 26, 27, 28, 32,
   39, 42, 50, 52, 65, 79, 80, 86, 90,
   109, 114, 117, 125, 127, 128, 131,
   132, 141

C

Calder, G. 113, 114–115, 116–117, 129
Callaghan, G. 3
Cameron, D. 75
Campbell's Law 44
Campbell's Law 44
Capita 46–47
capital 53, 71, 126
capitalism 22, 23–28, 32, 34, 35–36, 102,
   117, 140
Care Act 2014 59
care homes 60–61
care workers 59, 61, 127, 137–138
carers 138
Castellani, B. 34, 36, 54, 57, 69, 71, 127,
   139–140, 141
central government 64–65, 66
centralisation 73, 79, 83
Centre for Cities 75
Chakrabortty, A. 41
child development 79
child poverty 134
child wellbeing 133, 134
Children's Society 134
Christophers, B. 5, 23, 29, 30, 33, 37, 48,
   50, 76–77, 84, 85–86, 87, 89, 90, 92
Citizens Advice 90
citizenship 49
citizenship rights 24
City of London 37, 41, 49, 73, 74, 78, 92
civil rights 24
civil service 44–45

class ceiling, The (Friedman and
    Laurison) 116
class inequality 116–117
Clegg, N. 88
climate change 58–59
Coalition Agreement 40, 66
coalition government 40–43, 46, 66,
    83, 124
Coburn, D. 100
Community Care Act 1991 59
competition 55, 124, 128
competitive individualism 34–35, 102, 133
complex systems 52, 109, 151
complexity language 132
complexity theory 3–4, 20, 127
comprehensive university, The
    (Blackman) 123
computation 142
conservatism 141, 148
Conservative governments 66, 68, 87,
    122, 148
Conservative Party 63, 69, 79, 83
consolidation state 41–42
consumerism 49, 53–54
consumption 35–36
contract of government / submission 7
contracting out 44–45, 46–47, 59–60,
    119, 120–121, 146, 152
Cope, Z. 54
council housing *see* housing
COVID-19 crisis 33, 36, 46, 55, 57, 83
  care homes 60–61
  child wellbeing 134
  generational inequalities 131
  governance 120–121
  health inequalities 96, 97
  NHS Test and Trace 119–120
  public contracts 49–50
  public spending 148, 149, 150–151
  social contract 149–151
Cracknell, R. 63, 155n2(ch3)
Creasy, S. 120
credit 53
Cribb, J. 42, 59, 132
Crisp, R. 64, 66, 75, 83–84, 92
critical sociology 18
Crouch, C. 4, 23, 26, 27, 28, 29, 31, 32,
    33, 37, 39, 41, 42, 43, 48, 49, 50, 54,
    55, 56, 57, 59–60, 67, 68, 115, 139,
    140, 141, 142
Curtice, J. 146–148, 151
Curtis, S. 62, 106

D

Darwin, C. 37
Davis, A. 28, 33, 43, 44–45, 74, 75, 76,
    92, 119, 126
Dean, H. 35
debt 53, 54, 55, 56

Decent Homes Programme 89
deficit model 115, 118
DEFRA 58
deindustrialisation 27, 39–40, 67, 78, 79
Deloitte 120
democracy 48, 68, 148
Department for Work and Pensions 47
Department of Health and Social Care 58
dependency 35
dependency ratios 136
deprivation 76, 79, 80
deregulation 38, 56
devolution 19, 52, 62–66, 70, 105
difference principle 10
Disability Rights UK 47
discourse 139–140, 141
disposable income 4, 154n5(ch1)
diswelfares 2
Dodge, R. 134
Doward, J. 46
Doyal, L. 98, 103, 109
Dworkin, R. 111

E

Earle, J. 31
ecological dominance 53, 71, 92, 126
econocracy 31
economic imperialism 98
economic inequity 128
economy *see* global economy;
    political economy
Edminston, D. 41
education 65, 121–123, 125
Education Act 1944 122
Education and the working class (Jackson and
    Marsden) 118
efficiency 22–23, 30–31, 43
elitism 118
Elitist Britain (Social Mobility and Child
    Poverty Commission) 118
employment 27, 74, 78
equality 11–12, 14, 24, 95
    see also inequalities
equality of opportunity 117
equity 72
European Central Bank (ECB) 68
European Union (EU) 63, 66–69, 70–71
Exercise Cygnus 60

F

false universalism 27
families 114–115, 117, 121–122, 134, 138
Fazi, T. 13, 25, 26, 27, 28, 29, 30, 31, 33,
    54, 55, 68, 140, 142, 143
Fevre, R. 34–35, 37, 43, 44, 86, 99, 116,
    121, 122, 124, 128, 148
financial crisis 33, 36, 40–41, 55–57, 68,
    125, 132, 149
financial sector 38, 74

Finney, N. 90, 91
fiscal consolidation 56
'For public sociology' (Burawoy) 17–18
Fordism 25
Foresight land use futures project (Government Office for Science) 87
Fothergill, S. 78, 80
Fox Gotham, K. 55
Framework Institute 110
Fraser, N. 130, 133, 140, 142, 143, 149
freedom 14, 29, 154n2(ch2)
  negative 9
Friedman, S. 76, 115, 116, 118, 121, 127, 128

G

Gaebler, T. 45
Galbraith, J.K. 35
Gamble, A. 62
Gamsu, S. 123
gender inequality 27
general elections 42–43, 63, 68, 69, 79, 155n2(ch3)
general practitioners (GPs) 104–105
general will 11
Generation X 132
generational inequalities 131–132
gentrification 76
George, E. 78
Giovanni, A. 82
global capital 71
global competition 55
global economy 53–57, 70
global finance 32–33, 53
  see also international finance
global social governance 57–58
global social policy 57–62
globalisation 52, 53
Gough, J. 6, 7
governance 43, 45, 55, 57–58, 120–121
government deficits 54–55
Gray, M. 65–66, 80
Greece 68
green belts 87
Green, J. 98, 109
Greve, C. 74
Grimshaw, D. 66
Gross Domestic Product (GDP) 2
Grusky, D. 121
Guardian 46
Guilaume, C. 46

H

Haidt, J. 135
Hall, S. 73
Hamnett, C. 125
Han, B.-C. 35–36, 134
Hancock, M. 106, 111, 121, 155n1(ch6)
Harding, D.M., Baroness 119

Harris, T. 82
Hartz, E. 6, 7, 8, 9, 10, 11, 12, 154n8(ch1)
Harvey, M. 27, 108
Hay, C. 68
Hayek, F. 29, 34, 37, 100, 124
health 94–95, 95–97
  social determinants of 97, 98, 100, 104, 106, 107, 111
Health and Social Care Act 2012 105
health behaviours 106
Health equity in England (Marmot) 96–97
Health Gap, The (Marmot) 101
health inequalities 11–12, 15–16, 18, 94–98
  and health-related policy 102–108
  and place 79
  and political economy 98–102
  and social contract 108–112
health-maintenance activities 136
health-related policy 95, 102–108
healthcare 61, 152–153
Hemerijck, A. 53
High Speed 2 (HS2) 82–83
higher education 123–124
Hiley, D. 6, 8
Hill, M. 45, 53, 57, 65, 67, 138
Hills, J. 131–132, 137
Hirschman, A. 53
Hobbes, T. 7, 8, 9, 35, 37, 154n8(ch1)
Hobsbawm, E. 23
Hodge, G. 74
Holmwood, J. 24
Holt-White, E. 111
home ownership 132
Hood, A. 133
Hood, C. 43
household income 27, 76
housing 65, 76–77, 87–91, 92
Housing Act 1980 88–89
housing costs 132
Housing (Homeless Persons) Act 1977 87–88
housing wealth 125
How inequality runs in families (Calder) 114–115
human capital 126
Hunter, D. 103
Hunter, J. 82
Hupe, P. 45, 65
Hutton, W. 5, 12, 38, 41, 42, 62, 64, 75, 126

I

identity politics 139–141, 155n4(ch7)
ideology of power and the power of ideology, The (Therborn) 36
Illich, I. 96, 103
in-work poverty 127

income distribution 147
income inequalities 4–5, 30, 39, 125, 128, 132, 146
Independent Panel on Pandemic Preparedness and Response 60
individualism 1, 34–35, 53, 99, 102, 109, 110, 124, 133
inequalities 1–2
  Conservative government 15–16
  generational 131–132
  between nations 54
  New Labour 38, 40
  and place 72
  policy goals 151–152
  and taxation 57
  Thatcherism 38
  see also class inequality; equality; health inequalities; income inequalities; racial inequalities; spatial inequalities
inequities 26, 92
inflation 27
informal care 137–138
institutional racism 91
instrumental knowledge 18
intergenerational contract 130–144
  ageing 135–139
  routes and conditions for change 139–143
  younger generations 131–135
Intergovernmental Panel on Climate Change (IPCC) 58
international finance 126
  see also global finance
International Labour Office (ILO) 58
International Monetary Fund (IMF) 27, 28, 41, 53, 54, 57, 126, 131, 149
investor visa scheme 50
Italy 68

J

Jackson, B. 118
Jenkins, S. 77, 120
Jessop, B. 25, 28, 29, 39, 41, 44, 45, 49, 53, 55, 57–58, 60, 62, 64, 65, 66–67, 70, 71, 73, 74, 78, 92, 125, 132, 133
job guarantee 143
Johnson, B. 69, 74, 77, 83, 128
Johnson, P. 132
Jones, M. 66
Judge, L. 132
justice 11–12, 13

K

Kelly, M. 97
Kenny, M. 62, 63
Keynesian period 25–27
Khomami, N. 119
Kirton, G. 46
Klein, R. 104–105

knowledge 17–18
Kristofferson, K. 22

L

Labour Force Survey 116, 121
Labour governments 148
labour market 22
labour market participation 133
Labour Party 27, 37, 67, 87
  see also New Labour
Lamont, N. 78
Lancet Commissions 58, 59
land 84–87, 92, 155n3(ch4)
land tax 85
language 139
Laurison, D. 76, 115, 116, 118, 121, 127, 128
law 121
Lawson, N. 37
Leach, S. 64
Lees, L. 76
Lefebvre, H. 56
Leslie, J. 150
Lessnoff, M. 6, 9, 10
levelling up 66, 83
Leviathan (Hobbes) 9
liberalism 5, 29
life-cycle smoothing 138
life expectancy 97, 98, 101, 108, 110
Lindsay, J. 139, 155n4(ch7)
Littler, J. 125
local authorities / governments 42, 46, 64–66, 83–84, 105, 152–153
local government spending 59
Locke, J. 7
London 73–77, 77–78, 80–82, 138
loss allocation 2, 17
Lukianoff, G. 135
Lund, B. 86, 88, 89, 155n3(ch4)
Lupton, R. 39, 40, 122
Lynch, J. 98, 102, 109
Lyons Committee 2014 87

M

machine intelligence 142
Madgavkar, A. 57, 149, 150
Making housing affordable (Policy Exchange) 88
managerialism 43
Mandelson, P. 38
manufacturing 78
Marcuse, H. 35
marginalised groups 35
marginality 140
market justice 13
market logic 31
market rationality 44
market rule 29–30
markets 68, 126

Marmot, M. 18, 38, 66, 79, 80, 90, 94,
    96–97, 97–98, 100, 101, 103–104,
    105, 106, 107, 110, 111, 125, 127,
    134, 149–150
Marques, P. 82, 83
Marsden, D. 118
Marshall, T.H. 23–24, 25
Martin, R. 64, 72, 73, 75, 77, 78, 79,
    91, 92
Marx, K. 52
Marxism 19, 145
Mason, P. 10, 40, 55, 126, 140, 142
Massey, D. 22, 47–48, 72, 78
May, M. 14, 16, 65
May, T. 111
McCurdy, C. 138
McKinsey & Company 57
'me' intentionality 1
medical assessments 46–47
medicine 103, 121
meritocracy 116, 125
Merrick, R. 121
Meslin, E. 9
micro-class reproduction 121
middle classes 57, 131
migrant groups 90
Miliband, E. 41
Mill, J.S. 85
millennials 132, 134–135
minority ethnic households 90, 91
Minton, A. 88, 89, 90
Mitchell, W. 13, 25, 26, 27, 28, 29, 30,
    31, 33, 54, 55, 68, 140, 142, 143
Moreira, T. 136, 137
mortality 79
multinational corporations 32–33
    see also transnational companies
Murray, C. 35

N

National Audit Office (NAO) 42, 49–50,
    67, 119–120, 138
National Health Service (NHS) 103,
    104–105, 107, 111–112, 119–120
National Investment Bank 84
Navarro, V. 98, 99, 100, 102, 109
negative freedom 9
neoliberal diet 99
neoliberal psychopolitics 35–36
neoliberalism 5, 17, 23, 28–36, 148
    contradictions and inconsistencies 32–34,
        92
    ecological dominance 92
    key features 29
    and local governments 64–65
    and oil crises 27
    ongoing appeal 34–36
    and post-democracy 49, 50
    progressive 140

UK governments in the neoliberal
    era 37–43
New Economic Geography (NEG)
    77–78, 92
new institutional economics 43, 44
New Labour 38–40, 62, 78–79, 89, 101,
    110, 124, 148
New Public Governance 45
New Public Management (NPM) 43–45,
    46–48, 64
Newman, I. 38, 64
nexus 20, 62
NHS Test and Trace 119–120
Nielsen, C.F. 6, 7, 8, 9, 10, 11, 12,
    154n8(ch1)
Nixon, R.M. 53
Northern Ireland 63
northern powerhouse agenda 83
Nozick, R. 10, 66, 100

O

Oatley, T. 56
Obolenskaya, P. 122, 131–132
Observer 90
occupation structure 114
Office for National Statistics
    (ONS) 84, 137
oil crises 27
Open public services (HM Government,
    2011) 46
Organisation for Economic Co-operation
    and Development (OECD) 28, 57,
    70, 75, 131, 149
Osborne, D. 45
Osborne, S. 45
outsourcing 49–50, 120
    see also contracting out
Oven, K. 58
Owens, J. 125
Oxfam 54

P

Page, R. 15, 17
Paine, T. 85
Payne, G. 113, 114
Pearce, J. 80
Peck, J. 28–29, 30
Peel, E. 47
Pennell, I. 98, 103, 109
performance targets 43–44
personal independence payments
    (PIPs) 46–47, 50
phase shift 4, 154n6(ch1)
Phillips, D. 76, 78, 106
Pilling, S. 63, 155n2(ch3)
place 72
    see also spatial inequalities
pleasure principle 36
Pluckrose, H. 139, 155n4(ch7)

Polanyi, K. 7, 11
policy 16
policy sociology 18
political economy 2, 3–4, 13, 22–51
  conceptualisation 22
  global level 53–57
  and governance 55
  and health inequalities 98–102, 109–110
  neoliberal influence 28–36, 125
    contradictions and
      inconsistencies 32–34
    ongoing appeal 34–36
  New Public Management and
    governance 43–48
  post-democracy 48–50, 154n3(ch2)
  post-war welfare state 23–28, 64
  and social contract 51
  and social mobility 124–128
  and social policy 15, 20
  and spatial inequalities 72–93
    housing 87–91
    land 84–87
    London 73–77
    regional disparities 77–84
  UK governments in the neoliberal
    era 37–43
political rights 24
Porter, S. 42
possibility space 6
post-democracy 48–50, 154n3(ch2)
post-Fordism 5
post-industrialism 5
post-war welfare state 23–28, 64
post-work future 142–143
postmodernism 139
Poulantzas, N. 9
poverty 17, 24, 30, 35, 39, 42, 75–76,
  127, 134
Private Eye 47, 119
Private Finance Initiatives (PFIs) 74–75
private rental sector 90
private schools 119, 123
private sector 22–23, 33, 120
privatisation 5, 29, 30, 37, 44, 45–46,
  46–47, 85–86, 92, 146
  see also contracting out; right to buy
privatised Keynesianism 54
Probation Service 46
professional sociology 18
progress 2
progressive neoliberalism 140
proportionate universalism 66, 107–108
Public Contracts Regulations 49–50
public expenditure 25, 39, 40, 42, 44–45,
  59, **81**, 105–106, 138–139, 147–148,
  149, 150–151, 152
Public Health Act 1848 104
Public Health England (PHE) 58, 59, 60
public ownership 48

public sector 23, 30, 33, 42, 43–48, 49, 59
public services 45–46
public sociology 18
public spending cuts 54

Q

quasi-markets 44, 45

R

Race Audit 2017 91
race to the bottom 55, 57, 59, 70
racial inequalities 123
racialised social systems 91
Raikes, L. 73, 79, 82, 83
Randox 120
Rawls, J. 8, 9–10
reality 3
Reay, D. 115–116, 118, 119, 122, 123,
  124, 128
Reckless opportunists (Davis) 33
redistribution 16, 109, 110, 154n10(ch1)
redundancy 31
reflexive knowledge 18
regeneration 39
regional development 83–84
regional disparities 77–84
regulation 25
relative mobility 114
Resolution Foundation 132
retrenchment 45
revolting elite 71
Rhodes, R. 43, 44
right to buy 88–89
rise of the meritocracy, The (Young) 116
Robinson, J. 26
Rousseau, J.-J. 7, 8, 10–12, 14, 48, 95,
  141, 148
Ruane, S. 25, 26, 32, 39, 79, 80
Rubery, J. 66
Russia 50, 74

S

safety net 35
Salway, S. 98, 109
Sartorius, D. 95–96
Sayer, A. 4, 5, 22, 28, 31, 33, 38, 41, 53,
  54, 56, 74, 85, 86, 99, 133
Scambler, G. 18, 94, 98, 100, 101,
  109, 110
Scambler, S. 98, 100, 101, 109, 110
scholar activism 155n4(ch7)
Schrecker, T. 40, 53, 55, 78, 98, 99
Scotland 62–63
Scrutton, R. 63
securitisation 56
Serco 120
Sewell Convention 63
Shah, K. 150
Shankley, W. 90, 91

Shaxson, N. 74, 75
Simpson, P. 106, 132
Sinfield, A. 2, 17
Skills for Care 59
Slater, T. 88
Smith, A. 85, 86, 121–122
snowflake generation 134, 155n2(ch7)
social attitudes 146–148, 151
social care 46, 64, 70, 97, 137
social care homes 60–61
Social Care Institute for Excellence
    (SCIE) 59, 61, 137
social care services 58–60
social care workers *see* care workers
social class *see* class inequality; middle
    classes; underclass; working class
social contract 3, 6–14, 36, 48,
    145–146
  as analytical device 94
  and automation 142
  and capitalism 23
  COVID-19 crisis 149–151
  England 1–2, 2–3, 63, 64, 95
  European Union (EU) 68
  and global economy 55
  and health 96, 99, 100
  and health inequalities 108–112
  'me' intentionality 1
  and political economy 51
  proposals to improve 151–153
  and social mobility 113–118
  and social policy 16, 17
  see also intergenerational contract
social contract proper 7
social determinants of health 97, 98, 100,
    104, 106, 107, 111
social housing *see* housing
social investment 124, 133
social justice 9–10, 66
social justice activism 139, 141
social mobility 113–129, 153
  and political economy 124–128
  and social contract 113–118
  and social policy 118–124
  and wellbecoming 133
Social Mobility Commission 122, 132
social policy 2–3, 14–20, 145
  active ageing 136
  and discourse 140
  European Union (EU) 67
  and global economy 55
  global level 57–62
  health 95, 102–108
  life-cycle smoothing 138
  and neoliberalism 32
  New Labour 40
  and political economy 15, 20
  and social mobility 118–124
social policy analysis 17

social reproduction 130, 133, 139, 143
social rights 24, 30, 31, 125–126
social service state 24
social ties 10–11
society 57
socioeconomics 2
sociology 2, 15, 18, 42
spatial inequalities 72–93
  housing 87–91
  land 84–87, 92
  London 73–77
  regional disparities 77–84
Spencer, H. 35, 44, 124
Spicker, P. 14–15, 16
sponsored mobility 118
Srnicek, N. 2, 26, 27, 28, 29, 30, 34, 40,
    58, 67, 124, 125, 140, 142
St Croix, T. 125
stagflation 27
state capacity 42
state expenditure 32, 41
  see also public expenditure
State of the estate in 2012 (Cabinet Office,
    2013) 33
State of the nation (Social Mobility
    Commission) 122
Stewart, K. 67, 68
Stoker, G. 45
Stone, J. 88
Strathclyde Police Training and
    Recruitment Centre 74
Streeck, W. 1, 2, 3, 4, 13, 15, 22, 23, 25,
    26, 27, 33, 35, 36, 37, 41, 42, 46, 48,
    49, 53, 54, 55, 56, 68, 70, 98, 99,
    126, 133
structural inequities 26–27
structural racism 100
Sunday Mornin' Comin' Down
    (Kristofferson) 22
Suteanu, C. 3

T

tax reform 42
taxation 32, 33, 38, 55, 57, 85, 109, 110,
    133, 147–148, 152
Taylor-Gooby, P. 4, 42, 139
Telford, L. 39, 67, 69
temporary accommodation 90
Thane, P. 122
Thatcher, M. 44
Thatcherism 37–38, 86, 88–89, 98,
    99, 124
theory of social justice, the (Rawls) 9–10
Therborn, G. 17, 36, 48, 115, 116, 117
Third Way politics 39
Thomas, C. 106
Thompson, E. 50
Thompson, M. 1, 7, 10, 11, 141
Titmuss, R. 2, 17, 25, 82, 102

Tomaney, J. 65, 82, 83
trade unions 40, 41, 55
Transforming children and young people's mental health provision (DHSC and DfE, 2017) 15–16
transnational companies 57, 99
  see also multinational corporations
transport 82–83
Travers, T. 76
Treasury 75, 80, 83, 126
Truss, L. 50
Turner, T. 118

U

UK governments in the neoliberal era 37–43
UK Single Market Act 2020 63
UK2070 Commission 64, 66, 73, 75, 77, 80, 83, 120
underclass 35
unemployment 27, 30, 142
unions 40, 41, 55
United Kingdom Independence Party (UKIP) 63
United Nations (UN) 57
United Nations Special Rapporteur 42, 82, 148
universal basic income (UBI) 142
universalism 25
  false 27
  proportionate 66, 107–108
universities 123–124
Usmani, A. 26

V

Van Gunsteren, H. 24
Varoufakis, Y. 7, 68
Veblen, T. 35, 85
veil of ignorance 10
Verkerk, J. 45
Villadsen, K. 139
violent crime 79
Virdee, S. 26, 91

Vizard, P. 61, 105–106, 107, 136
von Mises, L. 29

W

Wales 63
Walker, A. 135–136, 138–139
Warren, J. 64, 65, 78
Warwick-Booth, L. 19
Waters, T. 133
'we thinking' 11
wealth gap 150, 152
wealth of nations, The (Smith) 121–122
Weeden, K. 121
welfare 16, 17, 66, 82
welfare benefits 80, 133
welfare reform 80
welfare spending 56
welfare states 4, 12, 23–28, 64, 90, 138
wellbecoming 133–135
wellbeing 133, 134, 135
Wilcox, Z. 75
Wilks, S. 119
will of all 11
Williams, A. 2, 26, 27, 28, 29, 30, 34, 40, 58, 67, 124, 125, 140, 142
Williams, F. 27
Wistow, J. 18, 39, 58–59, 60, 64, 65, 67, 69, 98, 104, 105, 109, 110, 111
Wlezien, C. 147
Wojcik, D. 73
woke generation 134, 155n1(ch7)
Work and Pensions Committee 47
working class 26, 27, 38, 50, 69, 79, 115–116, 118, 123
working week 22
World Bank 53, 54, 57, 126
World Health Organization (WHO) 57–58, 60, 136
World Trade Organization 53

Y

Yamamura, K. 35, 51, 53
Young, M. 116
younger generations 131–135

Lightning Source UK Ltd.
Milton Keynes UK
UKHW021507280622
405075UK00005B/1084